South African Politics

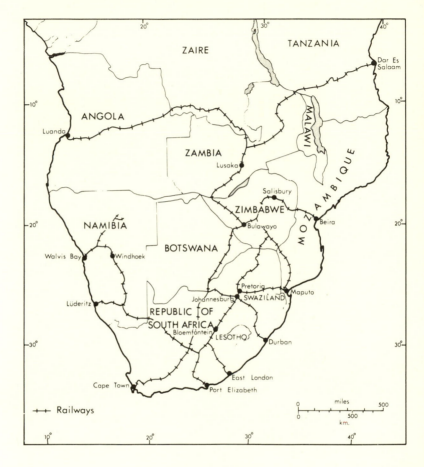

ZAIRE

TANZANIA

Dar Es
Salaam

ANGOLA

Luanda

MALAWI

ZAMBIA

Lusaka

Salisbury

ZIMBABWE

NAMIBIA

Bulawayo

MOZAMBIQUE

Beira

Walvis Bay

Windhoek

BOTSWANA

Lüderitz

Pretoria

Johannesburg

SWAZILAND

Maputo

REPUBLIC OF
SOUTH AFRICA

Bloemfontein

LESOTHO

Durban

Cape Town

East London

Port Elizabeth

+—+ Railways

miles

0   500

0   500
km.

Southern Africa

South African Politics

Leonard Thompson and
Andrew Prior

Yale University Press
New Haven and London

Published with the assistance of the
A. Whitney Griswold Publication Fund.

Designed by James J. Johnson
and set in Melior Roman.
Printed in the United States of America by
The Vail-Ballou Press, Binghamton, N.Y.

DT
770
.T46
1982

Library of Congress Cataloging in Publication Data

Thompson, Leonard Monteath.
    South African politics.

    Includes index.
    1. South Africa—Politics and government.
I. Prior, Andrew.   II. Title.
DT770.T46   320.968   81–14635
ISBN 0–300–02767–2   AACR2
ISBN 0–300–02779–6 (pbk.)

10 9 8 7 6 5 4 3 2 1

Contents

MAPS

List of Tables

Preface

The South African political system is unique; and its peculiar characteristics affect us all, whether we live inside or outside South Africa. "White" people of European origin, numbering one-sixth of the total population, monopolize the vital decision-making roles, except in small impoverished and underdeveloped reservations known as "homelands"; the rest of the population, most of whom are culturally and genetically related to the rulers and to the majority of the inhabitants of the other states of southern and central Africa, are restricted to subordinate roles and discriminated against in many aspects of life. South Africa also possesses by far the most powerful industrial economy in the African continent and is capable of producing nuclear weapons. Consequently, the country is a crucial part—indeed, a major promoter—of the racial tensions that continue to bedevil mankind.

The core of this book is a discussion of political power as it actually operates in the Republic of South Africa. We also explain the historical, demographic, economic, and international context and discuss the internal and external challenges to the racial order. Despite a rash of publications dealing with various aspects of South African affairs, none of them provides a similar description of the peculiarities of the South African system, based on the data and the scholarship of the early 1980s. This book will therefore be useful to anyone who wishes to have a succinct introduction to the subject, including students of history, political science, and international affairs inside as well as outside South Africa.

This book's predecessor was Leonard Thompson's *Politics in the Republic of South Africa*, which was published by Little, Brown and Company in 1966; it was reprinted five times before its data had become obsolete and was withdrawn in the mid-1970s. We use many of the analytical categories of the earlier book, which owed much to the inspiration and guidance of James S. Coleman. But much has happened in South Africa and its neighboring territories since 1966, and this present volume has been completely rewritten.

Many people have assisted us. The staffs of the Jagger Library, University of Cape Town, and the Sterling Memorial Library, Yale University, notably Moore Crossey of Yale, were particularly helpful in locating material and making it available. We are also grateful to the following persons who provided valuable information and comments: Heribert Adam, Win Armstrong, David Bleazard, Jenifer Dagut, John de Gruchy, Leonard Doob, André du Toit, Harvey Feinberg, William Foltz, Robert Harms, Anthony Heard, Dudley Horner, Barbara Lamb, Nic Olivier, Harald Sandstrom, Michael Savage, James Selfe, and Martin West. In New Haven, Marty Achilles, Pamela Baldwin, Claire Shindler, and Mary Whitney typed the final version for the press. Barbara Folsom, copyeditor, and Charles Grench, history editor, both of the Yale University Press, have been as efficient as ever in their handling of this book.

The Yale-Wesleyan Southern African Research Program, of which Leonard Thompson is director, provided Andrew Prior with an associate fellowship during the fall semester of 1980, which gave him access to Yale's many intellectual resources and made it possible for us to complete the work in close cooperation. We are grateful to the Ford Foundation and the National Endowment for the Humanities, the sponsors of that program.

New Haven, Connecticut   LEONARD THOMPSON
January 1981   ANDREW PRIOR

Chronology

Before A.D. 300	Ancestors of the African population begin to settle in South Africa
1652	Ancestors of the white population begin to settle in South Africa
1806	The British conquer the Cape Colony from the Dutch
1836–1854	The Great Trek: Afrikaners from the Cape Colony found republics in the Transvaal and the Orange Free State
1867	Diamond mining begins in Griqualand West
1886	Gold mining begins on the Witwatersrand
1898	Whites complete the conquest of the African population
1899–1902	The Boer War: Britain conquers the Afrikaner republics
1910	The Cape Colony, Natal, the Transvaal, and the Orange Free State join to form the Union of South Africa, a white-controlled, self-governing British Dominion
1912	Africans found the African National Congress (ANC)
1913	The South African parliament limits African landownership to the Reserves
1936	Parliament removes the African voters from the common electoral roll

1939	South Africa enters the war against Nazi Germany
1948	The Afrikaner National Party (NP) wins a general election and begins to apply its policy of apartheid
1952	The ANC and allies launch a passive resistance campaign
1955	The ANC and allies launch a Congress of the People campaign
1956	Parliament removes the Coloured voters from the common electoral roll
1958	Africans found the Pan-Africanist Congress (PAC)
1960	Police shoot 67 Africans at Sharpeville The government bans the ANC and the PAC The white representatives of African voters are removed from Parliament
1961	South Africa becomes a republic and leaves the Commonwealth
1966–1968	Lesotho, Botswana, and Swaziland become independent states and members of the UN
1968	The white representatives of Coloured voters are removed from Parliament
1971	The World Court rules that South Africa's administration of Namibia (South West Africa) is illegal
1974	Revolution in Portugal
1975–1976	Mozambique and Angola become independent states and members of the UN
1976–1977	Disturbances in Soweto and other cities result in at least 575 deaths
1976–1981	South Africa grants "independence" to the Transkei, Bophuthatswana, Venda, and Ciskei "homelands," but they are not recognized abroad

1977   The UN Security Council imposes a mandatory
                embargo on the supply of arms to South
                Africa
1978   P. W. Botha succeeds B. J. Vorster as prime
                minister
1980   Zimbabwe (previously Rhodesia) becomes
                independent and a UN member
1981   The NP wins its ninth successive general
                election

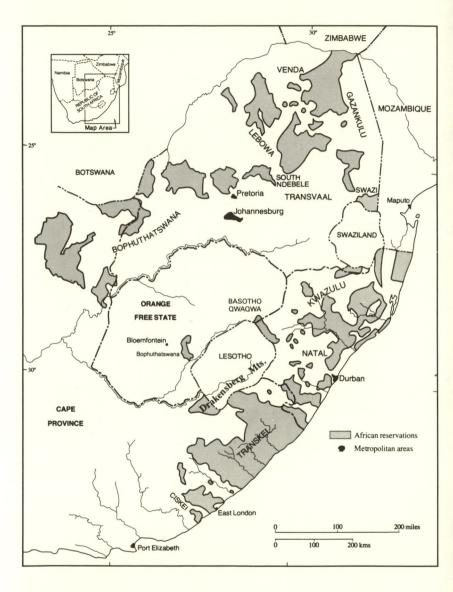

The African "Homelands" of the Republic of South Africa

1

Introduction

Scarcely a hundred years ago South Africa's sole significance to the outside world derived from its geographic location on the shortest sea route from Europe to Asia. This was the reason why the Dutch founded a refreshment station at the Cape of Good Hope in 1652 and maintained it as long as they could; and this was why the British conquered the Cape in 1795 and reconquered it in 1806.

South Africa now has the added significance of being a powerful industrial state in a partially developed continent. It is the world's largest producer of andalusite, chrome ore, gold, vanadium, and platinum; it ranks second in the production of manganese ore and third in antimony (metal), asbestos fibre, and gem and industrial diamonds. Besides these, it is a major producer of coal, iron ore, and uranium. It also has the largest estimated reserves of vanadium, platinum, chrome ore, manganese, gold, and fluospar, the second largest diamond reserves, and extensive reserves of coal and iron.[1] Although no exploitable quantities of oil have been discovered, its recoverable coal reserves, which are estimated at 61 billion tons, can be converted into energy resources of about 1,300 trillion megajoules. This compares favorably with Saudi Arabia's published proved re-

1. *Financial Mail* (Johannesburg), Mining Supplement, September 28, 1979, pp. 12–13.

serves of oil, which represent about 1,000 trillion megajoules.[2] South Africa's gross national product is 25 percent of the gross product of the entire African continent. The country produces 90 percent of the continent's steel and generates as much electricity as the rest of Africa put together. There are nearly as many automobiles and telephones in South Africa as in the rest of the continent.[3] There is a wide range of manufacturing and agricultural industries, and South Africa not only feeds itself but provides essential foodstuffs for other countries in the region as far north as Zambia. The communication system by road, rail, and air is efficient. The armed forces are among the best equipped and most disciplined in Africa. Thanks largely to gold exports, the balance of trade is usually favorable, and in 1980 there was a budget surplus of about 1,200 million Rand (approximately 1,500 million U.S. dollars). British, American, German, French, Italian, Japanese, and other foreigners have considerable investments in South Africa. Indeed, by all the recognized criteria, South Africa's economy is strong and self-sustaining, and its rate of development is rapid—illustrated by an average annual increase in the real gross domestic product of 4.8 percent for the entire post–World War II period.[4]

The South African ports are still important links in intercontinental trade. A large volume of shipping carrying necessary oil from the Middle East to Europe and the United States rounds the Cape each year: for although the Suez route between Europe and Asia is shorter, it is unable to cope with modern supertankers.

These geographical and economic factors do not in themselves make South Africa inordinately significant for mankind as a whole; yet the country does crucially affect the human destiny, and this is due almost entirely to its political system,

2. Ibid., Energy Supplement, June 29, 1979, p. 8.
3. Estimates derived from *Statistical Yearbook, 1977* (New York: United Nations, 1978).
4. *Statistical/Economic Review* (Pretoria: Government Printer, 1980), p. 6.

which is unique in the modern world. In no other system in a sovereign state is overriding power exercised by a minority racial group. In no other system is the maintenance of racial stratification—systematic and inescapable—the primary object of policy. In no other system are the leveling effects of industrialization and urbanization effectively countered by political processes.

The population of South Africa is officially divided into four main racial groups: White, Coloured, Asian, and African.[5] The Whites form 16.1 percent, Coloureds 9.2 percent, Asians 2.9 percent, and Africans 71.8 percent of the total population of 28 million.[6] The Whites have a monopoly of political power. Only Whites may be members of the South African Parliament and the South African Cabinet, which are sovereign over the entire Republic.[7] Economic power, too, is vested to an overwhelming extent in the hands of Whites who own most of the land and control all the major industries and businesses. According to a report of the Bureau of Market Research of the University of South Africa, in 1975 Whites accounted for 66.3 percent of personal disposable income, Africans for 15.3 percent, Coloured people for 12.8 percent, and Asians for 5.6 percent.[8] Every appreciable enterprise in the country employs Blacks,[9] most of whom do the unskilled work at low wages, whereas Whites do the skilled work at high wages. Thus, though members of all the racial groups participate in the economy and are dependent on

5. See note 9 below.
6. 1980 estimates. These figures include the populations of the "independent" Bantustans—the Transkei, Bophuthatswana, Venda, and the Ciskei.
7. The four territories named in note 6 are formally independent but have not been recognized by any other country except South Africa.
8. South African Institute of Race Relations, Survey of Race Relations in South Africa, 1978 (Johannesburg: SAIRR, 1979), p. 159.
9. The term "black" denotes all the South Africans who do not fall into the "white" group; it includes the African, Coloured, and Asian peoples of South Africa. The term "non-white," which was commonly used until about 1970, is avoided because it is offensive to identify a person in negative terms.

it, their opportunities, roles, and rewards are largely determined by their race.

South Africans rarely meet members of racial groups other than their own, except as white employers and black employees, white overseers and black laborers, or white officials and black subjects. Members of the racial groups live in different areas; they attend different schools and churches; when they are ill they are treated in different hospitals or different parts of the same hospital; and when they die they are carried in different hearses to different cemeteries. In most cases the facilities for Whites are greatly superior to the facilities for Blacks. Most of this separation is embodied in laws enacted by the sovereign all-white Parliament on the initiative of the all-white cabinet, applied by all-white courts and enforced by police under the orders of all-white senior officers.

South Africa is unique; and being unique it is isolated and threatened. The threat comes from without as well as within; for, since the transformation of Rhodesia into Zimbabwe was completed in early 1980, it is the one glaring example of a national political system devoted to the perpetuation of white domination in a period of history when racial domination is generally recognized to be morally indefensible; so long as that system exists, the independent governments which now control the rest of the African continent will regard their revolution as incomplete.

THE CASE FOR THE GOVERNMENT

The policy of the National Party (NP) which has ruled South Africa since May 1948 has been vigorously defended over the years by a succession of prime ministers, cabinet ministers, and Nationalist intellectuals. While this policy has undergone revisions—from an ill-disguised racial domination (baasskap) under Prime Ministers Malan and Strijdom to a more sophisticated "multinational development" in separate "homeland" states under Prime Ministers Verwoerd, Vorster, and Botha—its central core has remained unchanged.[10] The South African government's case may be summarized as follows.

The white South African nation has as much right to exist in South Africa as the American nation does in North America. Both trace their origins to the seventeenth century, both are fundamentally Christian nations derived from western Europe, both have struggled to become independent from Britain, and both have built up strong, prosperous countries in formerly primitive environments. South Africa has a more stable history than most African countries and has created a powerful economy whose benefits are shared by all sections of the population. What a former foreign minister said to the United Nations General Assembly in 1962 is still a constant refrain of Nationalist politicians:

> Per capita of our nonwhite population, more schools, both primary and secondary, are available for the nonwhites than in the countries of most of [tropical Africa]. . . . Per capita of our nonwhite populations, more beds are available for nonwhites in our hospitals than in any other state on the continent of Africa. . . . per capita of our nonwhite peoples more housing has been provided during the past years for nonwhite occupation than in many of the countries [of tropical Africa].[11]

White South Africa, under whose leadership these results are being achieved, has the right to survive as a nation. Its survival would be compromised by any policy which promoted the integration of the African people into the white political society. In the words of an Afrikaans intellectual: "An unquali-

---

10. P. van Duxton, "Bantu outside their Homelands," in *Yearbook of the South African Bureau of Racial Affairs* (Pretoria, 1972), p. 26. See also D. C. van der Spuy, ed., *South Africa 1976: Official Yearbook of the Republic of South Africa* (Pretoria: South African Department of Information, 1976), esp. chap. 12, "Multinational Development," and chap. 13, "The Black Man outside the Homelands."

11. E. H. Louw, Nov. 6, 1962, cited in H. H. Biermann, ed., *The Case for South Africa* (New York: McFadden Books, 1963), pp. 142–43.

fied democratic dispensation in white South Africa . . . will mean that the generally primitive and largely illiterate and socio-politically unsophisticated Bantu masses will by sheer weight of numbers determine the way of life and the value system that will obtain in the country."[12] Policies of universal suffrage, selective suffrage on color-blind criteria, or a political federation of races would sooner or later lead to black domination.

But just as the Whites have the right to national existence and self-fulfillment, so have the several black (African, Asian, and Coloured) communities which are embryonic nations. In the words of Dr. H. F. Verwoerd, a former prime minister and the recognized architect of "separate development":

We do not only seek and fight for a solution which will mean our survival as a white race, but we also seek a solution which will ensure the survival and full development—political and economic—to each of the other racial groups, and we are prepared to pay a high price out of our earnings to ensure their future. . . . We want each of our population groups to control and to govern themselves, as is the case with other Nations. Then they can co-operate as in a Commonwealth—in an economic association with the Republic and with each other. In the transition stage the guardian must teach and guide his ward. That is our policy of separate development. South Africa will proceed in all honesty and fairness to secure peace, prosperity and justice for all by means of political independence coupled with economic interdependence.[13]

This is a realistic policy of gradual withdrawal of white control over the African areas. The eventual outcome, in the formulation of Prime Minister P. W. Botha, will be a constellation of states, each politically autonomous while sharing common economic interests. Already much has been achieved. In 1976 the Transkei, the traditional homeland of the bulk of the Xhosa nation, became an independent state; the Tswana nation

12. N. Rhoodie, *Apartheid and Racial Partnership in South Africa* (Pretoria: Academica, 1969), p. 373.
13. H. F. Verwoerd's speech in London in May 1961, cited in Biermann, *The Case for South Africa*, p. 147.

achieved independence in 1978, the Venda in 1979, and the southern Xhosa in 1981. It is only a matter of time before the administrative and other obstacles are overcome and the other African nations (Tsonga, Swazi, Ndebele, Zulu, and so on) also become independent.

The Coloured and Asian groups will also be accommodated in the political dispensation of the future. It is unrealistic to grant them homelands because of their traditional close proximity to the Whites, so the government is devising a new conciliar system in which the interests of Coloureds and Asians as well as Whites will be articulated. This, too, is merely a question of administrative preparation before it will be translated into reality.

Overseas critics of separate development deliberately misrepresent this policy and see it as a racial issue, whereas it is, in fact, a matter of ethnic accommodation: "Should the Bantu of South Africa change into white-skinned beings overnight, the Xhosa would still be a Xhosa, and the Zulu would still be a Zulu. The Zulu is not a Zulu merely because he has a black skin—he is first of all a Zulu because of his socio-cultural characteristics and affiliation."[14]

Thus the separate development program is aimed at fulfilling the various ethnic groups' aspirations to separate nationhood and development. By granting to each group distinct political institutions, it will avoid the endemic ethnic conflicts which have become the bane of countries such as Lebanon and Northern Ireland, and many African countries.

The path to individual political advancement opens up dramatically once ethnic conflict is eliminated: "Even the shepherd boy on the hills overlooking the Transkeian capital, Umtata, can dream of the day when he is prime minister of his own land. In the integration model he will have to destroy his

---

14. Rhoodie, *Apartheid and Racial Partnership*, p. 379.

cultural make-up and personality in order to wage a battle in the field crammed with competitors from other groups."[15]

Far from denying political rights to the black people, the National party accords to each ethnic group the right to set up its own political institutions and legal and administrative machinery, and to regulate its own economic affairs. A political system that allows stronger ethnic groups to dominate and control others is not a viable long-term solution in South Africa; only a system that gives Africans a way of existing independently in specific geographical areas will lessen interethnic conflict and violence.

There are various reasons why critics of the National party deliberately misunderstand this policy. South Africa has become a scapegoat to appease the guilt of the former colonial powers for their centuries of racial exploitation; Western countries have opportunistically sided with the Arab and African countries to satisfy their needs for oil supplies and markets; and the partisan antigovernment English-language press in South Africa has provided fuel for foreign critics. Also, international communism is fomenting anarchy and upheaval with an eye to gaining access to South Africa's vast mineral wealth.[16]

Since the internal opposition has led to serious acts of sabotage, the government has been obliged to act with the utmost firmness to preserve law and order. Subversive organizations like the Communist party, the African National Congress, the Pan-Africanist Congress, the Christian Institute, and the various organs of the Black Consciousness Movement have been banned and steps have been taken to prevent their resurrection under different names. The government has also found it necessary to close down subversive publications such as the Soweto newspapers The World and Post and to place re-

15. Department of Information, Multinational Development in South Africa: The Reality (Pretoria: Government Printer, 1970), p. 9.
16. D. de Villiers, The Case for South Africa (London: Stacey, 1970), p. 143.

strictions on certain agitators who threaten national security.

While South Africa will have to brace itself for the total onslaught being planned against it now that Angola, Mozambique, and Zimbabwe are under black Marxist control, it is to be expected that in the long run the realistic policies of the government will improve the country's reputation. Already many Africans are cooperating in the homeland program; and those who are presently reluctant to do so are having their fears allayed by the benefits accruing from independence. Already many responsible Blacks realize that living conditions in South Africa are vastly superior to those in the African countries farther north, and that the policy of separate development holds out the promise of complete satisfaction for all the peoples of South Africa. These are the arguments in the case given by the National party that rules South Africa.

THE CASE AGAINST THE GOVERNMENT

Opposition to the ruling NP from within South Africa covers a wide spectrum, ranging from political parties which may contend for power within the sovereign parliamentary system, through political parties within the satellite and subordinate political institutions (the "homeland" legislatures, the former Coloured Persons Representative Council, and the South African Indian Council), to groups with no constitutional means of seeking political power.

There are three significant opposition parties which aspire to gain power at the center by constitutional means—that is to say, by winning a parliamentary majority from the existing white electorate. The Progressive Federal party, the official opposition, which won 26 out of the total of 165 seats in the 1981 general election, supports a policy of a common citizenship open to all regardless of color. It would, if it came to power, negotiate a new constitution in a national convention at which representatives of all ethnic groups would be present. The New Republic party, an offshoot of the United party which was dissolved in 1977, won eight seats in the 1981 general election. It advocates a loose federal approach, with maximum devolution of powers to local communities. Both the above parties draw most of their support from English-speaking urban constituencies. The Herstigte Nasionale party (HNP) is a right-wing offshoot of the National party. It favors continued white control of all of South Africa under Afrikaner direction and opposes any significant concessions to the Coloured people and the Asians as well as to the Africans. The HNP holds no seat in Parliament. Nevertheless, whereas in the 1977 general election it received only 3 percent of the votes cast, in the 1981 election it received over 13 percent. It is therefore a serious obstacle to reform and, if it continues to gain strength, will pose a threat to the hegemony of the NP.

The Liberal party, which supported a policy of extending the franchise to all South Africans, was formerly a constitutional contender for political power. In 1968 Parliament passed the Prohibition of Political Interference Act, which made it illegal for anyone to belong to a racially mixed political party. Rather than expel Blacks, the Liberal party disbanded. Before they were banned in 1960, there were also several organizations which, consisting for the most part of unenfranchised Blacks, sought to gain power by extraconstitutional means and, having done so, to inaugurate a nonracial democratic state "based on the will of the people." That remains the professed objective of African nationalists and their allies in other ethnic groups. Among several other former extraparliamentary political organizations, there was a small, multiracial Communist party of South Africa; it was banned in 1950. Despite their bannings, the African National Congress (ANC), the Pan-Africanist Congress (PAC), and the Communist party of South Africa (CPSA) maintain a presence in exile and promote revolutionary cadres inside South Africa.[17]

The Coloured Persons Representative Council (CPRC) operated within the official framework until the government disbanded it in 1980. Large numbers of the urbanized Coloured population had boycotted this council, regarding it as a puppet body. The Labour party, which consistently won the majority of seats in the council, stands for one-man–one-vote with direct parliamentary representation for all South Africans.[18]

Though these South African opponents of the government vary in many respects, all, with the exception of the HNP, criticize not merely the performance of the Nationalist government within the framework of the existing system, but the system itself. The common essence of their criticisms of the system may be summarized as follows.

The Afrikaner Nationalists have a distorted view of the nature of South African society. Whatever their antecedents may have been, the peoples of South Africa are not now separate

17. For documents illustrating the principles and programs of African political organizations, see T. Karis and G. Carter, *From Protest to Challenge: A Documentary History of African Politics in South Africa 1882–1964*, 4 vols. (Stanford: Hoover Institution Press, 1972, 1973, and 1977); G. M. Gerhart, *Black Power in South Africa* (Berkeley: University of California Press, 1978). On the National party, see H. Adam and H. Giliomee, *The Rise and Crisis of Afrikaner Power* (Cape Town: David Philip, 1979), reproduced in the United States as *Ethnic Power Mobilized: Can South Africa Change?* (New Haven: Yale University Press, 1979); N. Rhoodie, *South African Dialogue* (Pretoria: McGraw Hill, 1972). On the Progressive Federal party, see F. v. Z. Slabbert and D. Welsh, *South Africa's Options* (Cape Town: David Philip, 1979). On the Liberal party, see G. Carter, *The Politics of Inequality: South Africa since 1948* (London: Thames and Hudson, 1958). On the Communist party, see the *African Communist* (London, 1960–).

18. Criticized by the government for its noncooperative stance and by Blacks generally for having been part of the white-controlled political system, the Labour party feels the tensions from the Right and the Left. In 1980 it lost its political platform when the government disbanded the CPRC and replaced it with a nominated Coloured Persons Council.

nations which happen to have become temporarily and partially intermingled. Nearly all South Africans participate in one modern economic system controlled by one sovereign government, with the result that they have been molded into a single society and are irrevocably interdependent. That the Afrikaner Nationalist view of South African society is false is proved beyond all reasonable doubt by the fact that since 1948, while the NP government has been enacting and applying all sorts of separatist laws, the number and the proportion of South Africans of each racial group who live in the industrial towns and contribute to the white-controlled capitalist economy have persistently increased. Apartheid, in the sense of the separate development of separate races in separate areas, is therefore the very antithesis of what is happening in South Africa. The task of statesmanship is to accept, not to deny, these basic facts of South African life. Afrikaner nationalism, or any other nationalism which excludes masses of fellow South Africans, is a sectional and disruptive force; and there is no justification for discriminating against Blacks in seven-eighths of South Africa.

The separate development policy is fraudulent for the additional reason that the "Bantu Areas," forming the remaining one-eighth of South Africa, are small, scattered territories which could not conceivably become viable national homelands for anyone, let alone for twenty million Africans. At no stage has the government genuinely consulted with freely chosen representatives of the Coloured, Asian, or African communities. When the government has made a show of consultation, it has done so with carefully selected individuals and it has taken pains to manipulate the situation to its own advantage. Except for those who have succumbed to official patronage and intimidation—and they are remarkably few in the circumstances—nearly all black South Africans reject the entire political system as one that enables one-sixth of the inhabitants of South Africa to dominate the rest. This rejection is almost universal among the most highly educated and skilled Blacks, who would be the national leaders of South Africa if conditions of freedom obtained.

The withdrawal of moral allegiance from the existing political order was explicitly stated by Nelson Mandela, a leader of the banned African National Congress, in 1962, when he was on trial for inciting people to strike and for leaving the Republic without permission:

Your Worship, I would say that the whole life of any thinking African in this country drives him continuously to a conflict peculiar to this country. The law as it is applied, the law as it has been developed over a long period of history, and especially the law as it is written and designed by the Nationalist government, is a law which, in our view, *is immoral, unjust and intolerable.* Our consciences dictate that we must protest against it, that we must oppose it and that we must attempt to alter it. . . .

We have been conditioned by the history of white government in this country to accept the fact that Africans, when they make their demands strongly and powerfully enough for those demands to have some chance of success, will be met by force and terror on the part of the government. This is not something we have taught the African peoples, this is something the African people have learned from their own bitter experience. *Government violence can do only one thing and that is to breed counterviolence.* . . .

I hate the practice of race discrimination, and in doing so, in my hatred, I am sustained by the fact that the overwhelming majority of mankind hates it equally. . . . I hate the racial arrogance which decrees that the good things of life shall be retained as the exclusive right of a minority of the population, and which reduces the majority of the population to a subservience and inferiority, and maintains them as voteless chattels to work where they are told and behave as they are told by the ruling minority. Nothing that this Court can do will change in any way that hatred in me, which can only be removed by the removal of the injustice and the inhumanity which I have sought to remove from the political, social and economic life of this country.[19]

19. Karis and Carter, *From Protest to Challenge,* 3:771.

INTERNATIONAL REPERCUSSIONS

From a very early stage South Africa has been the object of criticism in the United Nations; and as the intensity of repressive racial legislation has stiffened and the number of Afro-Asian members of the United Nations has increased, the criticism has become more severe and the demands for active intervention more urgent.

In 1962, by a vote of 67 to 16 with 23 abstentions, the United Nations General Assembly recommended that member states break off diplomatic relations (if they had any) with South Africa, deny the use of their ports and air space to South African ships and aircraft, boycott South African goods and refrain from exporting goods to South Africa, and asked the Security Council to consider the expulsion of South Africa from the United Nations. This resolution was not mandatory, and it has not been strictly observed by some of the Afro-Asian countries which initiated it, while it has been largely ignored by the countries which opposed it, notably Britain, France, the United States, and South Africa's other principal trading partners. Nevertheless, boycotts of varying completeness have been imposed by many third world countries, the South African Airways had to reroute its flights to Europe via Las Palmas and Ilha do Sal in the Atlantic Ocean, and South Africa's trading potential with tropical Africa is not being fully realized.

By the mid-1960s South Africa was becoming isolated. The country left UNESCO in 1956 and resigned from the British Commonwealth in 1961, following scathing criticisms at a prime ministers' conference. It ceased to participate in the International Labour Organization and the World Health Organization and left the Food and Agricultural Organization of the United Nations, the Economic Commission for Africa, the Council for Technical Co-operation in Africa, and the Council for Science in Africa. Its athletes have been unable to take part in the Olympic Games since 1964, and in 1963 thirty heads of independent African states, meeting in conference at Addis Ababa, set up an African Liberation Committee consisting of representatives of nine states, with offices in Dar es Salaam, for the purpose of organizing the overthrow of the regimes in the then Portuguese territories of Angola and Mozambique and also in Rhodesia (Zimbabwe), South West Africa (Namibia), and South Africa.

By the early 1980s, South Africa's isolation had become quite perilous. This was largely because a series of internal explosions cast doubt on the capacity of the regime to adapt to changing circumstances. In 1976, African schoolchildren in Soweto, the principal African township serving Johannesburg, demonstrated against the government's insistence that Afrikaans should be used as a medium of instruction in the schools. The police opened fire and thus started a cycle of violence that spread to other urban areas and, according to an official report, resulted in the deaths of at least 575 people—494 of them Africans—and widespread damage. The government took drastic action, as it had done after a similar crisis when police shot 69 Africans at Sharpeville near Johannesburg in 1960. It arrested hundreds of people and banned seventeen movements that were affiliated to the Black Peoples' Convention, but it was not able to conceal the fact that many Blacks died in detention under suspicious circumstances and that police brutality certainly caused the death of Steve Biko, a popular young Black Consciousness leader. In 1980 there were further major disturbances, starting with protests by Coloured people against their educational system. By then the United Nations General Assembly had suspended South Africa from participation in its proceedings and had created a Special Committee on Apartheid and a Centre in the Secretariat that were giving publicity to the evils of South Africa. Until 1977, France, Great Britain, and the United States had used their vetoes in the Security Council to block resolutions aimed at imposing sanctions against South Africa. In that year, however, shortly after the death of Steve Biko and the banning of the Black Consciousness movements, these Western states joined the others in a unanimous resolution of the Security Council declaring the further acquisition of arms by South Africa to be a threat to world peace and requiring all states to refrain from supplying arms or related material that could be used for military or security purposes.

The isolation of the country was accentuated by the drastic changes that were taking place in the rest of southern Africa. Until 1974, South Africa was protected from invasion or infiltration from the north by buffer states with friendly governments. However, the revolution in Portugal in that year led to the establishment of radical black regimes in Angola and Mozambique; and in 1980 the guerrilla war in Rhodesia-Zimbabwe was brought to an end by a general election based on adult suffrage and the installation of another radical black regime in Salisbury. This transformation of the environment would be completed were Namibia (South West Africa) to be detached from South Africa's grasp, as seemed possible in the early 1980s.

Furthermore, the overthrow of the shah of Iran in 1979 deprived South Africa of its principal source of oil and made it face the permanent prospect of buying oil on the international spot market at dramatically increased prices, since OPEC was applying a boycott against South Africa. However, this was offset by a dramatic rise in the price of gold, a major source of revenue and foreign exchange, which averaged $308 an ounce in 1979, nearly double that in 1980, and over $400 in 1981. Also, the South African Coal, Oil, and Gas Corporation (SASOL) speeded up the construction of two additional plants which, when completed in the early 1980s, were expected to raise its production of oil from coal from 4 percent to between one-third and one-half of the country's needs.

Viewed from Pretoria, the external opposition to the South African system is largely Marxist inspired. The government reluctantly admits that South African Blacks have a genuine case for increased political rights, and it realizes that a black-white accommodation is essential if the country is to become politically stable. If black and white South Africans can present a united front to the world, it argues, they will be able to ward off any Marxist threat. But here it faces a dilemma: how is it to give the Blacks rights which are sufficient to satisfy their aspirations without, at the same time, jeopardizing the white hold on power and losing the support of the existing electorate? The government's answer has been to accelerate its homeland policy. Each African is to be a citizen of his ethnic "Bantustan," and there alone will he enjoy full political rights. To counteract the objection that the land area is inadequate—less than 13 percent of the country's surface—the government is considering enlarging it. In addition, the government has started to lift some of the restrictions on those Africans (an estimated 48 percent of the African population) who are established residents in the urban areas. The effect of this is to allow somewhat freer movement in a more open labor market, but without relinquishing control.[20] Self-governing "community councils" are intended to provide some political self-regulation for these people. The government hopes that its two-pronged policy of Bantustanization and the formation of a relatively privileged group of African urban dwellers will reduce conflict and abate foreign criticism.

The United States and its allies are faced with a difficult series of choices. On the one hand, white South Africans, like all human beings, deserve sympathy and understanding. White communities have dominated other societies elsewhere, without opprobrium, until very recently. The resistance to desegregation in the United States suggests that other communities, placed as the white South Africans are placed, might

20. These cautious and ambiguous changes have followed the reports of two investigative bodies which the government appointed in 1977: a Commission of Inquiry into Labour Legislation under the chairmanship of Professor Nic Wiehahn, and a Commission of Inquiry into Legislation affecting the Utilisation of Manpower under the chairmanship of Dr. P. J. Riekert.

have been just as uncompromising and no more capable of coming to terms with the modern world. Moreover, it is possible that the methods being used to maintain white supremacy in South Africa are so severe that many Blacks have become alienated to the point where they, in turn, would be unwilling to cooperate with Whites even if they were in a position to do so. If this is the case, we have the hallmarks of a classic revolutionary situation in South Africa; and the history of other revolutions reminds us that once violence is unleashed on a scale sufficient to destroy the existing order, the ultimate shape of South African society will be unpredictable. Moreover, the Western industrial countries have profitable investments in South Africa and are partially dependent on access to South Africa's mineral resources, and many of their military strategists regard the Cape sea route as having great strategic importance. These would seem to be potent reasons why the United States and its allies should refrain from becoming deeply involved in efforts to transform South Africa.

But these are not the only relevant considerations. The subjected African, Asian, and Coloured peoples of South Africa certainly deserve sympathy and understanding. Until recently most of their leaders hoped that South African society would become more egalitarian by peaceful evolution from within; but that hope has been denied. The freedom of South African Blacks has been curtailed and their human dignity has been outraged during the very period when their expectations have been raised by the passing of colonial systems elsewhere. It is now natural that they should regard the existing order as both evil and anachronistic, and that they should be highly suspicious of everyone who supports South Africa overtly or covertly. Moreover, the position of the United States and her Western European allies in the modern world is based, not merely on material power, but also—and more fundamentally—on an identification with freedom and justice. Asians and Africans are prone to regard the policy of the United States toward South

Africa as the acid test of its good faith. Further evasion of the issue by the United States would create the risk that the Soviet Union or the People's Republic of China might become the instrument of change in South Africa, and thereby the ultimate beneficiary of the entire African revolution.

Enough has been said to show why, during the coming years, South Africa is likely to generate a further series of crises, the outcome of which will not only determine the future of the local inhabitants but also have profound repercussions on the main course of international relations and on the place of the United States and its allies in the world.

The purpose of this book is to explain the basic facts concerning the peoples and the economy of South Africa, to show how the South African political system has become what it is, and to analyze the system as it operates today. These data will assist the reader to comprehend the complexity of the situation and the problem which is bound to be of concern to all.

2
The Context of the Political System

To understand a political system, we must know something about the context in which it operates. In this chapter, we review the historical background and the demographic and economic conditions of South Africa.

THE HISTORICAL BACKGROUND[1]

From time immemorial southern Africa has been the scene of interactions between diverse peoples. Knowledge about most of these processes is still meagre, but it is evident that by the

1. South African history is a controversial subject. General works in the Western liberal tradition include C. W. de Kiewiet, *A History of South Africa: Social and Economic* (Oxford: Clarendon Press, 1941), which, though dated, is still quite a useful brief introduction; T. R. H. Davenport, *South Africa: A Modern History*, 2d ed. (London and Toronto: Macmillan, 1978), which is very detailed on twentieth-century white politics; and Monica Wilson and Leonard Thompson, eds., *The Oxford History of South Africa* (hereafter cited as *OHSA*), 2 vols. (Oxford: Clarendon Press, 1969, 1971). A younger "radical" interpretation, largely Marxist in orientation, has not yet resulted in a general history of South Africa, but it is strongly represented in H. J. Simons and R. E. Simons, *Class and Colour in South Africa 1850–1950* (Baltimore: Penguin, 1969), and in articles in journals such as the *Journal of Southern African Studies*, published by the Oxford University Press. Harrison M. Wright, *The Burden of the Present: Liberal-Radical Controversy over Southern African History* (Cape Town: David Philip, 1977), discusses the relationship between these traditions. The best examples of Afrikaans historical scholarship are C. F. J. Muller, ed., *Five Hundred Years: A History of South Africa* (Pretoria: Academica, 1969), and F. A.

seventeenth century people earned their livelihood in the region in three different ways: by hunting, by herding, and by farming. Bands of hunters, the San, whom the Whites were to call Bushmen, had become confined to the more arid and mountainous areas; communities of transhumant herders of sheep and cattle, the Khoikhoi, whom the Whites were to call Hottentots, used the pastures in much of the western half of the country; and Bantu-speaking people (the ancestors of the present-day Africans), who owned cattle, raised grain, and used iron implements, occupied most of the better-watered eastern half of the region.[2]

The seventeenth-century position of the Bantu-speaking people of southern Africa represents the southern limit of a prolonged and complex expansive movement that probably began in the vicinity of eastern Nigeria before the beginning of the Christian era. By the seventeenth century, Bantu-speaking people were by far the most numerous and most powerful human element in southern Africa; and if Whites had not intervened, it is probable that they would eventually have completed their occupation of the entire region and conquered and absorbed most of its other inhabitants, as they had already done north of the Limpopo River.

---

van Jaarsveld, *Van van Riebeeck tot Verwoerd* (Johannesburg: Voortrekkerpers, 1971). For an African viewpoint, see W. M. Tsotsi, *From Chattel to Wage Slavery* (Maseru: Lesotho Printing and Publishing Company, 1981). Americans will be interested in George Fredrickson, *White Supremacy: A Comparative Study in American and South African History* (New York: Oxford University Press, 1981).

2. The names "Bushmen," "Hottentots," and "Bantu" are unsatisfactory for several reasons: (a) "Hottentots" and "Bantu" have acquired pejorative connotations and are rejected by present-day black South Africans; (b) though "Bushmen" and "Hottentots" may be regarded as ethnic terms, "Bantu" is essentially a linguistic term; and (c) it is a serious oversimplification to regard the precolonial population as consisting of three clear-cut types distinguished by ethnic, linguistic, and economic factors; these three factors are independent variables. R. R. Inskeep, *The Peopling of Southern Africa* (Cape Town: David Philip, 1978).

Before the nineteenth century the Bantu-speaking people of southern Africa were organized in small polities, varying from single villages with no more than a hundred members who were (or were deemed to be) biologically related to one another, to polities containing many villages and several thousand members. Though the total population increased over the years, most polities remained small because there was a tendency for new ones to be formed by secession from the old; the system as a whole was comparatively stable because wars were conducted within conventional limitations and because fresh land was available for occupation, either between existing settlements or beyond them, to the west and the southwest.

Each polity was ruled by a chief, who held office by virtue of some combination of hereditary and personal qualities. The powers of a chief were limited by well-established customs and by the fact that decisions could only be enforced if they had popular support. In fact, a chief made decisions in consultation with relatives—such as uncles, brothers, and sons—and with commoners who held key offices; and there were means for the rank and file to participate in the political process. For example, among the Sotho, who predominated on the plateau to the northwest of the escarpment, public meetings were quite frequent, and at some such meetings a man was able freely to criticize a decision and the men who made it.

The structure of society in much of southeastern Africa was transformed in the early nineteenth century. The change started among the Nguni, who predominated in the territory between the mountain escarpment and the Indian Ocean. First, Dingiswayo organized the men of his chiefdom into regimental age sets. And then Shaka, who acquired the chieftainship of the small Zulu clan in 1816, perfected the regimental system, introduced new weapons, and embarked upon unlimited wars of conquest.

Within a few years Shaka had created a large, militaristic "kingdom," stretching from the Pongola River in the north to the

Tugela River in the south, and from the sea to the mountain escarpment. His regiments disrupted numerous communities, whose survivors were either absorbed into his kingdom or ejected as refugees. In a chain reaction, destruction and reorganization were carried throughout most of southeastern Africa. Between the Vaal and the Limpopo rivers, Mzilikazi, starting as the leader of a small band of Nguni refugees from Shaka, created the Ndebele Kingdom on Zulu lines; elsewhere, local leaders amalgamated the survivors of other communities into defensive kingdoms, such as Moshweshwe's kingdom of Lesotho in the Caledon River valley. Thus, the political system which had prevailed for several centuries in much of southeastern Africa was transformed by 1836, when the Afrikaner *Voortrekkers* began to penetrate north and east from the Cape Colony.[3]

The white conquest of South Africa took place in two phases. In the first phase—roughly coterminous with the period of rule by the Dutch East India Company (1652–1795)—immigrants from the Netherlands, Germany, France, and other parts of northwestern Europe established themselves in southern Africa and became a distinct and fairly homogeneous community—the embryonic Afrikaner nation. They occupied the western half of the region, from the Cape northward toward the Orange River and eastward toward the Fish River; in the process they conquered the San and the Khoikhoi inhabitants of that area.

Some of the Khoikhoi retreated north of the Orange, where they were conquered in the nineteenth century; others were killed in occasional fighting or died from the ravages of diseases they had not encountered before, especially smallpox. However, many Khoikhoi remained within the expanding frontiers of white settlement, losing their land and their stock and their

3. Philip Curtin et al., *African History* (Boston: Little, Brown, 1978), chaps. 1, 9; Monica Wilson in *OHSA*, vol. 1, chaps. 3, 4; Leonard Thompson in *OHSA*, vol. 1, chap. 8, and *Survival in Two Worlds: Moshoeshoe of Lesotho 1786–1870* (Oxford: Clarendon Press, 1975).

social cohesion and becoming shepherds and cattleherders for the white farmers. Most of the San perished while attempting to resist the white advance; the survivors retreated to the north where they, too, were conquered during the nineteenth century. The Dutch East India Company also imported several thousand slaves into the Cape Colony—from tropical Africa, from Malagasy, and from Southeast Asia.

Miscegenation took place between members of the different communities in the colony, but white fathers did not usually take responsibility for their children by slave and Khoikhoi women, so that the colonial society consisted of a more or less "white" landowning population and "black" slaves of African and Asian origin and serfs of Khoikhoi and mixed descent. Later, after the slaves were emancipated (1834–38), these subordinate groups tended to merge with one another, and their descendants are known, comprehensively, as the Cape Coloured People.[4] Thus in South African terminology, unlike the American, the term "Coloured" is reserved for people of mixed descent.

During the second phase of white conquest, which roughly corresponds with the time of British ascendancy in South Africa (1795–1910), the African chiefdoms were conquered and white settlement was extended to its present limits.[5] In this period the

4. Richard Elphick, *Kraal and Castle: Khoikhoi and the Founding of White South Africa* (New Haven: Yale University Press, 1977); Richard Elphick and Hermann Giliomee, eds., *The Shaping of South African Society 1652–1820* (Cape Town: Longman, 1979).

5. The first significant armed clash between Whites and Bantu-speaking Africans—the Xhosa—took place in 1779; the first clear victory of Whites over Africans (Xhosa) was in 1812; the last African people in South Africa to be brought under white control were the Venda in the 1890s; and the last flicker of resistance on a traditional basis to the imposition of white control was the Zulu rebellion of 1906. Monica Wilson, "Co-operation and Conflict: The Eastern Frontier," in *OHSA*, vol. 1, chap. 6; Leonard Thompson, "The Subjection of the African Chiefdoms, 1870–1898," in *OHSA*, vol. 2, chap. 5; Shula Marks, *Reluctant Rebellion: The 1906–8 Disturbances in Natal* (Oxford: Clarendon Press, 1970); Howard Lamar and Leonard Thompson, eds., *The Frontier in History: North America and Southern Africa Compared* (New Haven: Yale University Press, 1981); D. M. Schreuder, *The Scramble for Southern Africa, 1877–1897* (Cambridge: Cambridge University Press, 1980).

white population was enlarged by further immigration, mainly from Britain, which began in 1820 and reached a considerable scale after the discovery of diamonds in Griqualand West (1867) and of gold on the Witwatersrand (1886). Nevertheless, the descendants of the seventeenth- and eighteenth-century white immigrants, who became known as Afrikaners, at all times outnumbered South Africans of British stock, and they managed to preserve their identity, partly because some of them—the Voortrekkers—left the Cape Colony in and after 1836 and founded independent republics in the interior: the Orange Free State (1854–1900) and the South African Republic, or Transvaal (1852–77 and 1881–1900).[6]

The Bantu-speaking people were conquered piecemeal: some by peaceful penetration, others by force of arms; some by British troops and colonial levies, others by Afrikaner commandos. While the Khoikhoi had lost control of their land, and with it their social and cultural autonomy, more or less abruptly in the process of conquest, the far more numerous and more formidable Bantu-speaking Africans managed to retain possession of enough land to preserve their social and cultural integrity. They kept all of modern Lesotho, most of modern Botswana, and about half of modern Swaziland (territories remaining under British control when the Union of South Africa was founded in 1910), as well as the lands that became the African reserves in the rest of South Africa. Nevertheless, these territories and reserves were not large enough to provide them with a subsistence, and they fell increasingly short of enabling the Africans to satisfy the new needs that were being fostered by traders and missionaries, and to pay the taxes that were being levied by governments. White farmers allowed, encouraged, and sometimes compelled African families to stay on their farms in order to provide them with labor or to pay rent, and when the mining industries developed, they employed large numbers of

6. Eric A. Walker, *The Great Trek* (London: Black, 1938).

Africans, who came from the reserves on short-term contracts and returned there when their contracts expired.[7] In addition, between 1860 and 1911 the Colony of Natal imported laborers from India to work on the coastal sugar estates. When their contracts expired, most of the Indians stayed in South Africa, becoming the nucleus of the present Asian community.[8]

As a result of these events, the economy of the entire southern African region has become closely integrated. The "white areas" draw labor from the surplus which is available in the no longer self-sufficient "homelands."

The Dutch Colonial Administration

During the Dutch period the Cape Colony was a minor dependency in a far-flung commercial empire, subordinate to the company directors in the Netherlands and the Council-of-the-Indies in Batavia, Java.[9] The company built forts and stationed garrisons in the Cape peninsula, which it valued as a stepping-stone on the sea route to Asia. From there, control over the entire colony was meant to be exercised by the governor and other senior officials, subject to instructions from Amsterdam and Batavia. The officials found it expedient to consult colonists when they were discussing colonial affairs, and in time it became accepted that colonists had the right to be consulted. Such consultation was achieved through "burgher councillors," who were appointed by the government from names supplied by the existing burgher councillors.

Beyond the Cape peninsula the government did little to make its authority effective. It established district headquarters at Stellenbosch (1679), Swellendam (1746), and Graaff-Reinet

7. Sheila van der Horst, *Native Labour in South Africa* (London: Oxford University Press, 1942); Francis Wilson, *Labour in the South African Gold Mines 1911–1969* (Cambridge: Cambridge University Press, 1972).

8. Mabel Palmer, *The History of Indians in Natal* (Cape Town: Oxford University Press, 1957).

9. On the Cape Colony during the Dutch period, see Elphick and Giliomee, *Shaping of South African Society*.

(1786) and appointed to each district an official (*Landdrost*) who, aided by one or two clerks and perhaps a handful of soldiers, was expected to keep order throughout a vast district. This he could do only with the cooperation of the white farmers, some of whom (*Heemraden*) were appointed to assist him with advice and to sit with him in hearing petty civil disputes, and others of whom (*Veltkornets*) had military responsibilities; but the only court with criminal jurisdiction in the entire colony was the Court of Justice in Cape Town, six hundred miles from the Fish River. Consequently, the farmers and, more particularly, the seminomadic pastoral farmers (*trekboers*) were very largely a law unto themselves. They improvised their own methods of attack and defense against San, and later against Bantu-speaking Africans; in the 1790s and again in the 1800s they drove the Landdrost out of Graaff-Reinet when he tried to moderate the activities of the commandos against the San, to preserve the peace with the Xhosa chiefdoms, and to take cognizance of the ill-treatment of Khoikhoi servants.[10]

The company built churches at Cape Town and elsewhere, appointed and paid their ministers (*predikants*), and exercised a veto over the appointments of deacons and elders as well as over the decisions of the church councils. Nearly all the white colonists were members of the Dutch Reformed Church. Most of them possessed Bibles, were married in church, and periodically traveled long distances when necessary to take communion (*nagmaal*). There was no private printing press in the colony and no high school, but elementary schools of sorts were attached to the churches. Some of the farmers were close enough to send their children to the schools, while others improvised as best they could to make their children literate.

10. On the trekboers, see P. J. van der Merwe, *Die Trekboer in die Gesbiedenis van die Kaapkolonie 1657–1842* (Cape Town: Nasionale Pers, 1938), and chapters by Leonard Guelke in Elphick and Giliomee, *Shaping of South African Society*, and by Hermann Giliomee and Robert Ross in Lamar and Thompson, *The Frontier in History*.

Thus in their formative days the embryonic Afrikaner people spread over a vast area and became a relatively self-sufficient, individualistic community. Since there were no great opportunities for amassing riches, each man considered himself as good as his fellows, but the racial practices of the Dutch East India Company, fortified by local conditions, caused them to look upon themselves as a distinct and superior community, innately superior to their slaves, their Khoikhoi servants, and their San and Bantu-speaking enemies.[11] While the Cape Colony was ruled by the Dutch East India Company in theory, in practice the company's writ was only effective over the Cape peninsula and some fifty miles inland, beyond which the vacuum was filled by the white farmers who, with their firearms, formed the dominant element in a loose-knit, preindustrial, racially stratified, plural society.

British Colonies and Boer Republics

To prevent the French from getting control of the sea route between Europe and Asia, the British conquered the Cape Colony in 1795 and again in 1806, and they retained it in the peace settlement of 1814–15. British administrators gradually amplified the institutions which the Dutch had created in the Cape Colony. They subdivided the districts into smaller units and applied the rule of law more effectively throughout the colony by sending judges on annual circuits to each district (1811 ff.). They changed the high court into a Supreme Court consisting of qualified lawyers, applying English rules of procedure, including the jury system in criminal cases, while retaining Roman-Dutch law as the common law of the colony (1827 ff.). They

11. I. D. MacCrone, *Race Attitudes in South Africa* (London: Oxford University Press, 1937), and chapters by Richard Elphick and Robert Shell in Elphick and Giliomee, *Shaping of South African Society*, by Hermann Giliomee and Robert Ross in Lamar and Thompson, *The Frontier in History*, and by Martin Legassick in Shula Marks and Anthony Atmore, eds., *Economy and Society in Pre-Industrial South Africa* (London: Longman, 1980).

freed the Khoikhoi from legal restrictions upon their movements (1828) and emancipated the slaves (1834–38).They introduced a system of public education for white children and paid missionary societies small subsidies for educational work among the Coloured and African peoples. They freed the Dutch Reformed Church from state control, and while encouraging other Christian denominations to operate, they refrained from creating an established church. After a sharp dispute, they allowed freedom for the press, subject to the law of libel (1828).

Moreover, having introduced a representative element in local government, in 1854 they created a colonial parliament, consisting of two Houses, both wholly elective by men who possessed a fairly low economic qualification, regardless of race or creed. In 1872, following the precedents set in Canada, Australia, and New Zealand, the parliament acquired control over the executive, subject to the overriding legal supremacy of the British Parliament. When, toward the end of the century, the Cape Colony incorporated the territories as far east as the Natal border at the Umzimvubu River, acquiring a large African population, the franchise qualifications remained color-blind, but the economic requirement was raised slightly and defined so that occupation of land on communal (i.e., customary African) tenure did not suffice, and a simple writing test in the English language was introduced.[12]

In practice the political system in the Cape Colony was always dominated by the white inhabitants whose political groupings tended to correspond with the Afrikaner-British division. No Coloured or African man ever sat in the Cape Parliament, and in 1909, on the eve of the foundation of the Union, when the colony contained about 582,000 Whites, 455,000 Coloured people, 8,000 Asians, and 1,520,000 Africans, 85 percent of the registered voters were white men, 10 percent were Coloured men, and fewer than 5 percent were African. Neverthe-

12. Davenport, *South Africa*, chap. 6.

less, the black voters were numerous enough to determine election results in several constituencies and to act as a moderating
influence over administration and legislation. Whether it was
fully realized or not, the system pointed logically toward the
progressive incorporation of members of the black communities
into the political process.[13]

In the colony of Natal the position was similar in form but
different in substance. The legal system and the institutions of
government were modeled on those of the Cape Colony. A parliament was created in 1856, and it gained control over the
executive in 1893. The fundamental difference lay in the fact
that, though the franchise was color-blind in theory, in practice
the Natal parliament legislated in 1864 to make it virtually
impossible for all but a handful of Africans to become voters and,
in 1896, absolutely to prevent Asians from acquiring the vote,
except for the few who already possessed it. In 1909, when Natal
contained about 98,000 white, 9,000 Coloured, 133,000 Asian,
and 953,000 African people, all the registered voters were white
except for 50 Coloured men, 150 Asians, and 6 Africans. The
consequence was that all branches of the Natal government
tended to operate exclusively in the interests of the white
community—and it was partisan tax laws, coupled with partisan administration, which led to a small but alarming African
rebellion in 1906.[14]

The Voortrekkers' first constitutional improvisations were
for the regulation of their own affairs as migrant communities,
and when they developed those improvisations into territorial
political systems, they ensured that they themselves should
remain dominant by confining participation in the political process to white men and, when necessary, by limiting the political

13. L. M. Thompson, The Unification of South Africa (Oxford: Clarendon
Press, 1960), pp. 109–10.
14. Ibid., pp. 110–11; David Welsh, The Roots of Segregation: Native Policy
in Colonial Natal (Cape Town: Oxford University Press, 1970); Marks, Reluctant
Rebellion.

powers of white men who were not the product of their own communities. Of the two major Boer republics, one—the Orange Free State—developed stability, and the other—the South African Republic—was always chronically unstable. Initially this difference was caused by the fact that the tougher and more factious *Voortrekkers* went farthest north; it persisted because the Orange Free State remained a simple agrarian society of Afrikaners and their African farm laborers, devoid of the complications of extensive African lands or major mining industries, whereas the South African Republic included large African-inhabited areas and also, ultimately, a great gold-mining industry, controlled by foreigners, and was the object of periodic British pressure.[15] The pressure came to a head in the war of 1899–1902, in which Great Britain conquered both the republics and incorporated them in the British Empire.[16]

Within six years from the end of the war, the British Liberals, having won a landslide victory from the Conservatives at the polls, gave the Transvaal and the Orange River Colony responsible government, with constitutions which excluded all but Whites from the franchise and enabled Afrikaner parties to come into power. Then, in 1908–09, a National Convention attended by delegates from the Cape Colony, Natal, the Transvaal, and the Orange River Colony[17]—all of them white men—unanimously

15. On the constitutional history of the Boer republics, see Leonard Thompson, "Constitutionalism in the South African Republics," in *Butterworth's South African Law Review* (Durban) (1954), pp. 49–72.

16. On the origins of the South African War, see Davenport, *South Africa*, chap. 8; J. S. Marais, *The Fall of Kruger's Republic* (Oxford: Clarendon Press, 1961); Ronald Robinson and John Gallagher, with Alice Denny, *Africa and the Victorians: The Official Mind of Imperialism* (London: Macmillan, 1961); Anthony Atmore and Shula Marks, "The Imperial Factor in South Africa in the Nineteenth Century: Towards a Reassessment," *The Journal of Imperial and Commonwealth History* 3 (October 1974): 105–39. Recent studies of the war itself include Thomas Pakenham, *The Boer War* (New York: Random House, 1979), and Peter Warwick, ed., *The South African War* (London: Longman, 1980).

17. The Orange Free State Republic of 1854–1900 became the Orange River Colony of 1900–1910 and the Orange Free State Province of 1910 on.

adopted a constitution for a united South Africa. The constitution was endorsed by the four colonial parliaments and enacted by the British Parliament, and the Union of South Africa came into being on May 31, 1910.[18] Since then, South African political history has been an evolutionary process, which is examined in the later chapters of this book.

Historical Mythologies

In order to understand a political system, historical background is important, not merely in the direct sense that it explains the origins of the social structure and of the institutional framework within which the system operates, but also in the indirect sense that the views people have of their past affect their present political attitudes and conduct. This is often particularly true of people whose values are being challenged and whose survival seems to be threatened, such as the Afrikaner nationalists who rule South Africa.

The principal deduction the more radical Afrikaner nationalists make from their history is that the rest of the world, so far as it has been concerned with them, has been hostile. They discern two sets of traditional enemies. One is composed of the British government and South Africans of British descent: the British government is seen as the oppressor of the Afrikaner people for as long as it had power in South Africa, and the British settlers, as its Trojan horse. British oppression reached its peak in the decade 1895–1905, when Joseph Chamberlain, colonial secretary, and Alfred Milner, high commissioner in South Africa, in collaboration with foreign mining capitalists, exploited the presence of the Uitlander community on the Witwatersrand to provoke a war. The British military commanders resorted to inhumane methods to crush the resistance of the Boer guerrillas,

18. On the origins of the South African constitution, see R. H. Brand, *The Union of South Africa* (Oxford: Clarendon Press, 1909); Nicholas Mansergh, *South Africa 1906–1961: The Price of Magnanimity* (New York: Praeger, 1962); Thompson, *Unification of South Africa*.

and Milner tried to denationalize the Afrikaners by swamping them with British immigrants and educating them into a British mold.

The other set of traditional enemies comprises the black people of southern Africa. San and Bantu-speaking Africans are seen as bloodthirsty savages who blindly resisted the spread of white Christian civilization. In the radical Afrikaner nationalist view of history, the central saga is the Great Trek, when both sets of enemies acted in conjunction. The *Voortrekkers* left the Cape Colony because the government had failed to control the Coloured people within the colony and the Africans on its eastern frontier; they then had to endure attacks by barbarous hordes under Mzilikazi and Dingane, and pursuit by Britain, which annexed their first republic of Natal and their settlements between the Orange and the Vaal rivers.

As is the case with other mythologies, this radical Afrikaner nationalist mythology has germs of truth in it. However, it is so selective, it so continuously imputes pure motives to one group and impure motives to others, that it is a grotesque distortion of the complex historical realities. The distortions are compounded as the mythology is projected from the past into the present and used to inflame present passions and justify present policies. To some Afrikaner nationalists, since Albion (England) was so perfidious throughout the nineteenth century, he cannot be trusted today, nor can other foreign powers with interests in South Africa; and since Africans were so savage, they must still be less than human beings.

From the African point of view, on the other hand, the central theme of recent South African history is white conquest and domination: the expropriation of African land, the perversion of authentic African political systems into subservient tools of the white regime, the reduction of all Blacks to thinly disguised serfdom, and the exclusion of all Blacks from any say in the central government. All else is secondary. The quarrels between the British government and South Africans of British descent are no more than the quarrels of robbers over the spoils.[19]

The irreconcilability of these different historical perspectives is a measure of the schism that exists in modern South Africa.

DEMOGRAPHIC CONDITIONS

South Africa has a racially stratified population, with a dominant white group and three black groups, which are officially designated Coloured, Asian, and African. The growth of these groups between the census of 1911 and the official estimate of 1980, and also an official projection for the year 2000, are shown in the following table.

The ethnic terminology used in South Africa has changed over the years, and today it does not correspond with the terminology used elsewhere. Whites (formerly called Europeans in South Africa) are people who are accepted as being exclusively of European or Caucasoid descent, though in fact a considerable proportion of them have at least one black ancestor. Coloureds are people with a wide variety of ethnic origins. Their ancestors include the slaves who were imported from Malagasy, tropical Africa, and Southeast Asia; local Khoikhoi and San; and white South Africans and white visitors to South Africa. The Asian group originated in the immigration of indentured laborers from India to Natal in the late nineteenth and early twentieth centuries. The Africans were formerly called Natives or Bantu by white South Africans and are called Africans or Blacks by themselves and by the rest of the world. In this book, except when

19. Marianne Cornevin, *Apartheid: Power and Historical Falsification* (Paris: UNESCO, 1980); "Mnguni," *Three Hundred Years*, 3 vols. in 2 (Cape Town: New Era Fellowship, 1952). A popular mythology among South Africans of British descent holds that Afrikaners are responsible for everything that is wrong with South Africa.

TABLE 1. Population of South Africa

Year	Africans		Asians		Coloureds		Whites		Totals
	1,000s	Percent	1,000s	Percent	1,000s	Percent	1,000s	Percent	1,000s
1911	4,019	67.3	152	2.5	525	8.8	1,276	21.4	5,972
1960	10,927	68.3	477	3.0	1,509	9.4	3,088	19.3	16,002
1980	19,955	71.9	795	2.8	2,554	9.2	4,453	16.1	27,757
2000 (est.)	37,300	74.2	1,200	2.4	4,900	9.7	6,900	13.7	50,300

NOTE: These figures include the populations of all the "homelands," including those that are officially independent.

SOURCES: Republic of South Africa, Population Census, 6th September 1960, vol. 1, Geographical Distribution of the Population (Pretoria: Government Printer, R.P. 62/1963), p. 2; Republic of South Africa, Department of Statistics, South African Statistics 1978, 1.6, Bulletin of Statistics, June 1979, and Statistical News Release, September 1980.

official South African terminology is necessarily followed, the terms employed are those in general use elsewhere—Whites, Coloureds, Asians, and Africans—and all but Whites are called, comprehensively, Blacks.

Before 1948 there were loosely defined racial categories which pertained to certain laws. These definitions did not always correspond with each other, and were made only for the purpose of the legislation concerned. After 1948 the government attempted to block mobility from one group to another ("passing") through the Population Registration Act of 1950, which provides for the compilation of a register of the entire population and for the issuing to every South African aged sixteen and over of an identity card specifying his or her race. Until 1962 acceptability by the community was the main test used by officials engaged in race classification, but an amendment of that year altered the definition of a "white" person, making it obligatory for appearance and acceptance to be considered together. A further amendment in 1967 introduced "descent" as the determining factor in race classification, and since then a person may be *accepted* as white and may *appear* to be white, but has to prove that both his parents were white before he can be *classified* as white.[20]

The difficulties that the government has met in giving effect to this crucial part of its program flow from the facts that race itself is an imprecise and, some would say, an unscientific concept, and that, over the centuries, there has been a large but indefinite amount of miscegenation in South Africa. Under the current system, miscegenation between Whites and Blacks, but not between the different black groups, is unlawful. The Immorality Act of 1957 (which replaced similar, earlier legislation) prohibits sexual intercourse between Whites and Blacks outside marriage, and the Prohibition of Mixed Marriages Act of 1949

20. M. Horrell, *Laws Affecting Race Relations in South Africa 1948–1976* (Johannesburg: South African Institute of Race Relations [SAIRR], 1978), pp. 16–17.

prohibits intermarriage between Whites and Blacks. Strenuous
efforts are made to enforce these laws. For example, between
July 1977 and June 1978, the police investigated 363 suspected
contraventions of the Immorality Act. Of these, 295 were
charged.[21] Consequently, so long as the present laws remain in
force, white and black South Africans will be two virtually
endogamous populations, except insofar as they are modified by
the effects of immigration.

The White Population

In a racially stratified society, demographic trends are of great
importance since they affect the relative strengths of the different racial groups. In South Africa the proportions which the
white group bears to the total population and which the Afrikaner community bears to the total white group are both crucial figures.

The white population increased almost fourfold between
1911 and 1980. This was partly due to immigration. From 1924
to 1977 inclusive, about 960,000 white people immigrated to
South Africa, with a peak in 1948 under the United party's
immigration scheme which was then scrapped by the
Nationalist government, and another steep rise during the
economic boom of the 1960s and early 1970s. Before 1948 over
half the white immigrants came from Britain; since then the
British proportion has dropped to about one-third. The balance
has normally come from continental Europe, but in recent years
there has been a large influx from African countries, especially
from Mozambique and Zimbabwe, as a consequence of decolonization. The department of immigration offers incentives to
white people with industrial skills to come to South Africa from
Europe, but with varying success. The immigration rate from
Europe declined for a while as a result of the 1976 disturbances

---

21. South African Institute of Race Relations, *Survey of Race Relations in
South Africa, 1979* (Johannesburg: SAIRR, 1980), p. 73.

in Soweto and elsewhere; but this was offset by an increase in the number of white immigrants from Mozambique and Zimbabwe.

There has always been a considerable emigration of Whites from South Africa. Although there was a net immigration of about 540,000 Whites between 1924 and 1977, some 420,000 left the country in those years. The number of emigrants exceeded the immigrants in 1960, 1977, and 1978, times of considerable political uncertainty. Among the emigrants were a high proportion of professional men, such as doctors and university teachers, and also considerable numbers of talented young South Africans.[22]

The primary cause of the increase in the white population is not immigration but a moderately high birthrate in conjunction with a very low deathrate. Recently, however, the rate of natural increase has declined and there has been an upward shift in the average age. If, as seems likely, present trends continue, the white proportion of the total population, which has already been declining, will decline still further. It is likely that it will fall below 14 percent by the end of the century.

Within the white population there are still two fairly distinct major communities, identifiable by their different home languages—Afrikaans and English. The Afrikaners have always been the more numerous and their preponderance is increasing. In 1936, 55.9 percent of the total white population spoke Afrikaans at home, and in 1976 an estimated 59 percent.[23] Immigration has strengthened the English-speaking community more than the Afrikaner, since many of the immigrants speak English and others—some even among those from the Netherlands—

22. For immigration and emigration statistics, 1924–58, see Union of South Africa, Union Statistics for Fifty Years (Pretoria: Government Printer, 1960), sec. C; for 1958–77, see South African Statistics, 1978 (Pretoria: Government Printer, 1979); for 1978–79, see Bulletin of Statistics (Pretoria: Government Printer), Quarter End, December 1979.
    23. Union Statistics for Fifty Years, p. A-18; South African Statistics, 1978, p. 1.29.

have moved into the English-speaking community in South Africa.

On the other hand, most of the white emigrants, too, have been English-speakers; few Afrikaners have emigrated. Nevertheless, the major cause of the increase in the Afrikaner numerical superiority is that the Afrikaner birthrate has been higher, which is related to the fact that a much higher proportion of Afrikaners than English-speaking Whites have always been rural. Over the years intermarriages have taken place between members of the two communities, so there are Afrikaans-speaking Smiths and English-speaking van Rynevelds, but intermarriages are still frowned upon in some quarters. The maintenance of the distinction between the two communities is promoted by the constitutional provision under which English and Afrikaans are both official languages of the Republic, and by the educational ordinances of the Transvaal, the Orange Free State, and the Cape Province, which compulsorily divide most of the white children into two groups, to attend Afrikaans- or English-medium public schools.

By 1911 white farmers owned nearly all the usable land outside the African reserves. Afrikaners owned most of it, the only substantial pockets of farmland owned by English-speaking whites being in the southeastern Cape Province and in Natal. Even then, 52 percent of the white population— including the large majority of the English-speakers and a small minority of the Afrikaners—lived in towns and villages, but the Witwatersrand gold-mining industry was still the only major industry in the country.[24]

Today much the same area remains in white hands, but there has been some expansion of Afrikaner holdings at the expense of English-speakers. The number of white people living on the land has declined since 1936, so that the entire increase in the white population since 1911—and more—has been ab-

24. *Union Statistics for Fifty Years*, p. A-10.

sorbed into the towns.[25] In 1960, 84 percent of the white population was urban (93 percent of the English-speakers and 76 percent of the Afrikaners); and Afrikaners formed 56 percent of the white urban population and 74 percent of the white rural population. In 1970, 86.8 percent of the white population was urban.[26] These trends are continuing. Afrikaners now comprise a clear majority of the white population in every rural area of the country except a portion of the southeastern Cape Province and central and southern Natal, and at least a substantial minority in every major industrial complex.

Throughout the white population, class and ethnicity are both important factors. Despite their massive movement to the towns since the 1920s, the Afrikaners still form a self-conscious ethnic community. Descended very largely from about a thousand people who were "free burghers" in the Cape Colony in 1691, they formerly possessed many of the characteristics of an extended family. The great grandfathers of nearly every living Afrikaner were farmers. To this day most Afrikaners are active members of a Dutch Reformed Church congregation; and there are many powerful institutions and voluntary associations which are dedicated to the promotion of Afrikaner ethnic interests. Nevertheless, there have always been considerable differences of wealth and status among Afrikaners, and these have been greatly accentuated by urbanization and industrialization during the last half century.[27] With South African ancestors dating back no further than 1820—and rarely so far—the English-speaking Whites are much more conscious of their external origins and links. In comparison with Afrikaners, they

25. The "white rural" population of South Africa was 696,471 in 1936, 571,014 in 1951, 522,707 in 1960, and 498,036 in 1970. *Population Census, 1960, Sample Tabulation No. 3*, p. 6; *South African Statistics, 1978*, 1.13.

26. *South African Statistics, 1978*, 1.13.

27. Hermann Giliomee, "The Growth of Afrikaner Identity" and "The Afrikaner Economic Advance," in Heribert Adam and Hermann Giliomee, *Ethnic Power Mobilized: Can South Africa Change?* (New Haven: Yale University Press, 1979), chaps. 4 and 6.

have always been very heterogeneous. Located in several separate pockets of settlement in South Africa, with diverse religious
affiliations and often conflicting economic interests, they have
never had a comparable sense of ethnic solidarity. Moreover,
though most of them are of British origin, about one in fifteen are
Jews. The people of Portuguese descent, who have flocked to
South Africa from Angola and Mozambique since 1974, are
culturally distinct from both the Afrikaner and the British communities.

The Coloured and Asian Populations

The Coloured population increased over fourfold between 1911
and 1980. This increase was not affected by migration, for practically all the Coloured people were born in South Africa and
few have left it. Nor has the increase been appreciably affected
by "passing," although until recently passing did take place into
the Coloured group from the Asian and the African, and out of
the Coloured group into the white. The rate of increase is essentially the result of a remarkably high birthrate in conjunction
with a moderately high deathrate. The Coloured group seems
likely to continue to increase more rapidly than the Whites for
some time to come, as their average age is still low, their birthrate remains high, and their deathrate is dropping.[28] If the laws
against miscegenation are repealed at some future date, ultimately the Coloured group would be likely to form a much
higher proportion of the total population.

The Coloured people have virtually no ties with traditional
black cultures, for the societies of their Khoikhoi ancestors disintegrated long ago, and their Malagasy, tropical African, and
Southeast Asian ancestors were removed from their own
societies when they were brought to South Africa in the seventeenth and eighteenth centuries. Indeed, most of the traits of the

28. *South African Statistics, 1978,* 3.7–3.32.

Coloured people are those of the Afrikaners, with whom they have always been intimately associated. Most of them speak Afrikaans at home; the remainder speak English.[29] Nearly all of them are Christians, with a preference for the Dutch Reformed churches, except for some 6.5 percent, known as the Cape Malays, who are Muslims and are treated in some respects as a separate subgroup.[30]

Ever since they began to emerge through the fusion of diverse stocks, the Coloured people have been part of a white-controlled society. Initially they were the slaves and the serfs of the Afrikaners in the preindustrial Cape Colony. Today most of them are still dependent on white employers; and most of them still live in the western part of the Cape Province, where they form a majority of the total population and there are relatively few Africans. Two-thirds of the Coloured people now live in towns.[31] Though most of them are very poor, there is a well-defined internal class system, status depending in part on educational and economic achievements and in part on skin color, with a light complexion carrying prestige. There is a considerable middle class, whose members have the tastes, the standards, and the aspirations of the middle classes in modern Western societies in Europe and America.

Between 1911 and 1980 the Asian population, too, multiplied more than fourfold. Like the Coloured population growth, the Asian was scarcely affected by migration in this period. The importation of indentured Indian laborers ceased in 1911 and, with very few exceptions, Asians have not been permitted to enter South Africa since 1913. Consequently, by 1980 practically the entire group was South-African born. In spite of the fact that until recently it was the policy of the South African government to treat Asians as temporary residents and to offer them inducements to return to India or Pakistan, few Asians ever

29. Ibid., 1.29.
30. Ibid., 1.30.
31. Ibid., 1.18.

made use of the opportunity,[32] and the government now ac-
knowledges that the Asians form a permanent element in the
South African population. The rapid increase in the Asian group
is essentially the result of a birthrate that is very high, though not
quite as high as the Coloured, in conjunction with a distinctly
lower deathrate than that of the Coloured people.[33] The birthrate
is now on the decline; between 1936–50 it was 3.14 percent, and
between 1951–70 it dropped to 2.88 percent.[34] The internal
structure of the Asian group is complex, with two superimposed
types of differences. First, though most of their ancestors came
as labor migrants from India, they came from different regions
and different castes. Though caste distinctions are no longer
significant among South African Asians, there are still fundamental religious distinctions among them. Second, during the
century since the Asians took root in South Africa, they have
been influenced in various ways through living as a minority
and subordinate group in a plural society. For example, while
most of them speak an Asian language at home, there are many
such languages (with Tamil, Hindi, Gujarati, Telegu, and Urdu
the most common); most Asians understand English also, and
about one-third speak English at home.[35] Again, while two-
thirds call themselves Hindus and one-fifth Muslims, Hinduism
and Islam bear many faces in South Africa, as elsewhere; 8
percent are Christians of one denomination or another.[36] Most
Asians are extremely poor, but there are many small traders and
clerks and a small peak of wealthy and educated people, among
whom the norms of the Western world tend to be dominant. Over
four-fifths of the Asians live in Natal, and most of the balance in
the Transvaal. Also, four-fifths of them now live in towns—half

32. *Union Statistics for Fifty Years*, p. A-24.
33. *Survey of Race Relations, 1979*, p. 71.
34. *South African Statistics, 1978*, 1.12.
35. Ibid., 1.29.
36. Ibid., 1.30.

of them in Durban, where they are the most numerous of the four racial groups.[37]

Although the Asian and Coloured groups have a similar status in South Africa, they differ in many respects. The Asians are a much more cohesive community than the Coloureds. For example, the rate of illegitimate births in the early 1970s was 43 percent among Coloureds and only 7 percent among Asians.[38]

The African Population

The African population multiplied by about four and a half times between 1911 and 1980. Other territories in southern Africa have contributed to this increase. Some of the immigrants entered South Africa under the auspices of the mining corporations' recruiting agencies and evaded repatriation when their contracts ended, but others came independently and for the most part their entry has not been recorded, so that the total volume is not known. The government estimates that in 1978 there were 576,043 "foreign Bantu" in the Republic.[39]

Vital statistics are not available for the African population of the Republic as a whole because there is still a serious under-registration of births and deaths, but there is evidence of a very high birthrate linked with a high deathrate—including exceptionally high infant mortality, much malnutrition, and periodic local famines. The result of these factors gives the Africans a much higher rate of increase than the other population groups. The minister of statistics estimated that in 1978 the African natural increase rate was 28.0 per thousand population; in 1977 the figure for Whites was 8.9 per thousand and for Coloureds and Asians 16.2 and 18.7 per thousand, re-

37. Ibid., 1.13.
38. Kogila A. Moodley, "South African Indians: The Wavering Minority," in Leonard Thompson and Jeffrey Butler, eds., *Change in Contemporary South Africa* (Berkeley: University of California Press, 1975), p. 252.
39. *South African Statistics, 1978*, 1.28.

spectively.[40] A rapid increase in the African population is to be expected, since diet and medical facilities are gradually improving. It is virtually certain that the Africans will continue to form over 70 percent of the total population of the Republic of South Africa, including the "homelands," and will approach three-quarters by the end of the century.

In southern Africa, traditional differences, such as those between the Nguni and the Sotho peoples, and those between chiefs and commoners, are no longer the principal determinants of the structure of the African population. The reason for this is that the Africans have experienced an exceptionally powerful alien impact, in terms of both duration and intensity. As early as the 1830s when, with a few exceptions, white activity in tropical Africa was still confined to the coastline, white missionaries in southern Africa were working among all the major African chiefdoms, and white settlers were moving into what became Natal, the Orange Free State, and the Transvaal. Fifty years later, when the scramble for tropical Africa was only just beginning, Whites had firm control over nearly all the traditional societies of southern Africa. And later still, white people were transforming the African societies of southern Africa far more radically than those of tropical Africa. White South African governments were reducing the chiefs to petty local officials—appointing them, paying them, controlling their public conduct in detail, and dismissing them at will—and white South African farmers and industrialists were drawing an ever-larger number of Africans into their service as laborers. Consequently, in tropical Africa most of the traditional societies remained relatively intact throughout the colonial epoch, and the postcolonial governments are experiencing great difficulties in welding the inhabitants of their states into nations. In South Africa the traditional societies have been thoroughly disrupted; in their place, the primary regional division among Africans is between

40. *Survey of Race Relations, 1979*, p. 71.

those who live in the "homelands," those who live in the "white rural areas," and those who live in the towns.

The "homelands"[41] are important in that they provide the territorial basis for the government's policy of apartheid, or separate development. They include those parts of the Republic that are reserved for African occupation. They represent what is left to the Africans of their ancestral landholdings after the disturbances of the Shaka period and after white conquest and settlement. In 1913, when about twenty-three million acres were occupied by Africans, the Natives Land Act gave Africans exclusive possession of those areas, prohibited Africans from acquiring possession of land outside them, and recommended that they should be enlarged. In 1936, by which time some three million acres had been added, the Native Trust and Land Act defined a number of "released areas" which were also to be added, but set no time limit for their transfer. Ultimately, if the 1936 act is fully implemented, the "homelands" will be about forty-one million acres, or 13.7 percent of the land area of the Republic; in 1976 they were actually about thirty-six million acres, or 12 percent of its area.[42]

The "homelands" form not one block of territory, nor even a few large blocks, but several hundred separate units, varying in size from the Transkei, with over eight million acres, to holdings of a few hundred acres surrounded by farms owned by white people. Viewed together, they take the shape of a fragmented horseshoe, the southeastern arm lying on the seaward side of the mountains between the Fish River and the Mozambique border and the northwestern arm on the plateau from the northern Cape, across the northern Transvaal to the Kruger National Park. Lesotho and Swaziland are contiguous with parts of the southern arm—Botswana with parts of the northern arm. Recently the government has been trying to consolidate the "homelands" by

41. See the map on page xiv.
42. *Survey of Race Relations, 1977*, p. 312.

a compulsory removal of Africans from "black spots" and resettlement on land acquired contiguous to existing larger units; however, the position is still one of intense fragmentation.[43]

Currently, only approximately nine million Africans are in the "homelands" at any given moment, and some eleven million are in the rest of the country—many in the rural areas, where most of them are farm laborers, but more than half in the towns, where most of them are industrial workers.[44] The farm laborers are the most static and depressed of the three subgroups. Scattered in tiny clusters over vast areas, they lack the facilities for community life that Africans have in the "homelands" and the opportunities for change that they have in the towns. The urban African population has been burgeoning throughout the twentieth century, increasing tenfold between 1911 and 1970. Many Africans, especially men of working age, still move at irregular intervals between the "homelands" and the towns, spending most of their working days in the towns, but maintaining a family in the "homelands" and keeping their right to share in the use of "tribal" land, to which they retire when they are no longer employable. Perhaps a million of the Africans who are in the towns fit into this category, and another one-third of a million are temporary immigrants from foreign countries;[45] but the number of Africans who have become essentially urbanized, having severed all connections elsewhere, has grown rapidly. In 1960 this was estimated at two and two-thirds millions; today this number has probably more than doubled.[46]

43. *Survey of Race Relations, 1978*, p. 268.
44. *Survey of Race Relations, 1979*, p. 71.
45. Ibid., p. 209.
46. The concept of permanent urbanization is a difficult one to define and still more difficult to apply statistically in any country, especially to the Africans in the Republic of South Africa. The South African Council of Scientific and Industrial Research made a sample survey of more than a thousand mine laborers, employees of public authorities, and industrial workers in and around Johannesburg in 1961 and found that 70 percent could be counted as industrial workers who had never reverted to rural employment, and 50 percent could be regarded as permanently urbanized in the sense that they had lived in town for at

TABLE 2. Populations of the "Homelands," 1977

People	"Homeland"	De Facto Population			De Jure Population	Population outside "Homeland" (%)
		African	Other	Total		
Tswana	Bophuthatswana	1,218,400	3,700	1,222,100	2,161,000	43.4
Xhosa	Transkei	2,419,500	14,500	2,434,000	4,032,200	39.6
Xhosa	Ciskei	530,600	4,300	534,900	995,800	46.3
Tsonga	Gazankulu	344,500	500	345,000	836,000	49
Zulu	KwaZulu	2,800,600	10,800	2,811,400	5,166,000	45.6
Swazi	KaNgwane	213,600	300	213,900	606,000	64.7
Pedi	Lebowa	1,432,200	3,300	1,435,500	2,066,000	30.5
S.Sotho	QwaQwa	92,700	200	92,900	1,745,000	94.7
Venda	Venda	348,400	700	349,100	461,000	24.3
Other*					1,104,000	
Totals		9,400,500	38,300	9,438,000	19,083,000	50.5

*Includes North and South Ndebele, foreign Africans, and Africans whose home tongue is English or Afrikaans. Since this table was compiled, the government has created a new "homeland" for the southern Ndebele. Its population is about 200,000 and is almost exclusively African.

Source: Loraine Gordon et al., comps., *Survey of Race Relations in South Africa, 1978* (Johannesburg, 1979), p. 272, citing the Bureau for Economic Research, Co-operation and Development.

In their home environment, nearly all Africans speak one of nine related Southern Bantu languages. The languages in the Nguni group are close enough for easy communication, as are those in the Sotho group; but a Nguni-speaker cannot easily communicate with a Sotho-speaker. By 1960 about 40 percent of the Africans were able to speak English or Afrikaans, and roughly the same number were able to read and write.[47] Since then both these proportions have been rising.

The effects of Christian missionaries in South Africa are reflected in the religious statistics. By 1970 two-thirds of the Africans professed to be Christians; three-fifths of these were members of churches with international affiliations (the most popular being the Methodist, Catholic, Anglican, Dutch Reformed, and Lutheran churches, in that order); and the remainder were members of separatist churches, of which there are legion.[48]

---

least five years, had their families with them, held no land rights in the "homelands," and never visited the rural areas. *Survey of Race Relations, 1962,* pp. 111–12. See also Francis Wilson, "The Political Implications for Blacks of Economic Changes Now Taking Place in South Africa," in Thompson and Butler, *Change in Contemporary South Africa,* chap. 7.

47. *South African Statistics, 1978,* 1.35.

48. Studies of African society in the major industrial centers of the Republic include: Philip Mayer, ed., *Xhosa in Town: Studies of the Bantu-speaking Population of East London, Cape Province,* 3 vols. (Cape Town: Oxford University Press, 1961–63); Philip Mayer, *Black Villages in an Industrial Society* (Cape Town: Oxford University Press, 1980), and "Class, Status and Ethnicity as Perceived by Johannesburg Africans," in Thompson and Butler, *Change in Contemporary South Africa,* chap. 6; Francis Wilson, *Labour in the South African Gold Mines* and *Migrant Labour: Report to the South African Council of Churches* (Johannesburg: Study Project on Christianity in Apartheid Society, 1972); M. Brandel-Syrier, *Reeftown Elite: A Study of Social Mobility in a Modern African Community on the Reef* (London: Routledge and Kegan Paul, 1971); M. Wilson and A. Mafeje, *Langa: A Study of Social Groups in an African Township* (Cape Town: Oxford University Press, 1963); M. West, *Bishops and Prophets in a Black City* (Cape Town: David Philip, 1975). There is also much relevant information in the works of African writers such as Ezekiel Mphahlele, *Down Second Avenue* (London: Faber and Faber, 1959, and later editions), and *The Unbroken Song, Selected Writings* (Johannesburg: Ravan Press, 1981); Naboth Mokgatle,

As these statistics suggest, besides the division between the "homelands," the "white rural areas," and the towns, the other main cleavage that runs through the African population involves conservatives and modernists. The more conservative African is likely to be rural, illiterate, and pagan; the more modern African is apt to be urban, educated, and Christian. There are all sorts of permutations and combinations of these qualities, including urban clusters of Africans who remain illiterate and pagan, and rural clusters who are educated and Christian. The trend, however, seems to be away from traditionalism, since in all parts of the country, including the "homelands," political autonomy and economic self-sufficiency, which were essential conditions of traditional African society, have completely disappeared. It is in the industrial centers, especially the Witwatersrand, where there are Africans from all parts of southern Africa, that a new urban culture is emerging—a culture shaped from the realities of modern industrial life. Among the urban Africans there is a growing middle class, composed largely of teachers, nurses, clergy, clerks, bus drivers, truckers, machine operators, and traders, who are comparable to their counterparts in other countries and to whom the "homelands" and their chiefs are relics of a bygone age.

This review of the demography of South Africa concludes with a consideration of the ethnic structures of the populations of the three main types of areas—"homeland," "white rural," and urban. Table 3 shows the distribution of the population when the 1980 census was taken.

The "homelands" are overwhelmingly African. They include a few thousand Whites, Coloureds, and Asians, as well as six and a half million Africans. Perhaps another half million Africans have homes in the "homelands" but were absent when the last census was taken. Most of the migrants are men, so that

---

The Autobiography of an Unknown South African (Berkeley: University of California Press, 1971); Can Themba, The Will to Die (London: Heinemann, 1972); and Nat Nakase, The World of Nat Nakase (Johannesburg: Ravan Press, 1975).

TABLE 3. Distribution of the South African Population, 1980

	"Homelands"*	"White Rural Areas"	Urban Areas	Totals
Whites	8,682	486,077	3,958,514	4,453,273
Coloureds	5,998	574,814	1,973,227	2,554,039
Asians	6,210	65,761	722,668	794,639
Africans	6,423,889	4,527,994	4,940,699	15,892,582

*Excluding Bophuthatswana, Transkei, and Venda. In 1980 the population of these three "independent homelands" totaled about 4 million people, nearly all of them Africans.

SOURCE: Republic of South Africa, Department of Statistics, *Statistical News Release,* September 1980.

there are always many more women than men in the "home-lands." The distribution of the Xhosa-speaking people is an interesting example. In 1977 there were about 5 million Xhosa, of whom 2.4 million were in the Transkeian "homeland," half a million were in the Ciskeian "homeland," and two million were in the "white" parts of the Republic—some as farm laborers, others as industrial workers, some as temporary migrants, others as permanent residents of farms and towns.[49]

The "white rural areas" are white in the sense that most of the land is owned by Whites, but not in the demographic sense. Indeed, Whites are fewer than one-ninth of their total population, and the overwhelming majority are black farm laborers— Africans in most parts of the country and Coloureds in the southwestern Cape Province.

In the towns, which are also regarded as white districts, the Whites number only about one out of every three persons. The populations of the principal urban areas recorded in the 1980 census were as follows.

49. *South African Statistics, 1978,* 1.15–1.16; *Survey of Race Relations, 1978,* p. 272.

TABLE 4. Urban Population of South Africa, 1980

	White	Coloured	Asian	African	Other	Total
Witwatersrand	1,175,241	150,703	69,788	1,851,934	6,732	3,254,398
Cape Town	427,692	660,321	11,536	174,566	1,281	1,275,666
Durban	232,626	44,062	154,943	224,314	688	656,633
Pretoria	351,590	14,746	14,867	146,766	438	528,207
Port Elizabeth	128,605	115,383	4,405	241,844	1,903	492,140
Vanderbijl Park Vereeniging	150,761	9,075	3,606	348,908	175	512,455
Sasolburg OFS Goldfields	59,860	5,374	0	238,972	0	304,206
Totals	2,526,375	999,664	259,145	3,227,304	11,217	7,023,705

SOURCE: Republic of South Africa, Department of Statistics, *Statistical News Release*, September 1980. Official figures such as these underestimate the number of Africans in the towns, for two reasons: town boundaries do not include all the de facto urbanized areas; and numerous de facto urbanized Africans evade census-takers because they are not legally entitled to be in towns. The Witwatersrand includes all magisterial districts from Randfontein in the west to Nigel in the east; Cape Town includes Wynberg, Simonstown, Bellville, and Kuils River; Durban includes Umlazi; and the OFS Goldfields are the districts of Odendaalsrus, Virginia, and Welkom.

The dynamic elements in South Africa are to be found in these towns. There most of the wealth of South Africa is produced. There, whatever the laws may be, complex and irreversible processes of cultural interaction are taking place. There the South African society of the future is being born. And there it is likely that the South African political struggle will be decided.

ECONOMIC CONDITIONS

Two facets of the South African economy are of great political significance.[50] The first is its strength: it is a strong economy by any standards and it is becoming stronger. The second is its inequality: there are exceptional inequalities of wealth in South Africa and those inequalities correspond closely with race.

The present South African economy is the cumulative product of four types of economic activity initiated at different times: subsistence farming, formerly practised by the Khoikhoi and African communities and by most of the white settlers;[51] farming to produce a significant surplus for local or overseas

50. A useful general account of the South African economy is in D. Hobart Houghton, The South African Economy, 4th ed. rev. (Cape Town: Oxford University Press, 1976). See also J. A. Lombard, ed., Economic Policy in South Africa (Cape Town: Hollandsch Afrikaansche Uitgevers Maatschappy, 1974). There are several official periodicals, including the quarterly Bulletin of Statistics of the South African Reserve Bank and the biennial South African Statistics; also nonofficial periodicals, The South African Journal of Economics and The Review of African Political Economy. Relevant articles appear in The Journal of Southern African Studies, published by the Oxford University Press, and the Journal of Modern African Studies, published by the Cambridge University Press.

51. To describe a community as comprised of subsistence farmers is not to deny that it had some internal specialization, or that it bartered or sold some of its produce. The African farming communities had specialized metal workers and bartered from village to village; and the Afrikaner trekboers sold some of their stock on the hoof to traveling butchers' agents from Cape Town, thus acquiring the means to buy a few necessities—such as guns, ammunition, sugar, coffee, and tea—from traveling traders.

markets, which was first practised by some of the early white settlers in the neighborhood of Cape Town but only became the practice of the majority of the white farmers during the late nineteenth century; mining, which began on an extensive scale in the late nineteenth century and is still an expanding activity; and manufacturing, which received its first strong impetus when overseas supplies declined during World War I and has expanded greatly, and more or less continuously, since about 1935.

Today the African "homelands" are a survival of the subsistence farming system of the Africans, modified by a great increase in the density of population and by the existence of a large and growing market for African labor in the rest of the Republic. Nearly all the African inhabitants of the "homelands" are wholly, or partly, mixed farmers, holding their land under communal tenure and producing very little for internal exchange and virtually nothing for sale outside the "homelands." These areas are overstocked with poor-quality cattle, sheep, and goats; their crops—mainly corn and millet—are of low yield and poor quality; and soil erosion is widespread. Road and rail communications are poor.

Rehabilitation schemes are beginning to improve the agriculture, at the cost of depriving many of the people of their traditional rights to land. However, scarcely any industrial opportunities exist for the displaced Africans in the "homelands," not only because their location is unfavorable, but also because the government prohibited private investment in the "homelands," by non-Africans until 1968, and is itself making only a small contribution to their development. The only town in the entire Transkei with a population of more than 5,000 is Umtata, which has about 25,000.[52] It is government policy to house many of the Africans who are removed from the land in new dormitory

52. Umtata is the capital and principal trading center of the Transkei. In 1970 it had a population of 20,229 Africans, 3,542 Whites, and 1,067 Coloureds. *Standard Encyclopedia of South Africa* (Cape Town: Nasau, 1975), 11:52.

townships just inside the borders of the "homelands" and to employ them in new private manufacturing industries just outside their borders, but the new industries are slow to develop.

The "homelands" are therefore backward by any standards and seem doomed to remain so for the foreseeable future. In the broader economic context they are reservoirs of labor for the expanding capitalist sector of the South African economy. In the broader political context, though the regions were originally proclaimed in part for the humanitarian purpose of saving for the Africans a portion of their ancestral land, they have for a long time provided white South Africans with a pretext for treating all Africans as temporary visitors elsewhere in the Republic, and are currently used as a pretext for depriving Africans of South African citizenship.[53]

The "white rural areas" are divided into about a hundred thousand farms with an average area of about two thousand acres. The farms are owned and managed by white people and operated by black laborers. Between 1924 and 1970 the gross value of arable farming and livestock products increased from 58 million Rand to 1,336 million Rand.[54] The principal field crops (in order of value) are corn (maize), fresh fruits, wheat, sugarcane, vegetables, tobacco, potatoes, vines, hay, and groundnuts; the principal livestock products are wool, milk and other dairy products, beef, mutton, poultry and poultry products, and pork.

53. On the economy of the "homelands," see Colin Bundy, The Rise and Fall of a South African Peasantry (London: Heinemann, 1979); Jeffrey Butler, Robert Rotberg, and John Adams, The Black Homelands of South Africa: The Political and Economic Development of Bophuthatswana and KwaZulu (Berkeley: University of California Press, 1977); Robin Palmer and Neil Parsons, eds., The Roots of Rural Poverty: Historical Essays on the Development of Underdevelopment in Central and Southern Africa (Berkeley: University of California Press, 1977); Republic of South Africa, Bantu Investment Corporation, Homelands: The Role of the Corporations in the Republic of South Africa (Pretoria: Government Printer, 1975); Ciskei Commission Report (Silverton, Transvaal: Conference Associates, 1980).
54. Houghton, The South African Economy, p. 263.

South Africa is virtually self-sufficient in foodstuffs and has a considerable surplus for export.

The principal mining industries produce the following:

TABLE 5. South African Mining Products, 1979

	Quantity Sold		Value of Sales
Gold	703,273	kilograms	R5,844,041,000
Coal	103,458,000	tons	1,145,878,000
Diamonds	8,395,000	carats	524,679,000
Asbestos	245,000	tons	107,044,000
Copper	196,000	tons	270,988,000
Manganese ore	5,208,000	tons	175,520,000
Iron ore	31,566,000	tons	293,830,000
Chrome	3,132,000	tons	88,743,000
Fluorspar	521,000	tons	30,126,000
Other minerals, (including the platinum group, uranium, and vanadium)			1,071,300,000

SOURCE: Republic of South Africa, *Bulletin of Statistics*, June 1980, 5.2, 5.3. The mid-1980 value of the Rand was US $1.32 or UK £0.54; at the end of 1981, it was US $1.02 or UK £0.54. The average London gold price was $308.16 an ounce in 1979 and $614 an ounce in 1980; at the end of 1981, it was ca. $410 an ounce.

The South African gold-mining industry has been the greatest in the world for nearly a century. Since the Second World War the techniques for extracting gold at deep levels and from low-grade ores have improved, and new mines have been brought into operation on the Far West Rand and in the Orange Free State. For several years prior to 1971, the price of gold had been fixed at $35 an ounce. Profits in the industry could only be maintained by increasing production, and the long-term future for the industry was bleak. This changed dramatically with the introduction of a free market price for gold in 1971. After that, the price of gold soared to much higher levels but became extremely volatile. It reached over $800 an ounce early in 1980 and dropped below $400 during part of 1981. These new levels had two important consequences for the gold-mining industry: they multiplied profits, and they extended the life expectancy of many mines which, under the previous price structure, would have ceased production.[55] In contrast to the earlier trend, the quantity of gold production declined from a peak of one million kilograms in 1970 to 702,000 kilograms in 1979. This reflected a policy decision to lengthen the life of the mines by reducing the grade of the ore treated. The fine gold content per ton of ore increased from 6.49 grams to a peak of 13.1 grams in 1968, after which it decreased to 8.4 grams in 1979.[56] With the higher gold prices, more mines were opened and the industry had the prospect for a long life. The profitability of the gold mines has been further enhanced by the important by-production of significant quantities of uranium.

The importance of the price of gold to the South African economy cannot be overestimated. A high price creates an economic boom, and a low price threatens recession. At an average price of over 600 dollars an ounce in 1980, the value of gold increased by 1700 percent in ten years in dollars and more than 1800 percent in Rands. Consumer prices in South Africa increased by about 250 percent over the same period. Therefore, at 600 dollars an ounce, the real price of gold was about fifteen times higher than in 1970.[57] The effects were remarkable. In 1980, South Africa probably had the highest growth rate of any country in the world, and the gold-mining industry provided the state with over R1,000 million in taxation. In the fiscal year

55. In 1963 gold sales totaled less than one billion Rands; in 1979 they totaled nearly six billion Rands (Monthly Bulletin of Statistics [July 1964], sec. D, and Bulletin of Statistics, Quarter End, June 1980, 5.2). Gold sales in 1980 were over ten billion Rands.

56. Focus on Key Economic Issues (Pretoria: Mercabank, March 25, 1980), p. 2.

57. Brian Kantor, Financial Mail, August 22, 1980, p. 845.

ending March 31, 1981, there was a budget surplus of about R1,200 million.[58] However, later in 1981 the price of gold fell to about $400 an ounce, and South Africa entered a recession.

South Africa's coal production has increased eightfold since 1910. Diamonds, too, are still an important product, but most South African diamonds are gems, and their production and sale are limited, to maintain price. South Africa also produces appreciable quantities of many other minerals, including a high proportion of the total world production of four of the other twenty-six minerals that are regarded as being of critical importance to the modern world economy: vanadium, the platinum group, chrome ore, and manganese ore.

Besides being a major producer of these minerals, South Africa also possesses significant reserves—reserves being the total amounts that have been identified in areas that have been well prospected. Estimates vary. The following table comes from the *Financial Mail* of Johannesburg:

TABLE 6. South Africa's Share of World Mineral Reserves (Estimated as a Percentage of Western World and World Reserves)

Mineral Commodity	Reserves (Metric Tons)	Western World Rank	%	World Rank	%
Vanadium (metal, 30m depth)	7,760,000	1	90	1	49
Platinum Group Metals (metal, 600m depth)	30,216	1	89	1	75

58. *Statistical/Economic Review, Budget 1980–81* (Cape Town: Government Printer, 1980).

Table 6 (Continued)

Mineral Commodity	Reserves (Metric Tons)	Western World Rank	%	World Rank	%
Chrome Ore (300m depth)	3,096,830,000	1	84	1	81
Manganese Ore (in situ)	12,139,800,000	1	93	1	78
Gold (metal)	16,500	1	64	1	51
Fluorspar (CaF$_2$ content)	31,400,000	1	46	1	35
Aluminum, Silicate refractories (andalusite, kyanite, sillimanite)	104,000,000	1	45	1	34
Diamonds (carats)	72,000,000	2	23	2	21
Vermiculite (crude)	73,000,000	2	30	n/a	n/a
Antimony (metal)	300,000	2	18	3	5
Uranium (metal up to $50/lb. U$_3O_8$)	391,000	2	18	n/a	n/a
Asbestos (fibre)	8,500,000	2	8	4	5
Phosphate (contained concentrate)	1,796,000,000	3	9	3	9
Zinc (metal)	12,067,000	4	10	5	8
Lead (metal)	6,157,000	4	5	5	4
Nickel (metal, 600m depth)	5,830,000	5	8	7	6
Titanium (metal)	15,037,000	5	8	6	7
Silver (metal)	8,690	5	6	6	4
Coal (largely bituminous, 300m depth)	32,341,000,000	5	4	8	2
Iron Ore (30m depth)	9,500,000,000	6	6	7	3
Copper (metal)	6,400,000	11	2	13	2
Tin (metal)	(confidential)	11	1	13	1

SOURCE: *Financial Mail* (Johannesburg), Mining Supplement, September 28, 1979, p. 13. For American estimates, see United States Senate, Subcommittee on African Affairs of the Committee on Foreign Relations, Committee Print, *Imports of Minerals from South Africa by the United States and the OECD Countries* (September 1980).

The manufacturing industry, like mining, is for the most part conducted by private enterprise; there are also several public corporations — notably, SASOL (South African Coal, Oil, and Gas Corporation), which produces oil from coal, and ISCOR (Iron and Steel Corporation), which makes steel. The railways, harbors, telecommunications, and much of the road transport are owned and operated by the public authorities.

When there was an industrial census in 1972, the production of manufacturing industry, including the public corporations but not the public authorities, was rated as follows:

TABLE 7. Value of Manufacturing Production, 1972

Manufacturing Industry	Rand 1,000
Food, drink, and tobacco	1,806,251
Textiles, clothing, footwear, and leather	1,074,525
Wood, cork, furniture	272,660
Paper, printing, publishing	584,991
Chemicals, rubber, and plastic products	1,348,710
Pottery, glass, and nonmetallic mineral products	412,608
Iron and steel basic industries, nonferrous metal basic industries, fabricated metal products	1,645,565
Machinery and electrical machinery	1,010,408
Motor vehicles and transport equipment	839,978
Professional equipment, photographic and other	159,623
	R9,155,319

Source: Republic of South Africa, South African Statistics, 1978, pp. 12 ff.

Since then, expansion has reached a very high rate, with the greatest increases in textiles, drink, paper, and publishing. Massive increases in chemicals and products of coal and petroleum can be expected in the 1980s.

Nevertheless, South Africa is still a heavy importer of machinery and transport equipment, and an exporter of raw materials, especially of gold. There is one striking exception to this general pattern: South Africa does not produce a drop of natural fuel oil. This is a grievous deficiency for an isolated state with an unpopular political system. The Republic imports only one-quarter of its energy needs, meeting most of the rest from locally mined coal. But this is a vital one-quarter—the oil that provides nearly all the liquid fuel requirements.

To overcome this deficit the government founded SASOL in the 1950s to convert coal to petrol and diesel fuel. Initially the capital costs were very high, but with the dramatic increase in the price of imported oil since 1973 the undertaking became financially viable. When the shah of Iran was overthrown in 1979, South Africa was forced to buy its oil from the international spot market at even higher prices. This spurred the government to hasten ahead with its SASOL additions. A second coal liquefaction plant came on stream in 1980 and a third will be completed by 1985. These combined operations are scheduled to produce about 140,000 barrels of oil a day— approximately half of the country's present liquid fuel requirements.[59] Extensive research programs are also under way to study the manufacture of alcohol fuels, derived from maize, sugar, and vegetable waste, as a substitute for imported oil. In addition, the discovery of offshore gas deposits has led to the investigation of methods of converting the gas into methanol for use as a petrol additive.

The first of South Africa's nuclear reactors, at Koeberg near Cape Town, will start generating electricity in 1982. Because of the refusal of the United States government to supply enriched uranium for the reactor, the South African Atomic Energy Board has built a small enrichment plant at Valindaba near Pretoria, to

59. *Financial Mail* (Johannesburg), Energy Supplement, June 29, 1979, p.31.

meet the requirements of at least two nuclear reactors.[60] Although extensive on and offshore prospecting for natural oil is in progress, no substantial finds have yet been made.

The following table analyzes South Africa's foreign trade in terms of commodities.

TABLE 8. Foreign Trade: Commodity Groups, 1976 (Excluding Gold Bullion and Oil) (Standard International Trade Classification); R million

Commodity Groups	Imports	Exports
Food and live animals	199.1	996.3
Inedible raw materials, except fuels	359.6	975.6
Chemicals	591.9	167.4
Manufactured goods and miscellaneous manufactured articles	1,328.1	1,379.5
Machinery and transport equipment	3,216.8	214.5
Agriculture, forestry, and fishing	139.1	608.2
Beverages, tobacco, mineral fuels and lubricants, animal and vegetable oils, and miscellaneous	540.3	209.1

Source: Republic of South Africa, *South African Statistics, 1978*, 16.7–16.9.

Britain has traditionally been South Africa's principal trading partner. However, in recent years the British proportion of the South African trade has declined as a result of increasing participation by the other European Common Market countries (especially West Germany), the United States, and Japan. South Africa's trade with Africa north of the Zambezi, on the other hand, is small. The following table shows an analysis of South Africa's foreign trade in terms of direction:

60. Ibid., p. 36.

TABLE 9. Foreign Trade: Direction of Trade, 1979 (Excluding
          Gold Bullion and Oil); R million

	Imports	Percent	Exports	Percent
United Kingdom	1,253.9	17.8	947.7	10.4
Other EEC countries	2,370.5	33.7	2,204.1	24.1
U.S.A. and Canada	1,341.2	19.1	1,543.4	16.9
African states	256.1	3.6	646.4	7.1
Rest of the world	1,816.7	25.8	3,787.2	41.5
	7,038.4	100.0	9,128.8	100.0

SOURCE: Republic of South Africa, *Statistical/Economic Review, Budget 1980–81* (1980), p. 15.

South Africa has one of the strongest economies of any country in Africa and it stands comparison with the economies of other rapidly developing countries, like Canada and Australia. Its strength lies in considerable and varied natural resources, a reserve of incompletely tapped potential manpower, and the capital investment and entrepreneurial experience that have accumulated during the century following the discovery of diamonds, which triggered the process of modernization. Thanks largely to the fact that South Africa is the source of over half the world's supply of gold, the country normally has a favorable balance of trade. The gross national product quadrupled between 1969 and 1979; and the real income per capita increased from R540 to R600 during the same period.[61]

The Republic is the dominant economic power in the entire southern African region. All the other territories are dependent on the Republic in important respects. For example, in 1980 about 44 percent of the 414,092 migrant workers in the gold

61. *Statistical/Economic Review, Budget 1980–81*, p. 6.

mines were recruited from neighboring countries, whose governments stipulate that their miners transfer a high proportion of their pay home. Lesotho, Mozambique, and Botswana are heavily dependant on revenue derived from migrants, and so are the "homelands," especially the "independent" Transkei.

TABLE 10. Sources of African Workers on the Gold-Mines (January–March 1980 Daily Average)

South Africans	
Transkei	115,106
Bophuthatswana	12,407
Other "Homelands"	53,062
"White" South Africa	51,180
Subtotal	231,755
Foreigners	
Lesotho	98,028
Mozambique	34,467
Botswana	17,672
Swaziland	8,047
Others	24,123
Subtotal	182,337
Total Africans	414,092

SOURCE: Merle Lipton,"Men of Two Worlds: Migrant Labour in South Africa," *Optima* (Johannesburg) 29, no. 2/3 (November 28, 1980): 94.

A tradition of conservative public financing has produced regular surpluses for the exchequer, and the 1980 budget showed a surplus of no less than 6.5 percent of gross domestic product.[62] Though there were crises of confidence among

62. Ibid., p. 4.

foreign investors after the Sharpeville shootings in 1960 and the Soweto unrest in 1976, the foreign reserves soon recovered and the capital required for continued development seems to be readily forthcoming from Britain, Western Europe, and the United States.

Industrial expansion continues to take place. During the 1980s SASOL will spend R6.2 billion on coal liquefaction plants; the Electricity Supply Commission will spend R7.75 billion on water schemes, and an undisclosed sum is being spent on a uranium enrichment plant.[63]

Racial Inequality

Racial inequality pervades the entire South African economy. According to official estimates, in 1978 the average monthly wages, excluding agriculture, of Whites was R588, of Asians R256, of Coloureds R192, and of Africans in the "white areas" R140.[64] No official estimate is made of wages paid to African farm laborers, but they are substantially less than in other economic sectors. In 1975 Africans in the "homelands" had an average per capita monthly income of R20.58.[65] In July 1979 about 12,000 Whites, 13,000 Coloureds, and 5,000 Asians were registered as unemployed in the main areas.[66] There is very serious unemployment among Africans. Problems of definition make it impossible to give a precise numerical figure; in 1978 Professor Gideon Jacobs of the University of the Witwatersrand estimated that it was as high as two million and was increasing because the labor market could not absorb the 200,000 African work-seekers coming to the market each year.[67] The following table gives the average number of persons employed and their average wages in the mining industries, the manufacturing industries, and the public services in 1979:

63. *Standard Bank Review*, November 1979, p. 5.

64. *Bulletin of Statistics*, Quarter End, March 1979, 2.3.

65. *Official Yearbook of the Republic of South Africa 1979* (Johannesburg: Chris van Rensburg Publishers, 1980), p. 237.

66. *Survey of Race Relations, 1979*, p. 197.

67. *Survey of Race Relations, 1978*, p. 171.

TABLE 11. Numbers Employed and Average Monthly Wages, 1979

	Mining	Wages	Manufacturing	Wages	Public Services*	Wages
Whites	99,866	R871	279,000	R630	469,094	R549
Coloureds	11,115	341	216,000	168	139,073	179
Asians	1,373	355	71,500	242	23,728	300
Africans	634,121	128†	704,600	177	488,362	157

*Public Services include the employees of the Republic, the railways and harbors administration, the post office, and the provincial and local administrations. The average wage rates cited are those in the public service of the Republic.

†African mine workers are also provided with food, medical treatment, accommodation, clothing, and other benefits. White mine workers receive even more considerable fringe benefits.

SOURCE: Loraine Gordon, ed., Survey of Race Relations in South Africa, 1979 (Johannesburg, 1980), pp. 221, 239, 240, 250–56.

Such inequalities exist partly because modern economic activities were pioneered in South Africa by white entrepreneurs, employing skilled white workers imported from Europe and black laborers who had no previous experience of modern industrial technology. In time, however, the correspondence of race with economic status might have been expected to diminish, as Blacks acquired industrial training and experience. There has, in fact, been a slight tendency in that direction, shown by the rise of a middle class among the Africans, as well as among the Asians and the Coloured people; but the tendency has been checked by a vast volume of white-made laws and white-imposed customs, which have gone a long way toward perpetuating inequality on a racial basis.[68]

First, there are laws that determine the ownership and occupation of land. Outside the "homelands" Africans may not own any land at all; in the "white rural areas," African occupation of land as labor-tenants is restricted by registration and licensing; and for residence in the urban areas, Africans other than domestic servants are confined to hostels or townships where they can have limited home-leasing rights. Moreover, under the 1950 Groups Areas Act and its amendments, which are being applied piecemeal by proclamation, all urban areas are being divided into zones; in each zone, members of one race—

68. On discriminatory legislation and practice in South Africa, see G. V. Doxey, The Industrial Colour Bar in South Africa (Cape Town: Oxford University Press, 1961); John Dugard, Human Rights and the South African Legal Order (Princeton: Princeton University Press, 1978); Stanley B. Greenberg, Race and State in Capitalist Development: Comparative Perspectives (New Haven: Yale University Press, 1980); Horrell, Laws Affecting Race Relations in South Africa 1948–1976; Frederick A. Johnstone, Class, Race and Gold: A Study of Class Relations and Racial Discrimination in South Africa (London: Routledge and Kegan Paul, 1976); A. S. Mathews, Law, Order and Liberty in South Africa (Cape Town: Juta, 1971; Berkeley: University of California Press, 1972); Albie Sachs, Justice in South Africa (Berkeley: University of California Press, 1973); S. van der Horst, ed., Race Discrimination in South Africa: A Review (Cape Town: David Philip, 1981); Francis Wilson, Labour in the South African Gold Mines 1911–1969.

and one only—may own real estate, reside, or conduct business. This law has been applied quite ruthlessly. Thousands of African, Coloured, and Asian families have been forcibly uprooted from their homes.

Second, there are the laws that restrict the movements of each African. Before 1964 no African had the right to be in an urban area unless he had resided there continuously since birth; or had worked there continuously for one employer for ten years or for different employers for fifteen years; or was the wife, unmarried daughter, or son under eighteen years of age of such a person; or had been given a permit to remain by the local authority. Permits were not valid for more than fourteen days, unless the African had obtained work. Furthermore, officials already had wide powers to banish Africans from towns, and such Africans had no right of appeal to the courts against a banishment order. These restrictions have not been substantially modified. Moreover, under the Bantu Laws Amendment Act (1964), officials may remove any African from any town at any time if they judge him or her to be "idle and undesirable." A further amendment of 1970 provides that an African who is illegally present in an urban area may be detained in a work colony and subjected to compulsory labor. Coloured people have considerable freedom of movement throughout the "white areas," but Asians may not settle in the Orange Free State or certain areas of northern Natal. On the other hand, Whites, Coloureds, and Asians may not enter African townships without a permit. In 1978, 272,887 Africans were arrested for alleged breaches of restrictions upon their movements.[69]

Third, the apprenticeship system, in combination with the educational system, puts obstacles in the way of Africans and many Coloureds and Asians from becoming trained as artisans. Fourth, employment in some skilled work in the mining industry in the "white areas" is reserved by law for Whites and

69. *Survey of Race Relations*, 1979, p. 390.

Coloureds. Fifth, until 1979 the Industrial Conciliation legislation discouraged African trade unions by failing to recognize them for the purposes of industrial conciliation, and it also discouraged the continuing existence of mixed white, Coloured, and Asian trade unions and prohibited the registration of new mixed unions. However, in 1979, amendments to the legislation permitted the recognition of African and mixed unions at the discretion of the Industrial Registrar. Since 1973 limited rights to strike have been granted to African workers.

Although the legal color bars in the workplace have been repealed in all except a few mining jobs, the effects of custom plus the color bars in other aspects of South African society still pervade the workplace. Education and technical training, mobility, and job security still correspond very closely with race, and there are still very few situations in which black workers have authority over Whites. Consequently, the South African economy has a serious weakness: a shortage of skilled workers.[70] This shortage is becoming more and more critical as the scale of the economy, and the size of the state bureaucracy required to apply the racial laws, expand. It will not disappear until the economic potential of the black population is released.

The two facets of the South African ecoomy—its strength and its inequality—are closely interrelated. Some Blacks, as well as Whites, are benefiting from economic growth, so the effects of economic inequality are to some extent offset by rising living standards and the expectation of further rises. The strength of the economy also enables the government to mobilize the resources required to suppress internal political opposition and to defy external opposition.[71]

70. Political and business leaders are keenly aware of this deficiency. For example, Owen Horwood, minister of finance, *Hansard*, vol. 2 (1980), (March 24–28, 1980), col. 3525, and D. Etheridge, chairman, Chamber of Mines, Annual Report, *Financial Mail* (Johannesburg), June 25, 1980.

71. See chaps. 5 and 6 below.

3

The Framework of Political Life

The constitution of the Republic of South Africa was enacted by the Parliament of the Union of South Africa and came into force on May 31, 1961.[1] But 1961 did not mark a break in South African constitutional and political continuity. The new constitution was merely the South Africa Act (which had been enacted by the British Parliament in 1909) as amended from time to time, and as revised at the time South Africa ceased to be a kingdom and became a republic, when all extant South African legislation not specifically repealed or amended by the new constitution remained in force. Consequently, South African politics are affected by many surviving statutes of the Union Parliament and by the relevant decisions of the Supreme Court of South Africa. Furthermore, in South Africa, as in other countries, the legal bases of politics are given life by the conventions and practices that have developed over the years.[2]

1. Republic of South Africa Constitution Act No. 32 of 1961. The basic commentary on the South African constitution is H. R. Hahlo and Ellison Kahn, *The Union of South Africa: The Development of Its Laws and Constitution* (London: Stevens, 1960), supplemented by Ellison Kahn, *The New Constitution: Being a Supplement to South Africa, the Development of Its Laws and Constitution* (London: Stevens, 1962), which includes a text of the constitution.
2. On the political and constitutional history of South Africa since 1910, see Heribert Adam and Hermann Giliomee, *Ethnic Power Mobilized: Can South Africa Change?* (New Haven and London: Yale University Press, 1979); Gwendolen M. Carter, *The Politics of Inequality: South Africa since 1948* (London: Thames and Hudson, 1958); K. Heard, *General Elections in South Africa 1943 –*

EXECUTIVE GOVERNMENT

The change to a republic necessitated the creation of a new head of state. Formerly the South African monarch was also the monarch of the other kingdoms in the British Commonwealth and, as in all of them except the United Kingdom, he was normally represented in South Africa by a governor-general. The monarch has been replaced by a "State President," who is elected by secret ballot by an electoral college consisting of the members of the House of Assembly, at a meeting presided over by the chief justice or his deputy. The state president holds office for seven years, unless he resigns or is removed for misconduct by resolution of the House of Assembly. The functions of the state president in South Africa remain similar to those of the king or queen in Britain; whereas in Britain the duties are determined largely by convention, in South Africa many, though not all, of the British conventions are spelled out in the written constitution.

The state president is declared to be the head of the republic and the commander-in-chief of the Defence Force, and to have power to convene and prorogue Parliament, to dissolve the House of Assembly, to make ministerial and other appointments, to confer honors, to pardon offenders, to appoint and receive ambassadors, to enter into and ratify treaties, to proclaim and terminate martial law, to declare peace and war, to perform the functions vested in him by other statutes, and to possess the prerogative powers formerly possessed by the

70 (London: Oxford University Press, 1974); W. K. Hancock, *Smuts: Vol. 1, The Sanguine Years*, and *Smuts: Vol. 2, The Fields of Force* (Cambridge: Cambridge University Press, 1962 and 1968); D. W. Krüger, *The Making of a Nation* (Johannesburg: Dagbreek, 1969); Nicholas Mansergh, *Survey of British Commonwealth Affairs*, 2 vols. (London: Oxford University Press, 1952–58), and *South Africa, 1906–1961: The Price of Magnanimity* (New York: Praeger, 1962); T. Dunbar Moodie, *The Rise of Afrikanerdom: Power, Apartheid and the Afrikaner Civil Religion* (Berkeley: University of California Press, 1975); Leonard Thompson and Jeffrey Butler, eds., *Change in Contemporary South Africa* (Berkeley: University of California Press, 1975); Monica Wilson and Leonard Thompson, eds., *The Oxford History of South Africa*, vol. 2 (Oxford: Clarendon Press, 1971).

queen.[3] However, the constitution also ensures that in exercising every one of these powers the state president is normally the creature of the Executive Council. Every official instrument signed by the state president requires the countersignature of a minister, and his every official action is required to be taken on the advice of the Executive Council, except only that he has discretion in appointing cabinet ministers, convening and proroguing Parliament, and dissolving the House of Assembly. Even in these cases he is declared to be bound by the existing (but undefined) constitutional conventions, which means that he is to act on ministerial advice whenever possible, and only in exceptional circumstances would he have any real discretionary power.[4] Such circumstances might arise if the ruling party disintegrated. For example, if a prime minister lost the confidence of the House of Assembly, and asked for its dissolution, the president might have a real choice between agreeing to a dissolution and attempting to find someone else capable of forming a government. That is what happened in 1939 when the United Party Cabinet and the Parliamentary party disintegrated on the war issue and Governor-General Sir Patrick Duncan refused Prime Minister J. B. M. Hertzog's request for a dissolution, and J. C. Smuts, previously deputy prime minister, formed a government.[5]

When the republican constitution was being debated in Parliament, Prime Minister H. F. Verwoerd said it was the government's intention that the State President should be above politics—a symbol of national dignity and pride.[6] For a country

3. In fact, many of the prerogative powers are spelled out in the constitution (these are included in the list above) and in other South African statutes. Among those covered by the general grant in the constitution and not listed elsewhere are some of political significance, notably the granting and renewal of passports.

4. Constitution, sections 7–23, 64.

5. Mansergh, *British Commonwealth Affairs*, vol. 1: *Problems of External Policy, 1931–39*, pp. 381–400.

6. *Senate Debates*, 1961, col. 3157. Before 1980 the state president was elected by a majority of votes of the senate and the House of Assembly. Since the abolition of the Senate, the election is by the House of Assembly alone. This ensures the appointment of the representative of the dominant party. Since 1961, all five state presidents have been Afrikaans-speaking politicians.

with cleavages as deep as those of South Africa, this ideal is virtually unrealizable.

In 1980, an amendment to the constitution created the office of vice state president. The provisions applying to the state president in respect of qualifications, election, period of office, and removal from office apply also to the vice state president. He is the chairman of the President's Council (see below, pp. 96–97), and he serves as acting state president in the event of this office being vacated.[7]

The constitution vests the real executive power in an Executive Council of not more than twenty ministers, each of whom is head of one or more departments of state. It also allows for the appointment of not more than six deputy ministers, without seats in the Executive Council, and provides that the ministers and deputy ministers shall not hold their appointments for more than twelve months without being members of the House of Assembly, and that they shall be appointed by the state president.[8] Though the words responsible government, Prime minister, cabinet, and party have no place in the written constitution, this means a system of responsible government as practised in the United Kingdom and most of the countries of the British Commonwealth—government by a cabinet, consisting of a prime minister and other ministers selected by him, and holding office by virtue of the prime minister's leadership of the party (or coalition of parties) that holds a majority of the seats in the dominant legislative chamber.

In South Africa the British doctrine of collective responsibility of the cabinet for every official action of every minister does not possess the strength that it has in the United Kingdom. Indeed, there are several clear-cut cases of independent action by ministers, as in 1936, when J. H. Hofmeyr, though minister of the interior, spoke and voted against a government bill to re-

---

7. Republic of South Africa Constitution Fifth Amendment Act, 1980, sec. 10A.

8. Constitution, secs. 16–23.

move African voters from the common electoral roll in the Cape Province. In 1978 Dr. C. Mulder, the minister of plural relations, resigned from the cabinet following a statement by Judge Mostert that he had received evidence of serious irregularities in the Department of Information, for which Dr. Mulder had carried responsibility. The official Opposition had called upon the entire cabinet to resign on the ground that it should take collective responsibility for what amounted to subversion of the parliamentary system. The government rejected this demand, claiming that other ministers had been exonerated from blame by the findings of a commission of inquiry under Judge Erasmus.

If a prime minister decides to rid himself of a colleague, he can easily do so (provided, as always, that he retains the confidence of a majority in the House of Assembly). Normally, the prime minister's request suffices, but if a colleague refuses to resign, the prime minister has only to tender his own resignation to the state president, who will then invite him to form a new cabinet from which he will exclude the recalcitrant minister, as Louis Botha did in 1912 when he excluded J. B. M. Hertzog.

At present there are two significant political parties represented in the House of Assembly, and each has a clearly defined intraparty machinery for selecting leaders. Consequently the person who should be prime minister is readily identifiable, and the state president has no option but to accept him and the colleagues he selects. This gives the prime minister immense strength in his relations with his own party, and the system has in fact produced an unbroken line of strong prime ministers in South Africa: Louis Botha (1910–19), J. C. Smuts (1919–24, 1939–48), J. B. M. Hertzog (1924–39), D. F. Malan (1948–54), J. G. Strijdom (1954–58), H. F. Verwoerd (1958–66), B. J. Vorster (1966–78), and P. W. Botha (1978–).

PARLIAMENT

The legislative power is vested in a parliament consisting of the state president and the House of Assembly.[9] The state presi-

9. Ibid., sec. 24.

dent's parliamentary functions are like those of the monarch of the United Kingdom. He formally opens each session of the House of Assembly, where he delivers a speech outlining the government's legislative program; but the speech is prepared by the cabinet. He assents to bills which have been passed by the House of Assembly, or withholds such assent—as advised by the cabinet.[10]

Before 1980, the constitution provided for a Senate, which was subordinated to the House of Assembly in much the same way as the British Parliament Act subordinates the House of Lords to the House of Commons. The Senate was abolished in 1980.[11] Its stormy history is discussed below.

The composition of the House of Assembly has changed over the years. Membership of the House has always been limited to white people who are qualified voters. The South Africa Act created a House of 121 elected members—51 from the Cape Province, 36 from the Transvaal, and 17 from the Orange Free State and from Natal—and provided a formula for the gradual increase in the size of the House to 150, and for the division of the 150 seats between the provinces thereafter in proportion to their numbers of white men. The House reached its total of 150 members in 1936. In the 1950s the basis of the division of the seats between the provinces was changed twice, and it is now

---

10. The constitutional provisions concerning assent to legislation are a good example of the way in which the president is deprived of effective discretion:

16. (2) Save where otherwise expressly stated or necessarily implied, any reference in this Act to the State President shall be deemed to be a reference to the State President acting on the advice of the Executive Council.

64. (1) When a Bill is presented to the State President for his assent, he shall declare according to his discretion, but subject to the provisions of this Act, that he assents thereto or that he withholds assent.

11. Republic of South Africa Constitution Fifth Amendment Act, 1980.

made in proportion to the numbers of registered white voters.[12]

During the 1970s the number of seats was increased to 165, made up of 55 from the Cape Province, 76 from the Transvaal, 20 from Natal, and 14 from the Orange Free State. In 1980 the constitution was amended to create 12 additional seats in the House of Assembly. Four of these are nominated by the state president, one from each province, and eight are elected by the House of Assembly according to the principle of proportional representation, each voter having one transferable vote.[13]

The South Africa Act also laid down a system for the periodic redelimitation of each province into electoral divisions. This, too, has been continued under the republican constitution. New delimitations are made at intervals of ten years by commissions of Supreme Court judges. The commissions are required to divide each province into its correct number of single-member electoral divisions, each containing approximately the same number of voters; but the commissions are entitled to allow a latitude of up to 15 percent either way from a provincial norm, and in so doing to give "due consideration" to five factors, including "sparsity or density of population."[14] In practice, delimitation commissions have always tended to give considerable emphasis to this last factor and to apply it in favor of rural areas, which have had between three and six more seats than they would on the basis of strict equality. Though the maximum latitude thus permitted is small by American standards, its political effects have been appreciable, since the party supported by the Afrikaner voters has always been overwhelmingly stronger in the rural areas.

Nevertheless, what has given Afrikaner parties their greatest advantage is the single-member constituency system itself, rather than the details of its application. This is due to the

12. Hahlo and Kahn, *Union of South Africa*, pp. 163–66.
13. Republic of South Africa Constitution Fifth Amendment Act, 1980, sec. 40.
14. Constitution, secs. 42–45.

fact that their own strength has been sufficiently spread throughout the rural constituencies and some urban ones, whereas a wastefully high proportion of their opponents' strength has always been concentrated in a few urban constituencies. The National party (NP) was able to come into power in 1948 primarily because of this, and to retain power in 1953, though on both occasions it was supported by fewer voters than the United party.[15] Even in the 1958 election, when the NP gained 103 seats to the Opposition's 53, it was estimated that if the uncontested seats had been considered, the anti-Nationalists would have led by 18,500 votes.[16] Only a system of proportional representation would have prevented the return of a minority government; such a system was in fact provided in the first report of the National Convention, before being abandoned in the final report of May 1909.[17]

The parliamentary franchise has always been a most contentious political issue in South Africa.[18] The initial compromise, under which the franchise laws of the four colonies remained in force in the respective provinces of the Union, survived for two decades, during which there was a slight increase in the number and the proportion of the black voters in the Cape Province. In 1929 there were 167,184 Whites, 25,618 Coloureds, and 15,780 Africans registered as voters in the Cape Province by virtue of their capacity to sign their names and write their addresses and occupations, and of their earning £50 a year or occupying a house and land together worth £75 (exclusive of the value of any land occupied under African customary tenure).

15. Carter, The Politics of Inequality, pp. 158–60.

16. South African Institute of Race Relations, Survey of Race Relations in South Africa, 1957–1958 (Johannesburg: SAIRR, 1958), p. 1.

17. Leonard M. Thompson, The Unification of South Africa, 1902–1910 (Oxford: Clarendon Press, 1960), pp. 122–34, 236–42, 369–74.

18. Hahlo and Kahn, Union of South Africa, pp. 164–66; Leonard M. Thompson, "The Non-European Franchise in the Union of South Africa," in Sydney D. Bailey, ed., Parliamentary Government in the Commonwealth (London: Hansard Society, 1951), pp. 166–77.

Then, in 1930 and 1931, the number of white voters was more than doubled by the enfranchisement of white (but not black) women and the elimination of the educational and economic qualifications for white (but not black) men in the Cape Province; at the same time, the qualification became applied more stringently to black applicants.[19] The result was that in 1935 there were 382,103 Whites, 24,793 Coloureds, and 10,628 Africans registered as voters in the Cape Province. In 1936 the African voters were removed from the ordinary voters' roll in the Cape Province and given the right to elect three Whites to represent them in the House of Assembly; this representation was abolished in 1960.[20]

The number of Coloured voters reached a peak of 54,134 in 1946 and then declined under stricter scrutiny of applicants, until the Separate Representation of Voters Act of 1951, validated and enforced in 1956, removed them from the common roll and gave them the right to elect four Whites to represent them in the House of Assembly. After that, the number of Coloured voters further declined to 24,306 in 1959. This indirect representation was abolished in 1968, which created, for the first time since Union in 1910, a parliament representing only Whites. Another act of the same year made it illegal for anyone to belong to a racially mixed political party. In 1958 the voting age for Whites was reduced from twenty-one to eighteen.[21]

The republican constitution of 1961 made no substantial changes in the franchise and electoral arrangements.[22] The House of Assembly created in 1981 contained 165 popularly elected members plus the extra 12 members provided for in the

19. Women's Enfranchisement Act, 1930; Franchise Laws Amendment Act, 1931.
20. Representation of Natives Act, 1936; Promotion of Bantu Self-Government Act, 1959.
21. Separate Representation of Voters Amendment Act, 1968; Prohibition of Political Interference Act, 1968; Electoral Laws Amendment Act, 1958.
22. Constitution, secs. 40–47.

1980 legislation (p. 76 above). All of them were Whites. All were elected or nominated exclusively by Whites.

The constitution provides that there shall be a session of the House of Assembly each year and that its maximum duration shall be five years. It also empowers the state president to dissolve the House of Assembly at any time.[23] Most sessions of the House of Assembly have lasted nearly the full five years, but the assembly elected in 1974 was dissolved in 1977 to enable the government to take advantage of the disarray in the Opposition following the dissolution of the United party, to obtain support for the new constitutional proposals and, as it later emerged, to prepare for an investigation into malpractices in the Information Department. Likewise, early in 1981 the government dissolved the House elected in 1977, in the hope of obtaining a strong mandate for some cautious reforms advocated by Prime Minister P. W. Botha.

The quorum for the House of Assembly is thirty.[24] The House elects from among its members a presiding officer, known as the Speaker, who has a casting vote but no deliberate vote.[25] The standing rules of the House of Assembly were originally derived from those of the British House of Commons, and in form British parliamentary procedure still prevails. The same distinction is made between public, private, and hybrid bills. A bill goes through the same stages. When it is introduced into the House of Assembly and read for the first time there is rarely any discussion. The second reading is the occasion for debate of the principle of the bill. That is followed by the committee stage, when the House resolves itself into a committee and goes through the bill clause by clause, considering amendments. The final stage is the third reading, when the bill as amended in committee is approved.

Apart from legislation, the most important business of the

23. Ibid., secs. 26, 29–30, 47, 53
24. Ibid., sec. 50.
25. Ibid., secs. 48–49, 51.

House of Assembly takes place when the House in Committee of Supply considers the budgetary proposals of the minister of finance and scrutinizes the conduct of each department as its appropriation is reviewed. As in the United Kingdom, question time is an important chance for the Opposition party: it occurs twice a week, when ministers give oral replies to questions, notice of which has been given in advance. On other days written replies are given. Strict time limits are imposed on nearly all speeches, precluding filibuster. When the majority party desires, it may, by majority vote, accelerate a decision on a motion in various ways: by continuing a debate throughout the night until the opposition has exhausted its members' time limits; by applying closure to the debate; or by imposing in advance specific time limits for each stage of a bill's progress. In the 1960s these expedients were frequently used when the government proposed a vast legislative program and was able to get most of it enacted.

The debating chambers are arranged on the British pattern, with "Government" and "Opposition" benches facing each other; unlike the British Parliament, however, each member has a seat for his exclusive use. Although standing committees and ad hoc committees of various sorts do exist, they do not perform the vital functions committees do in the U.S. Congress. Most important official business is conducted in open assembly. Nevertheless, party discipline is even stricter in South Africa than in Britain, with the result that it is not in the open House of Assembly but in the closed party caucus that individual opinion is freely expressed. Once a caucus—consisting of a party's members of the House of Assembly—has decided what line to take on a particular issue, its members will rarely disagree in the assembly, because to do so would incur the grave risk of expulsion from the party, with the almost certain sequel of defeat in the next election.

The typical debate in the House of Assembly is on a motion by a minister, with the Government benches supporting it, and the Opposition benches opposing it; the objective is not so much to clarify the issues and come to a demonstrably wise decision as to publicize and justify the decision which the caucus has already adopted. Debate is therefore often repetitious (in spite of rules against repetition) and replete with arguments *ad causam* and *ad hominem*; and the quality of debating humor in the Assembly, unlike the quality of Shakespeare's mercy, is very strained. The acrimony of debate often gives the uninitiated the impression that differences between the parties are fundamental, which is often not the case. In the House of Assembly elected in 1981, all members, being white representatives of white constituencies, had an interest in political stability and continuity. Both the Government and the Opposition considered that reforms, including constitutional changes, were necessary to fulfill these objectives; but they differed as to the nature of the reforms. The Government has no intention of allowing power over the greater part of South Africa to slip from white hands; while the Opposition advocates a federal scheme that would involve some genuine division of power among the races in the central government as well as between the center and the parts.

THE SUPREME COURT

Judicial authority in South Africa is vested in a single superior court, known as the Supreme Court of South Africa, which consists of the Appellate Division, presided over by the chief justice, Provincial Divisions, presided over by judge-presidents, and Local Divisions. The Appellate Division has appellate jurisdiction only; while the Provincial and Local Divisions are courts both of first instance and of appeal from inferior courts. The administration of the Department of Justice is under the control of a cabinet minister. Appointments to the bench are made by the state president on the recommendation of the cabinet, as advised by the minister of justice. Originally, the number of judges was fixed by statute, but since 1949 the government has had complete discretion, and there are now about a hundred judges and a number of acting judges sitting in eleven divisions, including Namibia, Transkei, Venda, and Bophuthatswana. Appointments to the Local and Provincial Divisions are usually made from among the senior practising advocates, but a few have been made from the public service. Nearly every appointment to the Appellate Division has been by promotion from another division.

Once appointed, a judge has effective security of tenure until he reaches the retiring age of seventy. He is removable by the state president only on receipt of an address from the House of Assembly pleading for the removal for misbehavior or incapacity; in actuality, no such address has ever been made and no removal has taken place in the Union or the Republic.

Though advocates who have been active in politics have often been appointed to the bench, the judiciary has a reputation for integrity and ability; the role of chief justices, at any rate from Lord de Villiers (1910–14) to Albert van de Sandt Centlivres (1950–57), has been distinguished. The judges have always tended to construe somewhat narrowly the powers that statutes have delegated to ministers and, where possible, they have applied the equitable principles of the Roman-Dutch law, regardless of persons. However, in recent years statutes have narrowed the scope for such action to a remarkable extent, and Professor John Dugard and others criticize the bench for accepting uncritically the doctrine of legal positivism.[26]

The inferior courts are in lesser repute. They are staffed by about a thousand magistrates spread over three hundred districts. These magistrates are invariably white men. Until recently few possessed legal training beyond the modest requirements for a public service examination. Today, however, in-

26. Ibid., secs. 94, 95; Hahlo and Kahn, Union of South Africa, pp. 249–67; John Dugard, Human Rights and the South African Legal Order (Princeton: Princeton University Press, 1978), p. 397.

creasing numbers have attended a university and have formal legal qualifications. Magistrates preside over criminal and civil cases and, in addition, exercise a wide range of administrative functions. They grant and pay African pensions, collect revenue, commit mental patients, administer farmers' relief schemes, control child welfare, issue maintenance orders, preside at civil marriages, and conduct general and by-elections. Except in Pretoria, the magistrate is the senior representative of the government in his district. Unlike the Supreme Court judge, the magistrate is, and is seen to be, a civil servant; his salary, conditions of employment, promotion, and transfer are under the direct control of the state.

A curious legacy of the colonial rivalries of 1908–09 is that the Republic still has no single capital city. Pretoria is the basic seat of government and administration, but the House of Assembly still meets a thousand miles away in Cape Town, which means that ministers and many public servants spend several months each year in each place. The Appellate Division of the Supreme Court sits in Bloemfontein.[27]

POWERS OF PARLIAMENT

The most important section of the Constitution concerns the powers of Parliament. It reads as follows:

59. (1) Parliament shall be the sovereign legislative authority in and over the Republic, and shall have full power to make laws for the peace, order and good government of the Republic.

(2) No court of law shall be competent to enquire into or to pronounce upon the validity of any Act passed by Parliament, other than an Act which repeals or amends or purports to repeal or amend the provisions of section one hundred and eight or one hundred and eighteen.

27. Constitution, secs. 23, 27, 94 (3).

Section 59 of the constitution is the outcome of a series of disputes extending over half a century. During most of that time controversy centered on the question of national status, and the basic process was the elimination of British power from South Africa. Initially, South Africa marched in step with the other Dominions, especially Canada. South Africa was separately represented at the Versailles Peace Conference and in the League of Nations. In the report of the Imperial Conference of 1926, the Dominions obtained a formal statement of their equality with the United Kingdom, and in the Statute of Westminster of 1931 some aspects of that statement were translated into British law.

Thereafter, however, South Africa took separate initiatives. In 1934 the Status of the Union Act provided that acts of the British Parliament were not valid unless they had been enacted by the South African Parliament, and that the governor-general must act on the advice of his South African ministers. In 1950 the Privy Council Appeals Act removed the right, which was already obsolescent, of appeal from the Supreme Court to the British Privy Council. Finally, in 1961, the Republic of South Africa Constitution Act eliminated the British monarchy from the South African legal system. Some people had hoped that South Africa would remain a member of the Commonwealth; but in the face of sharp attacks upon her racial policies at a Commonwealth Prime Minister's Conference in March 1961, Prime Minister Verwoerd withdrew his request for continued membership, so South Africa ceased to be a member of the Commonwealth when the Republic was inaugurated on May 31, 1961.

In eliminating the last legal vestiges of South Africa's colonial origins, the Afrikaner Nationalists displayed a combination of radicalism and legalism that is a distinctive mark of their performance in all controversies. During the 1950s there was a great struggle concerning the structure of the South African Parliament and the powers of the Supreme Court over South African legislation. This struggle, discussed in the succeeding pages, is a most instructive example of the South African political process.

From the first, the greater part of the South African Constitution was fully flexible. That is to say, most of its sections could be amended by the ordinary legislative process of bare majorities in the House of Assembly and the Senate, and the assent of the governor-general. There was no division of powers between the branches of the central government and nothing analogous to a bill of rights restraining the legislature from infringing the liberties of the individual.

Initially there were three types of exception to this general flexibility. Two of these—the complex of imperial controls and the few provisions that were specially safeguarded for the limited period of time in which they were to operate—had lapsed by the end of 1931. There remained a third type of exception: safeguards for the sections of the constitution which entitled qualified Blacks as well as Whites to vote in parliamentary and provincial council elections in the Cape Province, and which placed English and Dutch on the same footing as the official languages of the Union. These sections could only be amended by an act passed in a joint sitting of the Senate and the House of Assembly and, at the third reading, agreed to by two-thirds of the total membership of both Houses.

Before 1948 the South African government complied with these provisions when necessary. For example, when the language section was amended in 1925 to make Afrikaans an official language in place of Dutch, and when the franchise section was amended in 1936 to remove the Cape Province African voters from the common roll, the unicameral two-thirds majority procedure was used.[28] The Nationalist government which came into power in 1948 wished to remove the Cape Coloured voters from the common roll, although it did not possess a two-thirds

28. Official Languages of the Union Act, 1925; Representation of Natives Act, 1936.

majority. It found that the balance of legal opinion, in Britain as well as South Africa, held that since the enactment of the Statute of Westminster the safeguards had lost their legal efficacy and the South African Parliament, like the British Parliament, was competent to adopt any procedure it thought fit to pass valid legislation on any topic.

Consequently, in 1951 a Separate Representation of Voters Act purporting to remove the Cape Coloured voters from the common roll was passed through both Houses of Parliament by the ordinary bicameral procedure. But when this act was challenged in the Supreme Court, the Appellate Division decided that to legislate with effect in the fields covered by the entrenched sections, the South African Parliament was bound to comply with the requirements laid down in them. The Appellate Division therefore struck down the Separate Representation of Voters Act as invalid because it had not been enacted in the prescribed manner.[29]

Parliament then passed another act by the ordinary bicameral procedure, setting up a High Court consisting of the members of Parliament, and empowering it by a bare majority to review any judgments of the Appellate Division of the Supreme Court that invalidated acts of Parliament.[30] The High Court of Parliament then met and reversed the recent judgment of the Appellate Division. However, the act creating it was in turn declared invalid by the Appellate Division for the reason that the High Court was Parliament in disguise, and not the protection implicit in the constitution.[31]

After some delay, during which the government twice tried and failed to get a two-thirds majority in a joint sitting, in 1955 Parliament, by the ordinary bicameral procedure, passed an act requiring a quorum of eleven judges in the Appellate Division when the validity of an act of Parliament was in question, and

29. *Harris* v. *Minister of the Interior*, 1952(2) S.A. 429 (A.D.).
30. High Court of Parliament Act, 1952.
31. *Minister of the Interior* v. *Harris*, 1952(4) S.A. 769 (A.D.).

another act reconstituting the Senate in such a way as to give the government a two-thirds majority in a joint sitting.[32] The government then made the necessary additions to the Appellate Division, which had previously consisted of only six judges, and created the packed Senate. Finally, in 1956 parliament passed an act by the unicameral two-thirds majority procedure, revalidating the 1951 Separate Representation of Voters Act, disentrenching the franchise section of the constitution, and denying the courts the power to inquire into the validity of any act of Parliament save only an act affecting the equal status of the two official languages.

This constitutional amendment, too, was challenged in the Supreme Court, but the Appellate Division declared it valid by a ten to one majority, on the grounds that the Senate act did not tamper with the entrenched sections, while the act removing the Coloured voters from the common roll had been passed by the necessary two-thirds majority in a joint sitting of both Houses.[33] Thus, after a struggle lasting nearly two years, the government had contrived to circumvent the safeguard provided for the Cape Coloured people.[34]

Since the government abolished the Senate in 1980, a change in the status of the official languages—English and Afrikaans—requires a two-thirds majority in the House of Assembly.[35] With that exception, the party with a majority in the House of Assembly has virtually the same plenary powers in South Africa as the party with a majority in the House of Commons in Britain. Either body has the legal power to transform

32. Appellate Division Quorum Act, 1955; Senate Act, 1955.

33. *Collins* v. *Minister of the Interior*, 1957(1) S.A. 552 (A.D.).

34. For reviews of this legal struggle, see B. Beinart, "Parliament and the Courts," *Butterworth's South African Law Review* (1954), pp. 134–81; D. V. Cowen, *Parliamentary Sovereignty and the Entrenched Sections of the South Africa Act* (Cape Town: Juta, 1951), and "Legislature and Judiciary," *Modern Law Review* (July 1952), pp. 277–96, and (July 1953), pp. 273–98; Hahlo and Kahn, *Union of South Africa*, pp. 146–63; and Geoffrey Marshall, *Parliamentary Sovereignty and the Commonwealth* (Oxford: Clarendon Press, 1957), chap. xi.

35. Republic of South Africa Constitution Fifth Amendment Act, 1980.

any or every institution in the state, brushing aside any opposition. Neither the "unwritten" constitution of the United Kingdom nor the "written" constitution of South Africa provides effectively for legal impediments to such actions.

Nevertheless, the extralegal differences between the two cases are substantial. The House of Commons is elected by the mass of the British adult population, regardless of race: the House of Assembly is elected by a racial oligarchy comprising one-sixth of the total population of South Africa. Moreover, though political passions often run high in Great Britain, the party with a majority in the House of Commons continues to recognize the principal conventions they have developed over the years, if only because it would suffer politically if it ignored them. On the other hand, the party having a majority in the House of Assembly since 1948 has been able with impunity to ignore convention on several occasions, largely because the conventions themselves are not a local product but an importation from Britain. In British practice, the doctrine of parliamentary supremacy masks limitations upon the powers of the government of the day which are scarcely less effective for being extralegal; in South African practice, the doctrine has made Parliament little more than a convenient mechanism for giving legislative effect to the will of the prime minister and cabinet. The British system has been perverted in South Africa, and what remains is the empty shell of responsible parliamentary government.

REGIONAL GOVERNMENT

South Africa is a unitary state—that is to say, the central government is supreme over all the regional and local authorities. Of these the most important were previously the provinces, which coincide with the pre-Union colonies. Their system of government, which has not altered greatly since 1910, is set out in part 6 of the 1961 constitution.[36] It includes several original features that are of some interest to the student of government but can only be dealt with summarily here.

The chief executive officer of a province is an Administrator, appointed by the central government. He is chairman, with both a deliberative and casting vote, of an executive committee, the other four members of which are elected by the provincial council. Initially, the election was by proportional representation, the National Convention having assumed that party politics would not enter into provincial government. In fact, the national parties became involved in provincial elections from the very beginning, with the result that in the Transvaal and the Cape Province the executive committees always included members of more than one party, and the same was often the case in Natal and the Orange Free State. This awkward situation was terminated in 1962; since then a party with a majority in a provincial council has been able to elect all four of the elected members of the executive committee.[37] Both the Administrator and the executive committee hold office for a fixed term of five years. Since the Administrator is appointed by the central government and neither he nor the elected members of the executive committee are dismissable by the provincial council, the system of responsible government does not exist in the provinces.

A provincial council contains as many members as the province has in the House of Assembly, or twice that number in special circumstances. In 1981 the Cape Provincial Council had 55 members, Transvaal 76, Natal 20, and the Orange Free State 28. They are elected in single-member electoral divisions by the voters who possess the parliamentary franchise. Since 1970 provincial council elections have been held at the same time as parliamentary elections; the duration of each provincial council is the same as that of the House of Assembly. When the African

36. Secs. 66–93; Hahlo and Kahn, *Union of South Africa*, pp. 175–82.
37. Provincial Executive Committees Act, 1962.

voters were removed from the common roll in 1936, they were given the right to elect two white provincial councillors in the Cape Province, but those seats were abolished in 1960.[38] When the Coloured voters were removed from the common roll in 1956, they too were given the right to elect two white provincial councillors in the Cape Province.[39] This was abolished in 1968. So long as there were African or Coloured voters on the common roll, they were eligible for election to the Cape Provincial Council, and one African and two Coloured men were, in fact, elected. But the provincial councillors who represented the African and Coloured voters were not permitted to take part in the election of senators—the one function of the provincial councils that affected the composition of Parliament.

Provincial councils have the power to make ordinances in a number of fields specified in the constitution. The most significant are direct taxation, hospitals, municipal and other local institutions, local (as distinct from national) roads and other local public works, and the school education of Whites (as distinct from the education of Blacks and as distinct from university, technical, and adult education). Within these fields provincial legislation is subject to the approval of the central government. Moreover, Parliament may freely legislate, expressly or implicitly, in any of these fields, and in the event of a conflict, acts of Parliament always prevail over provincial ordinances. Parliament may at any time restrict the competence of the provincial councils or change the system of provincial government.[40] In fact, the powers of the provinces have diminished

38. Representation of Natives Act, 1936; Promotion of Bantu Self-Government Act, 1959 (effective June 30, 1960).

39. South Africa Act Amendment Act, 1956, and Separate Representation of Voters Amendment Act, 1956, validating and amending the Separate Representation of Voters Act, 1951.

40. The constitution still includes a provision that Parliament shall not alter the boundaries of a province, nor abolish any provincial council, nor abridge its legislative powers, except upon petition from the provincial council concerned (sec. 114); but this provision has no legal efficacy.

over the years. The central government has narrowed their tax-
ing powers,[41] it has taken from them the control of African and
Coloured school education,[42] and it has established the basic
legal patterns of urban life.[43] In addition, the provinces have
always been handicapped by an insufficiency of revenue for the
performance of their obligations, and they are now heavily dependent on subsidy from the central government.

The National party now has majorities in the provincial
councils of the Transvaal, the Cape Province, and the Orange
Free State, and consequently all the members of their executive
committees are Nationalists. In Natal, on the other hand, the
Administrator is a Nationalist nominee and the other members
of the executive committee are members of the New Republic
party.

THE "HOMELANDS" POLICY

The Cape colonial government began to create a system of district councils in the African reserves of the colony at the end of
the nineteenth century. These district councils included both
nominated and elected members. They were chaired by white
officials and had advisory powers over the allocation of local
taxes for roads, schools, hospitals, and other public works. The
South African government extended the practice to the other
provinces. In addition, in 1931 it created a general council for
the Transkei, and in 1936 a country-wide Natives Representative
Council. These bodies, too, were chaired by white officials and
contained nominated as well as elected Africans; and their powers, also, were only advisory.[44]

41. For example, by the Financial Relations Act, 1913; the Financial Relations Consolidation and Amendment Act, 1945; and the Financial Relations
Amendment Act, 1957.

42. Bantu Education Act, 1953; Coloured Persons Education Act, 1963.

43. For example, Group Areas Act, 1950, and its many amendments.

44. J. Butler et al., The Black Homelands of South Africa (Berkeley: University of California Press, 1977), pp. 24–28.

Since coming into power in 1948 the National party government has applied the doctrine that the African population is composed of ten different "nations." It has grouped the former "native reserves," set aside for Africans' use by the Natives Land Act of 1913 and its amendment of 1936, into ten "homelands," where each African "nation" is to be given political and civic rights denied to it in the "white areas" of the country. In the 1950s, the government abolished the Natives Representative Council, and with it the principle of country-wide African political institutions, substituting a new system of "Bantu Authorities" from the "tribal" to the "homeland" level. Each council was dominated by chiefs subject, initially, to white supervision. Finally, the Bantu Homelands Citizenship Act of 1970 provides that every African in the Republic shall not be a citizen of South Africa but of a "homeland," irrespective of whether he was born there or resides there or has ever been there; and the Bantu Homelands Constitution Act of 1971 empowers the government to grant independence to any "homeland."[45]

The Transkei was the first territory to complete the process envisaged in these laws. It became "self-governing" in 1963 and "independent" in 1976, under conditions that ensured its control by collaborative chiefs.[46] Bophuthatswana followed in 1977, Venda in 1979, and Ciskei in 1981. The governments of South Africa and these four "homelands" are the only ones in the world that recognize the validity of these grants of independence. The South African government wishes to confer "independence" on the remaining six "homelands" in the near future, but many of them may decline to accept it. In particular, whereas Chief Kaiser Matanzima of the Transkei, Chief Lucas Mangope of Bophuthatswana, Chief Patrick Mphephu of Venda, and Chief Lennox Sebe of Ciskei have accepted "independence," Chief Gatsha Buthelezi of KwaZulu has refused the offer of indepen-

45. Ibid., pp. 28–39.
46. Newell M. Stultz, *Transkei's Half Loaf: Race Separation in South Africa* (New Haven: Yale University Press, 1979).

dence but uses his office as a platform for demanding more rights for Blacks throughout South Africa. Moreover, most urban Blacks attack the "homeland" policy as an instrument for extending and perpetuating white domination.

South African spokesmen claim that each African ethnic group has its own "homeland." This is not consistently so. Pedi and North Ndebele share the Lebowa "homeland," and the Xhosa are divided between the Ciskei and the Transkei. Moreover, every "homeland" consists of more than one portion of territory, separated by white farming land. The most severely divided are KwaZulu, which is made up of 29 major and 41 minor fragments, and Bophuthatswana, which has 19 fragments, some of them hundreds of miles apart. Even if the proposed consolidations are completed, Bophuthatswana will be six noncontiguous areas and KwaZulu, ten.[47]

In the face of international opprobrium and the total absence of international recognition, the "homelands" policy is likely to undergo some modifications. "Community Councils" now allow limited self-government in African urban areas, and there are plans to set up a nominated African body with the task of advising the white government on matters concerning Africans.[48] Further land additions are likely to be made to some "homelands," and the status of Africans in "white areas" may improve through the desegregation of some facilities. But it is unlikely that the government will grant anything but superficial changes, at least in the near future. In particular, the government may be expected to persist in rejecting African claims to a share in the common South African citizenship. Nevertheless, most Africans will continue to contribute their labor to white industry and agriculture, and the impoverished "homelands" will remain convenient labor reservoirs for the Republic, while their

47. *Survey of Race Relations, 1977*, p. 312.
48. In 1980 the government planned an African advisory body as an adjunct to the President's Council. It was never implemented because of African opposition.

"self-governing" or "independent" status will serve as a pretext for discriminating against Africans.

COLOURED AND ASIAN COUNCILS

When the National party came to power in 1948, it had three immediate objectives with regard to the Coloured population. The first was to segregate the Coloured people biologically, which it did by prohibiting Coloured-white intermarriage and sexual relations.[49] The second was to segregate Coloured residential areas, which it achieved under the Groups Areas Act of 1951. This act resulted in the shifting of thousands of Coloured families from areas which became defined as white. It bore unequally on the Coloured and the white communities: the former were moved from desirable areas close to the city of Cape Town to the windswept, sandy parts of the Cape Flats; whereas Whites gained control of the areas thus lost to Coloureds. The third objective was to segregate the Coloured people politically. As explained above, this process was completed in 1968, when they were deprived of any say in the composition of Parliament and of the right to be members of the same political parties as Whites. Instead, the government created a "Coloured Persons Representative Council" (CPRC), partially elected by Coloured people throughout the Republic on the basis of general adult franchise, and partially appointed by the government.[50] This legislation provoked a crisis in the Coloured population. Many of them had hoped that they would not experience the full impact of apartheid and that the Whites would eventually incorporate them into their own dominant community. The 1968 legislation destroyed this illusion.

49. Prohibition of Mixed Marriages Act No. 55, 1949.
50. Prohibition of Political Interference Act, 1968; Separate Representation of Voters Amendment Act, 1968; Coloured Persons Representative Council Act, 1968.

From 1969 to 1980 the Coloured population was divided over the attitude they should take toward the CPRC. All recognized that the CPRC was a subordinate political institution and that Parliament could repeal or amend the powers it had delegated to the Council. Some Coloured people rejected collaboration outright. They denounced as "quislings," betrayers of democracy, and supporters of racism anybody who was involved directly or indirectly in the CPRC.[51] Others, self-defined "realists," while recognizing that the CPRC was set up by the government to avoid democratic representation in Parliament, were prepared to use it as a forum for expressing their views. On this ticket the Labour party (LP) contested the inaugural election of the CPRC and won most of the seats in the council.[52] A third group accepted the National party's claim that the Coloureds have an "identity" separate from the Whites, and the principle of "positive equal development." This group, the Federal Coloured Peoples party (renamed the Freedom party in 1978), was prepared to accept the political separation of Coloured and White, and to work within the framework of the CPRC.[53]

From its inception the CPRC received only limited Coloured support. At the inaugural election in 1969, only 35.7 percent of the potential electorate voted, and this dropped to 25.3 percent in 1975. Most apathetic were the upper-income, better-educated urban dwellers, who were sharply aware of the impotence of the council.

51. On this, see the constitution of the *Anti-Coloured Representative Council Committee*, which campaigned for the boycott of the 1975 CPRC elections, in P. Hugo, *Quislings or Realists: A Documentary Study of "Coloured" Politics in South Africa* (Johannesburg: Ravan Press, 1976), p. 473.

52. See the 1968 statement by the founder of the Labour party, M. D. Arendse: "The Labour Party's rejection of Apartheid is written into its constitution. It wishes to use all legal means and machinery to destroy the idea that the Coloured people as a whole accept Apartheid. To do this it must enter the political field and fight the elections on the basis of the present set-up. This it regrets exceedingly, but it sees no practicable alternative." "Statement on the Formation of the Labour Party," in Hugo, *Quislings or Realists*, p. 129.

53. "Federal Coloured Peoples Party: Constitution," in ibid., p. 279.

In 1980, recognizing that the CPRC was not an effective political instrument for its purposes, the government dissolved it and announced that it would substitute a wholly nominated Coloured Persons Council.[54] Later in 1980 the government abandoned its intention to set up such a council when it became apparent that it would receive no significant support. Instead, the government created another nominated consultative body, the President's Council.

The "separate development" program for the Asians encountered similar problems to that for the Coloureds, since the Asians, too, lacked a potential "homeland." In 1981 the first election was held for a fully elective South African Indian Council, but the vast majority of the Asians boycotted the election.

THE PRESIDENT'S COUNCIL

On February 3, 1981, Marais Viljoen, the state president, formally inaugurated a new body, the President's council.[55] This council is presided over by a new titleholder—the state vice president, who was elected by the House of Assembly for the purpose. The other sixty members of the council are all nominated by the government. Most of them are white; the rest are Coloured and Asian.

The government has defined the council's responsibilities as follows:

At this stage the Council's activities are largely directed towards contributing to the process of constitutional development by means of investigations, negotiations and recommendations. As a new constitutional dispensation has a bearing on every facet of society, the members of the President's Council have been divided into a Constitutional

54. South African Coloured Persons Council Act, 1980.
55. The President's Council was created by the Republic of South Africa Constitution Fifth Amendment Act, 1980, secs. 102 and 103.

Committee, a Science Committee and a Planning Committee, as well as Committees on Economic Affairs and on Community Relations.[56]

Prime Minister Pieter W. Botha and his colleagues have predicted great things of the council. They have stressed that it is the first time people of different racial groups have been brought together to deliberate on the future of the country, and they have given the public to expect that the council's advice will lead to significant changes in the South African political system.

Nevertheless, the President's Council labors under serious political constraints. The government has adamantly refused to include Africans in the council; largely for this reason, most of the effective organizations and substantial leaders among the Coloured and Asian peoples have boycotted it. Consequently, it has no discernible mandate to negotiate on behalf of the Coloured and Asian peoples, to say nothing of the Africans. Moreover, the increase in the voting strength of the unequivocally racist Herstigte Nasionale party (Reestablished National party, HNP) in the general election held on April 29, 1981, has limited the capacity of the National party government to institute radical reforms even if the President's Council were to recommend them.

BLACK LOCAL GOVERNMENT

Under 1962 and 1963 legislation the government established advisory bodies known as Urban Bantu Councils (UBCs) with elected majorities and minorities composed of representatives of tribal chiefs. These bodies were meant to advise local white authorities in the day-to-day administration of local government. By 1976 these councils had ceased to play any significant role in local affairs. During the Soweto unrest of that year, it was

56. Address by the state president on the occasion of the opening of the fifth session of the Sixth Parliament of the Republic of South Africa, January 23, 1981, *South African Digest*, January 30, 1981.

apparent that the UBCs enjoyed neither the support of the residents nor the power to influence the government.

In 1977 the government abolished the UBCs and replaced them with elected Community Councils (CCs), which fall directly under the control of the minister of co-operation and development.[57] Allowance is made in the legislation for a CC to make recommendations on housing, transportation, and recreation. By 1979, 198 CCs had been established, and a government spokesman declared that they would eventually receive the same status, powers, and responsibilities as white municipalities.[58]

In 1963 a management committee system, under the control of the minister of community development, was set up in Indian and Coloured areas. The government indicated that it would give these bodies increasing powers in the administration of local affairs. However, by 1980, after the establishment of about 122 Coloured and 8 Indian management committees, they remained little more than advisory appendages to white town and city councils, with almost no executive powers. Dissatisfaction with the system was widespread, and the Association of Management Committees called on the responsible minister to scrap the system and to give all South Africans equal representation on town and city councils, irrespective of race.[59]

These changes in the administration of Blacks have resulted in the undermining of the power of the old hierarchy of provincial and municipal authorities and have increased the power of the central government. Previously the provincial and municipal authorities were responsible for the local administration of all the inhabitants. Now all control over Blacks emanates either directly from the central government or from political institutions dominated by it. The Department of Co-operation and Development controls all Africans in urban areas; the Department

57. Community Councils Act No. 125, 1977.
58. *Survey of Race Relations, 1975*, pp. 408–09.
59. *Argus*, 26 August 1980.

of Community Development controls Coloureds directly or through management committees; it also controls Indians directly or through the SAIC.

There are still many problems to be solved before such a system can be effective. For example, the CCs enjoy little credibility in the African urban areas, as is seen from participation in Soweto elections as low as 5.6 percent.[60] In whatever way Blacks are incorporated into the white political structures, there is one point which cannot be emphasized too strongly: unless there is a fundamental change in the status of the subordinate political institutions, absolute legal power will continue to be exercised over black affairs by the white Parliament. There is nothing in the government's plans as announced in 1980 to suggest that Parliament will cease to retain sovereign legal power to legislate as it wishes on any topic over any area outside the "homelands" for the African, Coloured, and Asian communities. This means that, notwithstanding the proliferation of subordinate authorities and advisory bodies, there is in 87 percent of South Africa only one political process of vital significance: the process that determines the composition of Parliament, a process from which all Blacks—Asians, Coloureds, and Africans alike—are wholly excluded.

POLITICAL PARTIES

Since the parliamentary electorate has always been overwhelmingly white, South African political divisions have been divisions within the white community, its basic historic and cultural cleavage being between the Afrikaners and the South Africans of British descent. There have been three main types of political parties: parties led by Afrikaners, consisting almost exclusively of Afrikaners and dedicated to the promotion of the interests of

60. *Survey of Race Relations, 1978*, p. 341.

Afrikaners; parties led by British South Africans, consisting almost wholly of British South Africans and dedicated to the promotion of their interests; and middle parties comprising both Afrikaners and British South Africans and dedicated to the reduction of the historic tensions between the two groups and the creation of a united white South African nation.

Because the British South Africans have always been a minority within the white South African population and have been hampered by an unfavorable demographic distribution and by unfavorable delimitations, no British party has ever looked as though it would obtain a parliamentary majority. The main struggle has therefore been between Afrikaner parties and middle parties. British voters have often had no effective alternative to supporting a middle party, whereas Afrikaners have normally had an effective choice between a middle party and an Afrikaner party. Politics have thus been determined primarily by the conduct of the Afrikaner voters. In effect, an Afrikaner party has been able to prevail when it has been supported by about two-thirds of the Afrikaner voters, while a middle party has required the support of at least one-third of the Afrikaners as well as virtually all the British voters.

The political history of South Africa since 1910 falls into two periods, each of which started with middle-party government and developed into Afrikaner government. The first was terminated by the Great Depression and the second is still in progress. From 1910 to 1924 the dominant party was the South African party (SAP)—a middle party led by Louis Botha (d. 1919) and J. C. Smuts, Afrikaners whose policy was to create a united white South African nation through the gradual fusion of the two stocks, to develop South Africa's material resources within the capitalistic framework, to advance South Africa's autonomy within the evolving British Commonwealth, and to cooperate with Britain in international affairs. Initially the official opposition was the Unionist party—a British party led by L. S. Jameson; in 1913 the first Afrikaner party was founded by

J. B. M. Hertzog, who feared that the policy of the Botha government (of which he had formerly been a member) would result in the virtual absorption of the Afrikaners by the British, and the subordination of the interests of the white urban workers to the capitalists, and of South Africa to Britain.

Assisted by the Afrikaner reaction against South Africa's participation in World War I (which included a small-scale rebellion), Hertzog's National party (NP) whittled more and more Afrikaners away from the SAP in successive elections. The SAP became increasingly dependent on British support, so that it formed a coalition with the Unionist party in 1915 and absorbed it in 1921. By that time the basic Afrikaner party– middle-party alignment was being distorted by the existence of a white Labour party, consisting largely of urban workers of British descent who were concerned about obtaining protection both from management and from black competition. The SAP government supported management in industrial disturbances on the Witwatersrand, so the NP was able to obtain the cooperation of the Labour party and form within it a coalition government in 1924. In 1929, however, the NP won a clear majority of the seats in the House of Assembly, and if the depression had not followed, the NP might have maintained its control indefinitely.

As it was, the depression threw South African politics— like the politics of many other countries—into a state of confusion. The government lost support largely because of factors beyond its control, but also because of its doctrinaire and inexpedient decision to remain on the gold standard after Britain had left it. In the 1933 election, the NP lost seats for the first time since its foundation, though it remained the strongest party in the House of Assembly. By that time, however, Hertzog had reached the conclusion that the raison d'être for an exclusive Afrikaner party had disappeared. He believed that the protective legislation his government had sponsored had ensured that the Afrikaner people could cooperate with the British South Africans without endangering their cultural identity, and that it was desirable that the two streams of the white South African nation should cooperate to protect themselves against the Africans. Accordingly, in 1933 the SAP and the first NP formed a coalition government, and in 1934 they fused to found the United party (UP), with Hertzog as prime minister and Smuts as deputy prime minister.

At its birth the UP had a large majority in Parliament. However, a small British group, led by Colonel C. F. Stallard, refused to follow Smuts and formed the Dominion party, while a somewhat larger number of Afrikaners, under D. F. Malan, also rejected Hertzog as a leader and became a second National party (NP). Malan aimed to preserve the identity of the Afrikaner people pure and unsullied by British influence, and by constitutional means to achieve an Afrikaner domination of South Africa, thus completing the work that, however well he had begun it, Hertzog was deemed to have compromised by the fusion.

The Second World War had effects similar to the First. After winning the war debate in the House of Assembly, Smuts formed a coalition government of the diminished UP and the Labour and Dominion parties, all of which increased their strength in the 1943 election. For a time the Afrikaners who were opposed to South Africa's participation in the war were fragmented between the NP, which pursued a constitutional course, and several lesser organizations such as the Ossewabrandwag and the New Order, which prepared for the expected Nazi victory. Malan applied himself doggedly to the task of uniting the fragments and winning Afrikaners away from the UP, while the UP absorbed the Dominion party as the SAP had previously absorbed the Unionist party.

The 1948 election was decisive. It enabled the NP to form a government in alliance with the small Afrikaner party. Soon afterward, third parties were temporarily eliminated, as the NP absorbed the Afrikaner party and the UP extinguished what remained of the Labour party. The Nationalist government improved its position by granting parliamentary representation to the white voters of South West Africa (Namibia); by placing the Coloured voters firstly on a separate roll (1956), then scrapping this separate representation entirely (1968); by removing the white representatives of Africans from Parliament (1960); by reducing the minimum voting age for Whites from twenty-one to eighteen; and by securing skillful delimitations. In 1981, it won a vast majority of the Afrikaner votes; and it increased its strength in the House of Assembly from 73 seats in 1948 to 131 in 1981, while the combined seats of opposition parties dropped from 65 in 1948 to 34 in 1981.

Before the Second World War the color question was never a major determinant of South African party allegiance. All the main parties were agreed on the maintenance of white supremacy, all of them, when in power, sponsored legislation for this purpose, and there was no serious challenge to the dominant position of the Whites from inside or outside South Africa. Even so, one of the factors in the rise of the first NP was its success in presenting itself to the electorate as the party which was best able to maintain white supremacy. It was Hertzog who labeled his policy toward the Africans as one of segregation; one of the conditions of the fusion of 1934 was that UP should promote this policy by removing the Cape African voters from the common roll.

After the Second World War, white supremacy became more difficult to maintain in the face of the involvement of vast numbers of Africans in the urban economy and black demands for radical concessions, at a time when tropical Africa was being decolonized and the new Asian and African states were beginning to use the United Nations as a forum for criticism of South Africa. The second NP came into power in 1948 largely because it insisted that segregation as applied by the UP was no longer enough, and a more far-reaching policy, labeled "apartheid" (separateness), was needed if white supremacy was to be maintained in South Africa in the postwar world. Since then, apartheid has been the major substance of political controversy in South Africa. It was a major cause of the triumphs of the NP under the leadership of D. F. Malan and J. G. Strijdom. Under H. F. Verwoerd, B. J. Vorster, and P. W. Botha, the policy was modified and given the new label "separate development." The UP, led first by J. G. N. Strauss and then by Sir D. P. de Villiers Graaff after the death of Smuts in 1950, was continuously on the defensive, based on the assumption that to oppose white supremacy would be politically disastrous. It tried to find points of difference from the NP within the framework of white supremacy, and over the years it moved closer and closer to the Nationalist position. By 1977, the UP had suffered so much through defections and loss of support that the party dissolved and the majority of its parliamentary members formed another party—the New Republic party, which did not succeed in regaining the lost power and prestige.

Between elections the UP had lost several of its parliamentary members—some hiving off toward the NP and eventually joining it, others moving in the other direction, only to be eliminated from Parliament in the next election. The most notable secession was of eleven members in 1959; they broke with the UP and founded the Progressive party, which had the goals of repealing discriminatory laws, gradually incorporating Blacks in the common roll electorate subject to educational and economic qualifications, and providing protection for all in a rigid constitution with a Bill of Rights. But in the 1961 election all of them except Mrs. Suzman were defeated by UP candidates. In 1974 this party (renamed the Progressive Reform party) won seven parliamentary seats; and in the 1977 election, in which the New Republic party fared badly, it became the official Opposition, with 17 seats. In the 1981 election, now named the Progressive Federal party, it increased its seats to 26.

The present distribution of seats in the House of Assembly represents the logical working out of South Africa's political arithmetic. The ruling NP has consistently applied the only formula for success under the South African political system: an appeal to the Afrikaner voters as Afrikaners, combined with an appeal to the British voters as Whites.

By the middle of the 1960s the National party had consolidated its position to the extent that it could only be dislodged by some major catastrophe. Since then, the most alarming threat to the NP has come from the Right. During a parliamentary sitting in 1969, Albert Hertzog, a former cabinet minister, accused the NP of deviating from its original principles. He labeled English-speaking white South Africans as liberals, and maintained that only Calvinist Afrikaners could be entrusted to rule South Africa.[61] Later that year, B. J. Vorster, the prime minister, announced his intention to weed out the "rebels" by calling a general election and expelling Hertzog from the party. Hertzog retaliated by forming the Herstigte Nasionale party (HNP), which stood for national unity around the core of Afrikanerdom. It regarded English speakers as "Afrikaners in making" and declared that Afrikaans should be the sole national language. It described the National party's economic policies as opportunistic and contended that economic gain should not stand in the way of racial segregation. In the 1969 election it made a poor showing. The HNP won 3.59 percent of the votes cast and the NP's share was 54.86 percent, as compared with 58.6 percent in the 1966 general election.[62] In the 1981 election, the HNP increased its share of the votes cast to 14.1 percent, and about 30 percent of the Afrikaners who voted did so for the HNP. Although the HNP did not win any seats in Parliament, its increased support turned many previously safe NP seats into marginal constituencies which it might win in future elections. Consequently, the NP is weighed down by fears of Afrikaner disunity and concerned about the pressure from the Right within its own ethnic base. The irony is that, if the NP were to

61. *Hansard*, vol. 11 (1969), cols. 4506–07.
62. *Survey of Race Relations, 1970*, p. 4.

attempt to introduce changes sufficiently radical to ensure a peaceful settlement of conflict within South Africa, it would probably do so at the cost of its own position.

In the 1981 election the NP held all the seats for the Orange Free State, all the Cape seats except twelve in the English-speaking areas of the southwestern and the eastern Cape, all of the Transvaal seats except nine on the Witwatersrand, and seven of the Natal seats. The PFP had a strong footing on the Witwatersrand, in Natal, and in the southwestern and eastern Cape Province. With the exception of one seat in the eastern Cape, the NRP was confined to Natal.

TABLE 12. The State of the Parties after the 1981 General
         Election

Party	Cape Province	Natal	Orange Free State	Transvaal	Totals
National Party	43	7	14	67	131
Progressive Federal Party	11	6	—	9	26
New Republic Party	1	7	—	—	8

4

How the System Works

Reduced to the simplest meaningful terms, South African society may be represented thus:

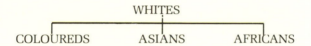

This shows graphically that the major cleavages in South African society are racial rather than class cleavages, and that one "race," labeled white, dominates the others. There are firm social boundaries between these four primary divisions of South African society and they are protected partly by law and partly by custom. In particular, the dominant white division is wholly endogamous by law—that is to say, it is a crime for a white person to have sexual relations outside the white division; while each of the subject divisions is almost entirely endogamous by custom rather than by law. There are, of course, different social classes within each of the four divisions, based on education, occupation, and wealth. For these reasons, we shall call South Africa a caste society, and the Whites, the Coloureds, the Asians, and the Africans the four South African castes.[1]

1. The South African case is somewhat similar to the early twentieth-century American South, as analyzed by John Dollard in *Caste and Class in a Southern Town* (New Haven: Yale University Press, 1937), especially pp. 62–97. We are grateful to Leonard Doob and William Foltz for this reference and for their corroboration of our usage.

Within each South African caste, one of the persistent lines of division is ethnic in character. In the white caste there are Afrikaner and English-speaking communities; in the Coloured caste, Christian and Muslim communities; in the Asian caste, Hindu and Muslim communities; and in the African caste, the traditional Xhosa, Zulu, Sotho, and other ethnic communities are still discernible. While the caste lines are extremely rigid, the community lines within each caste are flexible. There is individual mobility from one community to another and a tendency for class stratifications, based upon individual attainment, to supersede the old community divisions within each caste.

In a modern society a man has numerous loyalties— subnational, national, and even supranational—and no one loyalty absolutely subsumes all the others. Loyalty to the nation comprising all the citizens of the territorial state transcends and moderates, without destroying, loyalties to subnational communities, classes, institutions, and associations; and supranational loyalties in turn transcend and moderate nationalism. In a caste society, too, a man may have many loyalties, but loyalty to caste tends to dominate and subsume all others. The dominant caste equates itself with the "nation"; the symbols of the dominant caste become the authorized "national" symbols; and caste loyalty is the overriding loyalty that members of the dominant caste, and their educational and even religious institutions, transmit to their children, by example and by manifest indoctrination. When we analyze the political socialization process in such a society, we are studying the social techniques by which a dominant caste seeks to preserve its power. The principal technique is the avoidance or even the prevention of intercaste contacts, except between master and servant, ruler and ruled. Therefore, in the model caste society the dominant caste coexists with others in the same social, political, and economic system, but without mutual understanding or a sense of shared humanity.

The South African case approximates this model rather closely. Few members of the dominant caste dream of egalitarian association with members of other castes, and fewer still practise it. But in South Africa there is the further complication that the dominant caste itself contains two ethnocultural communities between which there is a long tradition of competition and hostility. Moreover, within the dominant caste there are still two rival traditions concerning the relations between the two communities: according to one tradition they should fuse into a single white "nation"; according to the other, the integrity of the Afrikaner "nation" must be preserved and any fusing that takes place must be on Afrikaner terms, amounting to the enlargement of the Afrikaner nation through its absorption of the English-speaking white community.

THE POLITICAL SOCIALIZATION PROCESS

In this section we shall consider the socializing experiences of members of the different South African castes and communities which take place in the family and in educational and religious institutions. The contributions that voluntary associations, communications media, and political parties make to the political socialization process will be dealt with later.

Afrikaans- and English-speaking Whites

The nuclear white South African family has two special characteristics. The first is that it almost invariably employs one or more black domestic servants. In his earliest years a white child will often be left in charge of a black servant; if he is a farm child he may have playmates among the children of the black farm laborers. As his social awareness develops, the white child perceives that the Black is treated by his parents and his older brothers and sisters as an inferior, attached to but not of the family. Thus family life inculcates an early familiarity with individual Blacks, which is soon overlaid with a consciousness of difference and superiority.

The second special characteristic of the white South African family is that its members are usually drawn exclusively from either the Afrikaner or the English-speaking community, and the other community is simply not encountered in the family situation. If by chance some relative has married outside his community, the fact will certainly be a matter of comment, and probably adverse comment. In this or some other way the child will at an early age become aware of the existence of the other community as an object of rivalry and hostility.

The white child is required by law to attend school and in most cases he goes to a public school, where education is free. There his experiences confirm and strengthen the attitudes he has acquired in his home. His school environment is as exclusive as his home environment. His teachers and fellow pupils are drawn almost entirely from his own community; the only Blacks to be found on the school premises are servants; and the major loyalty inculcated by the school is to the community or, at most, to the white caste.

Formerly there were a number of schools which catered for both white communities, partly as a matter of convenience in areas where they lived intermingled, and partly because it was United party policy to encourage such schools as a means of reducing community exclusiveness.[2] This policy was opposed by the National party, which feared that Afrikaner children would become denationalized in such schools. In 1948 the Instituut vir Christelik-Nasionale Onderwys (Institute for Christian National Education) of the Federasie van Afrikaanse Kultuurverenigings (Federation of Afrikaner Cultural Associations) produced a tract called *CNO-Beleid* (Christian National Education Policy).[3] Its basic thesis was that each of the white com-

2. B. Rose and R. Tumner, *Documents in South African Education* (Johannesburg: Ad Donker, 1975); B. Rose, ed., *Education in Southern Africa* (Johannesburg: Collier-Macmillan, 1970); F. E. Auerbach, *The Power of Prejudice in South African Education* (Cape Town: Balkema, 1965).
3. *CNO-Beleid* was published in Johannesburg in 1948. It is a pamphlet of

munities should provide children with an education that would preserve and perpetuate its own peculiar heritage, and that the Afrikaner schools should "be imbued with the Christian-National spiritual and cultural material of our nation. . . . We wish to have no mixing of languages, no mixing of cultures, no mixing of religions and no mixing of races."[4]

In such schools religion should be the key subject and all secular subjects should be taught in a "Christian" spirit: history as a revelation of the purposes of God, who has "willed separate nations and peoples," and the natural sciences so that "There shall be no attempt to reconcile or abolish the fundamental oppositions."[5] The parents should have the decisive say in the appointment and control of teachers, and the church in supervising the youngsters' faith. This document was approved by the synods of the Dutch Reformed churches, and although it has never been officially adopted by the National party, its principles have been applied in varying degrees in the different provinces.

In all of the provinces, with the exception of Natal, it is compulsory for the white child to be educated through the medium of home language, Afrikaans or English. This is defined as the language better known by the pupil and it is up to the principal of the school to decide which language that is.

In 1967, the government passed two Education acts which placed the control of educational policy for Whites in the hands of the minister of national education, but left the administration in the hands of the provinces. Dr. Connie Mulder spelt out the purpose of the legislation during the parliamentary debate:

---

thirty-one pages, containing a foreword by J. C. van Rooy, chairman of the FAK, and fifteen Articles.
  4. Ibid., p. 6.
  5. Ibid., Articles 2. 6, and 11.

Everything loses its meaning when the spirit of the nation is killed. Our schools must be able to make . . . [the children] proud of this their only fatherland which the Creator has given them. Therefore our education must be national . . . fostering a love for those things which are one's own; . . . love for their flag, their freedom and their national anthem must be impressed upon them daily. To the child those things must be beautiful and precious.[6]

A new subject, "Youth Preparedness," has been added to the curriculum, with a syllabus and textbooks that inculcate a militaristic attitude and indoctrinate in apartheid:

Our forefathers believed, and we still believe today, that God himself made the diversity of peoples on earth. . . . Inter-racial residence and intermarriage are not only a disgrace, but are also forbidden by law.
It is, however, not only the skin of the white South African that differs from that of the non-white. The White stands on a much higher plane of civilization and is more developed. Whites must so live, learn and work that we shall not sink to the cultural level of the non-Whites. Only thus can the government of our country remain in the hands of the Whites.[7]

Whereas in most countries the educational system is a means of incorporating all children into a common nationalism, the South African educational system aims to develop and perpetuate ethnocultural differences. This is found most noticeably in the division between White and Black, but also between English and Afrikaans. The Afrikaans text of a code of honor printed in 1965, *Pupils' Study Diary*, urges the pupil to strive "always and at all times to serve *my* country and *my* people [volk]." The word *volk* when thus used in Afrikaans excludes all

6. C. Mulder, quoted in Rose and Tumner, *Documents*, p. 129.
7. L. C. Becker and G. J. Potgieter, *Voorligting vir Standerd VI* (Johannesburg, 1960), pp. 30–31.

other population groups in South Africa.[8] The English version reads, "to serve my country and *its* people at all times."

On leaving school a white student who has passed the matriculation (twelfth) grade examination may, if he wishes, proceed to a university. There are ten residential universities for white students in South Africa, all of them semiautonomous institutions. They charge low fees because they receive heavy state subsidies, based on their enrollment, with the result that a high proportion of white South Africans receive a university education. In the universities of Cape Town, the Witwatersrand, Natal, and Rhodes University, the medium of instruction is English; in the universities of Stellenbosch, Pretoria, and the Orange Free State, Potchefstroom University for Christian Higher Education, and the Rand Afrikaans University, the medium is Afrikaans. The University of Port Elizabeth, founded in 1965, is dual-medium; so is the University of South Africa, a nonresidential correspondence university which caters for all racial groups. There is no legal compulsion on the white student to enroll in the university where his home language is the medium of instruction, but the number who do not is small. The Afrikaner youth who attends an English-medium university defies strong social pressures and weakens his prospects of joining the administrative and political establishment.

The tone of the English-medium universities is cosmopolitan. Their faculties are recruited from outside as well as inside South Africa and they strive for universal standards of teaching and research. However, their circumstances are increasingly adverse. The Afrikaans-medium universities are staffed almost entirely by Afrikaners, and some of their teaching and research in the social sciences is limited by myopia, if not marred by serious bias.[9] Thus the limitations of the family as an agent of

8. Auerbach, *Power of Prejudice*, p. x.
9. See, for example, Leonard M. Thompson, "Afrikaner Nationalist His-

socialization in a plural society are shared by the school and the university.

For many white South Africans another major socializing agent is the church or synagogue. Nearly all Afrikaners are members of one of the three Dutch Reformed churches: the Nederduitse Gereformeerde Kerk (NGK), which is the strongest in all parts of South Africa; the Nederduitsch Hervormde Kerk (NHK), whose main strength is in the Transvaal; and the Gereformeerde Kerk van Suid-Africa (GKSA), the smallest but most fundamentalist of the three, and the one that controls the Potchefstroom University for Christian Higher Education.[10] All three churches are derived from the same Dutch colonial institution and each is today a completely autonomous body. The Dutch Reformed churches limit their membership to Whites although they do admit a few Coloured congregations. The separate Dutch Reformed Mission churches are open to all races, but very few Whites actually belong to them. The Dutch Reformed churches have been intimately associated with the rise and triumph of Afrikaner nationalism. Many *predikants* (clergy) were staunch opponents of Milner's anglicization policy and have propagated the ideal of an exclusive Afrikaner nation with a divine mission. Consequently, the typical Dutch Reformed church congregation is as much a racial corporation as the Afrikaner family or school—a racial corporation with a special function of invoking the awe-inspiring rituals and sanctions of fundamental Calvinism in support of the separation of South African society into racial units.

---

toriography and the Policy of Apartheid," *Journal of African History* 3, no. 1 (1962): 125–41; John Sharp, "Two Separate Developments: Anthropology in South Africa," *Royal Anthropological Institute Newsletter*, no. 36 (1980); H. W. van der Merwe and David Welsh, eds., *The Future of the University in Southern Africa* (Cape Town: David Philip, 1977).

10. In 1976 John de Gruchy estimated that 34.7 percent of the white population were members of the NGK; 5.2 percent, of the NHK; and 2.7 percent, of the GKSA (*The Church Struggle in South Africa*, p. 240).

Most English-speaking white South Africans profess to be members of Protestant churches (notably Anglican, Methodist, and Presbyterian), and there are sizable minorities of Catholics and Jews.[11] Unlike the Dutch Reformed churches, the English-speaking religious organizations are branches of, or closely associated with, international bodies. In a series of pronouncements all of them have condemned apartheid. Nevertheless, all of them practise racial separation to some extent. Most English-speaking white churchgoers are members of all-white congregations. This is not because of church policy but is a result of legislation which divides residential areas on racial lines. Consequently, church congregations are, for the most part, racially divided. Leaders such as Catholic and Anglican archbishops have tried to eliminate racist practices and promote genuinely multiracial Christian congregations and schools, but in so doing they have risked the loss of white lay support.

The socialization experiences of the Afrikaner are all of a piece—in family, school and university, and church the same values are cherished, and these are the values that preserve the domination of the white caste and the autonomy of the Afrikaner community. On the other hand, the socialization experiences of English-speaking white South Africans reveal a dichotomy between ideal and actuality. The Afrikaner, therefore, tends to possess a singular sense of moral and intellectual rectitude, even when his conduct is abhorrent to the rest of mankind, whereas the English-speaking white South African is prone to cynicism.

Africans, Coloureds, Asians
A major problem for a ruling caste is how to reconcile the members of the subordinate castes to their place in the social

11. Estimates made in 1976 based on the 1970 census are as follows: the Anglican church, 400,000 white members; the Methodist church, 360,000; Roman Catholic, 305,000; and Presbyterian church, 120,000 (ibid., p. 240). At the time of the 1970 census there were 118,000 Jews in South Africa. *South African Statistics, 1978,* 1:30.

order. In this process, education has a key role. In South Africa, as elsewhere in the continent, Christian missionaries took the initiative in introducing Western education to African peoples. By 1948 there were over five thousand mission schools in South Africa, and they received considerable subsidies from the state. Most of the missionaries were of European rather than South African origin, affiliation, and outlook, and they regarded it as their purpose as educators to transmit modern knowledge rather than to attempt to adapt it to the peculiar circumstances of subject peoples. From the National party's point of view, this was dangerous; for while the party leaders recognized that the economic system demanded that some modern education should be provided for the subordinate castes, they wished to prevent it from making them dissatisfied with their subordinate roles. As Hendrik Frensch Verwoerd saw it:

good racial relations are spoilt when the correct education is not given. Above all, good racial relations cannot exist when the education is given under the control of people who create wrong expectations on the part of the Native himself. . . . It is therefore necessary that Native education should be controlled in such a way that it should be in accord with the policy of the State.[12]

Accordingly, following the report of a commission under the chairmanship of Werner W. M. Eiselen, then secretary for native affairs,[13] Parliament in 1953 passed the Bantu Education Act, which started a radical transformation of African school education.

The transformation is almost complete.[14] African education is dealt with and, for the most part, controlled by a central government department, the Department of Education and Training (formerly Bantu Education), which is distinct from the

12. *House of Assembly Debates, 1953*, col. 3576.
13. Union of South Africa, *Report of the Commission on Native Education, 1949–51: U. G. 53/1951* (Pretoria: Government Printer, 1951).
14. Muriel Horrell, *A Decade of Bantu Education* (Johannesburg: South African Institute of Race Relations, 1964).

Department of National Education that concerns itself with white education. No private college for training African teachers is allowed to exist, so that the training of African teachers is now conducted exclusively in government colleges. No private school for Africans may exist without obtaining a license from the government. In several cases the government has refused to grant licenses—for example, to the School of Christ the King in Sophiatown, Johannesburg, which was formerly controlled by the Anglican Community of the Resurrection, and to Adams College in Natal, a distinguished high school founded by American missionaries in 1853.

In most cases it has not been necessary to refuse licenses because the private schools no longer receive state subsidies. The withdrawal of these funds was a lethal blow to missionary education. Most of the missionary schools have now been transferred to the government. By 1980 fewer than a hundred schools, with an enrollment of about fifteen thousand pupils, remained under private control. Most of these were Roman Catholic schools. The Catholic church raised funds to continue its educational work after the withdrawal of the subsidy, but financial difficulties eventually resulted in the transfer of most of its schools to government control.

The Department of Education and Training provides some elementary education for most African children and secondary education for a few, and it controls the content of their education at all levels. The most conspicuous pedagogical changes made by the National party government concern languages. Most of the mission schools used English as the medium of instruction after the first year or two, so that English was the main literary language of the African population and seemed likely to become the lingua franca. Between 1953 and 1979, the African language of an area was the sole medium of instruction in public schools until standard 6 (eighth grade); today, parents can choose between English and Afrikaans as a medium of instruction after standard 2. As a result there was a period of a marked decline in the transmission of English—the one South African language that is a universal language—and an erection of further barriers between Africans.[15]

Before 1963 the education of Coloured and Asian children was a provincial matter, conducted for the most part in state-aided schools run by missionary and other private organizations, and to a lesser but increasing extent in government schools. Asians themselves subscribed large sums of money for building schools, which they handed over to the provinces for administration. Most Coloured and Asian children received at least an elementary education. It was compulsory for Coloured children in Natal, and the Cape Provincial Council had accepted the principle of compulsion for both Coloured and Asian children and was applying it where practicable.[16] In 1963, however, Parliament passed a law transferring Coloured school education to the central government's Department of Coloured Affairs, and the transfer was followed by the same sort of process that has been applied to African schools—the elimination of the private schools and the tightening of controls over teachers and syllabuses.[17] A similar step took place in the case of Asian education.

In 1978–79 a total of R253 million was allocated to African education, which resulted in an expenditure of an average of R71 per pupil. Each racial group is expected to pay for its own education and this results in a vast disparity in the funds spent on education for the different groups. The following table illustrates the overall differences in education expenditure for the various groups, and shows that the gap began to narrow after 1975 but is still enormous.

15. This process was, however, reversed in the "homelands," where secondary education always took place through the medium of English.

16. For summaries of the state of Coloured and Indian education of the time, see South African Institute of Race Relations, *Survey of Race Relations*, 1961, pp. 241–47, 1962, pp. 188–94, and 1963, pp. 229–35.

17. Coloured Persons Education Act, 1963.

TABLE 13. Government Expenditure per School Pupil,
1953−1979

Year	White		Indian		Coloured		African	
	R	%	R	%	R	%	R	%
1953	128	100.0	40	31.0	40	31.0	18	14.0
1960	145	100.0	—	—	59	41.0	12.5	8.6
1968	228	100.0	70	31.0	—	—	14.5	6.4
1975	644	100.0	190	28.0	150	22.0	42	6.5
1977	654	100.0	220	33.6	158	24.1	49	7.5
1979	724	100.0	357	49.3	225	31.0	71	9.8

SOURCE: F. E. Auerbach, *Discrimination in Education* (Cape Town: Centre for Intergroup Studies, 1976); Loraine Gordon et al., comps., *Survey of Race Relations in South Africa, 1978* (Johannesburg, 1979), p. 399; *Intergroup* (Cape Town: Centre for Intergroup Studies), June 1980.

The inequalities in the educational system are further reflected in the teacher-pupil ratios. In 1979 the white ratio was 1:19.6; Coloured 1:29.6; Asian 1:26.2; and African 1:47.6.

In 1976 and 1977 widespread rioting and unrest were triggered by the introduction of Afrikaans as a medium of education in African schools, and it became apparent that the entire system of "Bantu education" was unacceptable to young Africans. The government discontinued the compulsory use of Afrikaans and introduced a limited universal education as a result of the protests. Nevertheless, in 1980 pupils at Coloured schools boycotted classes and denounced their inadequate school facilities and inferior educational system. Despite the fact that the government promised to make more money available to Coloured schools, dissatisfaction persisted with the fundamental disparities in the educational system. These are: the separate government departments for white, African, and Coloured education; the vast discrepancy between money spent on schooling for the different groups; and the racial exclusiveness of the schools and universities.

Apartheid is now applied in a far-reaching way at the university level. Until 1959 the South African universities were free to determine whom to admit as students: the universities of Cape Town and the Witwatersrand admitted Blacks as well as Whites and taught them in mixed classes. In 1959, 12 percent of the Cape Town students and 6 percent of the Witwatersrand students were black. The University of Natal admitted Blacks to the Durban but not to the Pietermaritzburg campus but taught them in separate classes. In 1959, 21 percent of the Natal students were black. The other five full-fledged universities that then existed enrolled white students only; while the University College of Fort Hare, a former mission institution affiliated with Rhodes University, was attended by Coloured, Asian, and African students.[18]

In 1959, Parliament passed legislation making it unlawful for Blacks who were not previously registered as students in the established universities to register there in the future without special permission from the government, empowering the government to create new "university colleges" for black students, and transferring Fort Hare to the government as such a college. In the next few years the number of black students at the established universities declined, admission to Fort Hare was limited to Xhosa-speaking Africans, and four new universities were founded for Zulu-speaking Africans, Sotho-speaking Africans, Asians, and Coloured people. In 1976 the government also established a Medical University of South Africa to provide medical, dental, and veterinary training for Africans; thenceforward, no Africans were to be admitted to the previously existing university medical faculties.

18. *Survey of Race Relations, 1961*, p. 252.

During the 1960s and 1970s there was a vast increase in the number of university places in South Africa. The total number of students in the residential universities increased from about 30,000 in 1959 to over 104,000 in 1980 and those in the nonresidential University of South Africa, from 9,171 to 56,174. In recent years, moreover, the government has permitted considerable numbers of black students to study in those "white" universities that are willing to admit them, mainly on the ground that the courses they wish to take are not available in their segregated institutions. In 1980, Blacks formed 11 percent of the student body in the University of Cape Town, 10 percent in the University of Natal, 9 percent in the University of the Witwatersrand, and 7 percent in Rhodes University; and some people were predicting that those universities would become predominantly black within the next generation. While most of those black students were Coloureds and Asians, they included 734 Africans. Even Stellenbosch, which had no black students at all as recently as 1976, admitted 81 Coloured, 4 Indian, 1 Chinese, and 7 African students in 1980, and the other Afrikaans-medium universities are now admitting a trickle of black students to their postgraduate programs.[19]

In 1980 the composition of the student bodies was as follows (see table 14).

The present effects of the recent changes in black university education are limited. The government continues to insist that it has no intention of returning to the "white" universities the control over admissions they lost in 1959. Black students continue to experience discrimination in the "white" universities, where they are not permitted to live in the established student residences nor to take part in some of the social activities. In the black universities, students are subject to stringent controls. Their organizations require the approval of the rectors, who may

19. *Survey of Race Relations, 1980*, p. 538. On this subject, see especially Hendrik W. van der Merwe and David Welsh, eds., *The Future of the University in South Africa* (Cape Town: David Philip, 1977).

TABLE 14. University Enrollment, 1980

Residential Universities	White	Coloured	Indian	Chinese	African	Totals
Cape Town	9,334	846	230	25	71	10,506
Durban Westville	76	36	4,756	—	7	4,875
Fort Hare	26	2	—	—	2,698	2,726
Natal	7,547	179	656	13	376	8,771
The North (Turfloop)	28	2	—	—	2,722	2,752
Orange Free State	8,320	2	—	—	10	8,332
Port Elizabeth	2,938	39	6	27	28	3,038
Potchefstroom	6,687	3	2	—	6	6,698
Pretoria	16,658	2	—	—	—	16,660
Rand Afrikaans	4,795	2	4	—	3	4,804
Rhodes	2,701	53	82	35	44	2,915
Stellenbosch	11,858	81	4	1	7	11,954
Western Cape	20	3,963	152	—	18	4,153

Witwatersrand	11,897	169	643	174	243	13,126
Zululand	1	2	—	—	1,509	1,512
Subtotals	82,886	5,381	6,535	275	7,742	102,822
Nonresidential University						
University of South Africa	37,404	10,687	5,144	117	2,822	56,174
Totals	120,290	16,068	11,679	392	10,564	158,996

SOURCE: Adapted from South African Institute of Race Relations, *Survey of Race Relations in South Africa, 1980* (Johannesburg: SAIRR, 1981), p. 538, which is derived from information supplied by the registrars of the universities. At Stellenbosch University, 3 students were not classified by race; hence the total differs by 3 from the sum of the racial lists. There were also 322 students in the Medical University of South Africa, 909 students in the University of the Transkei, and approximately 200 in the University of Bophuthatswana; nearly all of these were Africans.

dismiss students who infringe the regulations. In 1980, 70 percent of the faculties in the black universities were white and only 2 percent of the faculties in the white universities were black.

Students in black universities have consistently opposed government policies. In 1976 and 1977 nationwide protest against "Bantu education" was expressed particularly strongly in these universities and, as was to be expected, the government struck back vigorously: in 1976 it detained many black students in terms of security legislation, and in 1977 it banned the black South African Student Organization. Because of the systematic victimization of their leaders, black students are reluctant to make themselves available for positions of leadership and cynicism pervades the black universities.

It is difficult to assess the full psychological and political consequences of the present educational arrangements for South African Blacks. There have been numerous disturbances in the black South African schools and colleges under the present regime. During 1976, Fort Hare, the University of Zululand, Lovedale Teachers Training College, and the University of the Western Cape were all extensively damaged by arson. This, coupled with student boycotts, made black universities close for long periods during the year. The government presumably hoped that its educational policy would mold the minds of the subordinate castes into an acceptance of apartheid between White and Black, between Coloured and Asian, and between Xhosa, Zulu, and Sotho. Recent events have shown that this is not what is happening.

In colonial situations Western education always tended to corrode traditional particularism, however carefully it may have been controlled by the colonial power. This is also the case in South Africa. Among the host of impediments to the indoctrination of black youth in South African schools is the fact that nearly all the teachers are necessarily Blacks, who are themselves very conscious of the differences between their own conditions of employment and the conditions of employment of

white teachers in South Africa, and who cannot easily be perverted into reliable propagators of the ruling philosophy.

Moreover, the government cannot control the other socializing experiences of Blacks to the same extent that it controls their
education. Among rural Africans, and even among Africans who
have spent most of their lives in towns, there are still many
conservatives who reject Western cultural influences. In contrast, there are also many who have turned their backs upon the
past and think and act essentially (though not necessarily exclusively) as members of a contemporary proletariat.[20] The former,
in rejecting modernity, go a long way toward meeting the requirements of the ruling caste; the latter, in accepting modernity, do not. Continually confronted with the contrast between their own poverty, insecurity, and powerlessness, and the
wealth, the freedom, and the power of the Whites, they are
bound to conclude that social morality and South African law
are irreconcilable and that their own hardships are due to the
political system, and to transmit these conclusions to the next
generation.[21] The same is true of many Coloureds and Asians.[22]

Some Christian churches in South Africa, especially the
Dutch Reformed churches, reflect the structure of South African
society and encourage their black members to accept their subordinate lot. Others, however, do not conceal from their black
members their rejection of the caste principle and their abhorrence of its practical effects, while the separatist, African-
controlled churches have a wide range of attitudes toward the

20. Philip Mayer, *Townsmen or Tribesmen: Conservatism and the Process
of Urbanization in a South African City* (Cape Town: Oxford University Press,
1961); Monica Wilson and Archie Mafeje, *Langa: A Study of Social Groups in an
African Township* (Cape Town: Oxford University Press, 1963).

21. For example, Naboth Mokgatle, *The Autobiography of an Unknown
South African* (Berkeley: University of California Press, 1971); Mtutuzele Mat-
shoba, *Call Me Not a Man* (Johannesburg: Ravan Press, 1979).

22. For example, Ahmed Essop, *The Haji and Other Stories* (Johannesburg:
Ravan Press, 1979).

state and society—including, in some cases, radical opposition.[23]

The struggle that is taking place for the minds of the black peoples of South Africa is not, of course, a simple struggle between "traditionalism" and "modernity." The essence of traditional societies cannot be recreated in South Africa, for the conditions in which traditional societies flourished—political, economic, and psychological self-sufficiency—no longer exist anywhere in the Republic. Nor is the government trying to recreate traditional societies in their original form. What it *is* attempting is a form of neotraditionalism, to be achieved by cementing alliances with the most conservative elements in each of the subordinate castes and communities. Of these, the African chiefs and their heirs in the "homelands" are the most important. The "homeland" leaders who cooperate with the government in Pretoria may obtain material comforts, the satisfaction of exercising power at the local level, and the illusion of autonomy. On the other hand, conformist chiefs are under strong pressure from below and are liable either to throw in their lot with the group of modernists, or to try to translate the illusion of power into reality.

Furthermore, in South Africa as in other countries, modernity takes many forms. First, there are great variations in the extent to which black South Africans have experienced alien influences. Most of the Coloured people and Asians have had a long, intense, and continuous exposure. Africans whose ancestors lived near the eastern frontier of the old Cape Colony—such as the Xhosa and the Mfengu—have had a more protracted exposure, and in general a more concentrated one, than those of Zulu or Sotho origin. Also, Blacks who have always worked and lived in towns have experienced a more intense exposure to

23. G. B. Sundkler, *Bantu Prophets in South Africa* (London: Oxford University Press, 1961), and *Zulu Zion* (London: Oxford University Press, 1976); Martin West, *Bishops and Prophets in a Black City: African Independent Churches in Soweto, Johannesburg* (Cape Town: David Philip, 1975).

alien influences than Coloured and African labor tenants on white farms and Africans who migrate periodically between the "homelands"and the towns. Second, Blacks have gained very different impressions from their contacts with members of the ruling caste. To some, the dominant impression has been the paternalism of a responsible employer; to others, the seemingly capricious conduct of a policeman. Third, black South Africans make many different types of selections from the modern elements around them. Some try to create stable, middle-class homes; others turn to criminality.

The Effects of Political Socialization
The present generation of South African whites has absorbed the mystique of a dominant caste, but in varying degrees. The main internal cleavage within the dominant caste corresponds with its ethnocultural division into an Afrikaans- and an English-speaking community. In the Afrikaner community the mystique is effectively transmitted because family, school, university, and church combine to promote it, with comparatively few exceptions. In the English-speaking community the mystique is less effectively transmitted because the churches, the universities, some of the schools, and even a sizable minority of the families do not wholly accept the validity of the caste principle, even though they may tend to conform in practice. In the 1980s, however, the superior numbers, cohesion, and political power of the Afrikaners, and the growing challenge of the Blacks and the external world to the existing political system are weakening the anticaste influences on the English-speaking white community. White South Africans have become apprehensive of the future, and their disagreements are mainly over how best to preserve their security in the transformed world of the late twentieth century.

White South Africans are not able to control the socialization experience of Blacks. Although the scope of law has been extended to make egalitarian contacts between members of the white and the black castes extremely difficult, and although the educational system has been remodeled with the purpose of reconciling Blacks to subordination, the continuous absorption of more and more Blacks into the modern sector of the economy produces rising expectations that are only partly satisfied by minor advances in material prosperity. The decolonization of Angola, Mozambique, and Zimbabwe, and the antiracial climate of world opinion strengthen black South African resentments against the effects of apartheid. These expectations and resentments are transmitted in black families, in black churches, and even, sub rosa, in the government-controlled black schools and universities.

RECRUITMENT TO POLITICAL ROLES

In South Africa outside of the "homelands," all powerful executive, legislative, judicial, administrative, and military roles are limited by law to members of the white caste, and the overwhelming majority of the members of the cabinet, of the majority side in the legislature, of the judiciary, and of the senior echelons in the bureaucracy and the armed forces, are drawn in practice from the Afrikaner community. That is to say, ascriptive criteria set out in law define an outer oligarchy from which recruitment to authoritative governmental roles may take place; and further ascriptive criteria of an extralegal character determine an inner oligarchy from which most of the decisive roles are filled. Within the inner oligarchy—the Afrikaner community—on the other hand, individuals are recruited and promoted by criteria of achievement. Thus, nearly all the key political positions in South Africa are filled by well-educated Afrikaners who have given long and efficient service to the Afrikaner community.

The Afrikaner Leadership

Only Afrikaners were members of the cabinets of Daniel François Malan, Johannes G. Strijdom and Hendrich Frensch Verwoerd before 1961, when Verwoerd appointed two conservative white South Africans of British descent to junior ministries as a step toward the consolidation of the white caste under Afrikaner leadership. Since then it has been customary for there to be one or two English-speaking ministers, as a token representation of the English-speaking members of the National party. At the beginning of 1981 the state president was an Afrikaner; nineteen of the twenty cabinet ministers were Afrikaners, and the six deputy ministers were Afrikaners.

The State President, Cabinet Ministers and Deputy Ministers (1981)

M. Viljoen	State President
P. W. Botha	Prime Minister
S. P. Botha	Minister of Manpower Utilization
P. G. J. Koornhof	Minister of Co-operation and Development
H. Schoeman	Minister of Transport Affairs
O. P. F. Horwood	Minister of Finance
J. C. Heunis	Minister of Internal Affairs
H. H. Smit	Minister of Posts and Telecommunications
R. F. Botha	Minister of Foreign Affairs and Information (also responsible for the SABC)
F. W. de Klerk	Minister of Mineral and Energy Affairs
L. Le Grange	Minister of Police
A. P. Treurnicht	Minister of State Administration and of Statistics
L. A. P. A. Munnik	Minister of Health, Welfare, and Pensions
F. Hartzenberg	Minister of Education and Training (for Blacks)
C. V. van der Merwe	Minister of Water Affairs, Forestry, and Environmental Conservation
G. v. N. Viljoen	Minister of National Education
M. A. de M. Malan	Minister of Defence
P. T. C. Du Plessis	Minister of Agriculture and Fisheries

D. de Villiers	Minister of Industries, Commerce, and Tourism
H. J. Coetsee	Minister of Justice
S. F. Kotze	Minister of Community Development and State Auxiliary Services
S. A. S. Hayward	Deputy Minister of Agriculture
G. de V. Morrison	Deputy Minister of Co-operation
J. J. G. Wentzel	Deputy Minister of Development
P. Cronjé	Deputy Minister of State Auxiliary Services
P. J. Badenhorst	Deputy Minister of Internal Affairs
D. W. Steyn	Deputy Minister of Finance, Industries, and Commerce

As these men, with the exception of Horwood, are representative of the ruling Afrikaner elite, an analysis of their backgrounds provides insight toward understanding their motives and actions. All but Horwood and one other were born into the Afrikaner community in South Africa. The exception is S. P. Botha, who was born in Zambia but from an early age received his education at Afrikaans schools in South Africa. Most were born on farms or in country towns; the leadership is overwhelmingly of rural origin.

The Afrikaner leaders are the product of a community that is more egalitarian than most industrial societies. Insofar as there was an Afrikaner elite a half-century ago, it was an elite of achievement, consisting of predikants, politicians, lawyers, teachers, and successful capitalist farmers. Nearly all the present generation of cabinet ministers are sons of men who practised one of these occupations; two-thirds of them were landowners or farmers, pure and simple. Notably absent from the list are industrial occupations, on both the management and the labor sides. Sixty years ago nearly all the successful entrepreneurs and skilled artisans of South Africa were members of the English-speaking white community. Afrikaner penetration into commerce and industry, which accelerated dramatically after 1948, has still to be felt in the upper echelons of political leadership.

Born between 1915 (M. Viljoen) and 1940 (D. de Villiers),

these political leaders were either directly associated with the struggle for the protection of the Afrikaner community from anglicization or were imbued with it by their parents and community. By the 1950s this battle was won with the political ascendancy of the Afrikaner, and anglophobia was replaced by negrophobia, the major concern of the present cabinet.

The Afrikaner leaders are well educated. All graduated from high school and all except Kotze and Wentzel attended a university. Eight hold university doctorates, three of which are medical degrees. The overwhelming majority attended Afrikaans-medium universities. Stellenbosch was the most popular—indeed, all South African prime ministers except Louis Botha (who was innocent of formal education) and P. W. Botha were students at Stellenbosch. Three studied abroad— Koornhof was a Rhodes Scholar at Oxford where he earned a D.Phil., Schoeman studied agriculture in the United States, and Malan worked with the United States Army at Fort Leavenworth. This contrasts with six ministers of the 1960 Verwoerd cabinet who had studied abroad and is a reflection of the expansion of higher education in South Africa. Perhaps only five of the total cabinet had traveled widely before they entered Parliament.

Prior to entering politics, six of the twenty-six were farmers (S. P. Botha, Schoeman, Du Plessis, Hartzenberg, Hayward, Wentzel) and several others combined farming with a profession. Four were lawyers (Heunis, Le Grange, Coetsee, de Klerk). Koornhof was a research officer with the Department of Bantu Affairs, R. F. Botha and de Villiers were in the Diplomatic Service, Smit a journalist, and P. W. Botha and Kotze were employed as party organizers by the National party. De Villiers (a former South African rugby captain) and Treurnicht (who later became a newspaper editor) are ordained ministers of religion. G. Viljoen is a former rector of the Rand Afrikaans University and administrator general of South West Africa, and is a former head of the Afrikaner Broederbond. In this last capacity he had unbridled access to the entire Afrikaner elite. Malan was a professional soldier and chief of the South African Defence Force. A notable absentee from this list is anybody who has had experience in commerce, at either a practical or a theoretical level. Indeed, the only cabinet exception is the English-speaking Horwood, who was once a university lecturer in commerce and then a professor of economics.

All these Afrikaner politicians have been politically active for many years, and none of them has experienced any brand of Afrikaner nationalism save that of Daniel F. Malan and his successors. Most have taken the traditional route to political leadership, starting with service on local party committees and graduating to a provincial committee and parliamentary candidature. Exceptions to this are Malan, who was recruited from the army, and G. Viljoen who, as mentioned above, was a university principal and government administrator. Others first became politically prominent through paid or unpaid service in organizations connected with the party.

None of the Afrikaans-speaking cabinet members has had the salutary experience of being a member of the Opposition as distinct from the Government side in Parliament. All of them entered Parliament after 1947 (the earliest was Pieter W. Botha in 1948, and the most recent were Munnik, de Villiers, and de Klerk in 1972, and G. Viljoen and Malan in 1980). As students, M. Viljoen and Smit were active in the Nasionale Jeugbond, Koornhof was active in SABRA (South African Bureau of Racial Affairs) and the FAK (Federation of Afrikaner Cultural Organizations), and all without exception are members of the Broederbond.

There has been one outstanding addition to the material interests of many of the leaders since they entered politics. In spite of the fact that none of them came into politics from mining, manufacturing, or commercial backgrounds, many have been drawn into the business world as directors of companies. This growing personal involvement of the political leadership in capitalist enterprises is a factor of political significance. Formerly the National party represented the white rural interest and the white urban worker's interest and was distinctly suspicious of big business. That is no longer the case. As the Afrikaner share of industrial, commercial, and financial management has increased, the leaders of the National party, notwithstanding their rural origins and their anticapitalist traditions, have become personally involved in the capitalist interest.

South African public servants are protected by statute against arbitrary dismissal, but appointments and promotions are vested in cabinet ministers, provided they consider the recommendations of the Public Service Commission and similar bodies.[24] In the early years of the Union most senior posts were held by English-speaking white South Africans, but the Hertzog government aimed at establishing equality between the two white communities, and the governments of Malan, Strijdom, Verwoerd, Vorster, and Botha have almost invariably appointed Afrikaners to senior posts. The transformation is now virtually complete. By 1980 over 80 percent of the civil servants were Afrikaners and the Afrikaans language prevails in the Union buildings to such an extent that it is surprising to hear English being spoken. This has vital political significance. The civil service has burgeoned since 1948, and by 1980 over 40 percent of employed Afrikaners were on the payroll of state or parastatal institutions. Many of them are operators of apartheid apparatus and therefore have a direct interest in the status quo.

In 1980 the director general of the South African Defence Force and the chiefs of staff of the army and air force were Afrikaners. The chief of the navy, Rear-Admiral R. Edwards, was English-speaking. This reflects the membership of the military

24. B. Beinart, "The Legal Relationship between the Government and Its Employees," *Butterworth's South African Law Review* (1955), pp. 21–72; H. R. Hahlo and Ellison Kahn, *The Union of South Africa: The Development of Its Laws and Constitution* (London: Stevens, 1960), pp. 185–86.

as a whole: the permanent members of the army and air force are predominantly Afrikaans-speaking, while the navy is divided equally between English and Afrikaans speakers. Blacks were always employed as unarmed auxiliaries in the Defence Force, but in the 1970s the exclusive racial character of the combat units was changed with the formation of African, Indian, and Coloured units. The military follows a policy of equal treatment in pay and status for all groups, and has had no difficulty in finding black recruits. In 1979 there were 4,000 Blacks in the forces out of a total number of about 65,500, and Coloureds and Indians made up 20 percent of the 5,500 permanent force personnel in the navy.[25]

The upper echelons of the military have had virtually no experience of conventional warfare: of the chiefs of staff only Major General A. M. Muller saw combat in the Korean War. However, since the early 1970s, when the South African Defence Force replaced the South African police in the Caprivi strip and Ovamboland, they have had extensive experience of counterinsurgency operations, including the invasion of Angola in 1974 and 1975 when combat units penetrated to about a thousand kilometers north of the Namibian border. The present military leaders are relatively young, and most were appointed by P. W. Botha either while he was minister of defence or when he combined the offices of prime minister and defence.

The present minister of defence, General Magnus André de Merindol Malan, is the former chief of the Defence Force. He comes from a staunch Afrikaner Nationalist family. The academic career of his father, a university professor, was cut short because of his opposition to South Africa's participation in World War II; he later became a National party member of Parliament and Speaker of the House of Assembly. Magnus Malan

25. Survey of Race Relations, 1979, p. 83; cf. C. Legum, ed., Africa Contemporary Record 1978–1979.

sees himself as continuing his father's struggle for Afrikaner survival. He observed the Algerian War at first hand while on secondment to the French army, and he also studied with the United States Army shortly before the Vietnam War. He maintains regular contact with the military establishments of Israel and the Chinese Nationalists in Taiwan, and he has studied the Nationalist Chinese concept of "political war" by which they hope to undermine the Communist regime of the People's Republic of China. Under his direction the South African military has prepared to wage a counterinsurgency war. This has a number of components, corresponding to the range of "threats" to South Africa: diplomatic, psychological, semantic, cultural, economic, military, political, and intelligence. Malan sees his task as minister of defence as one of coordinating strategies to counteract these threats. As chief of the Defence Force he was the chairman of the coordinating committee of the army, the navy, the air force, and the state-owned and controlled armaments industry, Armscor. In addition, he has improved contacts between the military and private industry.

The threat of armed incursions into South Africa has resulted in an expansion of the role of the military in political decision-making. In 1972 a State Security Council was created. Meeting barely six times during Vorster's twelve years as prime minister, in 1980 it met fortnightly under the chairmanship of Prime Minister Botha. The director general of the Defence Force is a permanent member of this council, which plays a pivotal role in harmonizing national economic and political policies with the interests of military strategy. Other permanent members of the council include the head of the National Intelligence Service, the minister of police, and the commissioner of police. The State Security Council gives the military command direct access to the political system and, should the armed struggle intensify, the armed forces would have constitutional means for intervening directly in political matters.

In 1978 there were about nineteen thousand white and sixteen thousand black members of the police force. Nearly all the senior police officers are Afrikaners. There are relatively few English-speaking police; in recent years an attempt was made to recruit them, but it met with little success.[26]

The present intake into all branches of the public service is overwhelmingly Afrikaner. A young English-speaking white South African comes from a community with a strong industrial and commercial tradition, and he knows he can easily be absorbed into the private sector of the economy with good prospects for promotion and material success, while he also suspects that if he were to join the public service his prospects of promotion would be poor. A young Afrikaner, on the other hand, assumes that he will find the atmosphere in public service congenial and his prospects good. Consequently, the Afrikaner community has as complete control over the bureaucracy, the police, and the armed forces as it has over the Parliament and the cabinet.

The Black Leadership

The leaders of black political organizations have always been drawn from the modern elements in the black community. The leadership, internally and abroad, is in the hands of people with a good modern education and extensive experience of political activism. Nearly all the top people in the African National Congress (ANC) and the Pan-Africanist Congress (PAC), which cannot operate overtly in South Africa, are university-trained men, who, at one time or another, were held or jailed by the South African police. Nelson Mandela, the president of the ANC, who has been serving a life sentence on Robben Island since 1963, is a qualified lawyer. Robert Sobukwe, president of the PAC until his death in 1977, was a lecturer in Bantu languages at the Univer-

26. *Survey of Race Relations, 1979,* p. 105.

sity of Witwatersrand before his arrest in 1960, and after being released in 1969, he too qualified as a lawyer. Most of the "homeland" leaders, too, such as Gatsha Buthelezi of KwaZulu and the Matanzima brothers of the Transkei, have had university training; so have the urban African leaders, such as Steven Biko, the founder of the South African Students' Organization who was killed by the police in 1977, Dr. Nthatho Motlana of the Soweto Committee of Ten, and Bishop Desmond Tutu, general secretary of the South African Council of Churches. Beyond that, it is difficult to generalize. The African leaders come from the most varied ethnic, regional, and class backgrounds. All the "homeland" leaders are of chiefly lineages; so are some other African leaders, including Nelson Mandela, but most of them are commoners by traditional criteria. These Africans started life in all parts of South Africa and all three categories of land— "homelands," "white rural areas," and towns—though nearly all except the "homeland" leaders have lived for long periods in the towns.

The cleavages among black political organizations, and their diverse strategies, are dealt with in chapter 5. Courage has always been a prerequisite for political activity among black South Africans. Since 1960, with overt activity outside the "homeland" institutions and the government-created African, Indian, and Coloured councils banned or harassed, this is truer than ever.

THE COMMUNICATIONS SYSTEM

The first modern political communications in South Africa were created by Whites for Whites and from an early stage two parallel sets of publications developed: books and newspapers in English for the English-speaking white community, and an Afrikaans medium set for the Afrikaners.[27] In time, however, the caste line became more and more remote from the line dividing South Africans who use modern communications media from those who do not.

The modern communications network is necessarily fragmented in South Africa; some of this is due to geographical factors. People live at different distances from the major population centers where modern communications are most readily available and therefore experience different intensities of exposure; and the great distances between the main population centers create regional variations. But the importance of geographical differentials is diminishing, for radio and television reception extends to every part of the country and most English-language daily newspapers are very much the same in all the main centers, relying on the same news services and expressing similar political views, and the Afrikaans dailies are also similar to one another. Fragmentation is mainly due to differences of interest and, above all, of language.

With the growth in the number and the variety of the users of modern communications, there has been an increase in the range of services available. Newspapers are now produced in many languages for the different black communities. But since the newspapers designed primarily for Whites have by far the best news coverage, they are read by the better-educated Blacks, for whom special editions, emphasizing black community news, are printed; and because the English-language papers are at least to some extent critical of the government, Blacks prefer the English to the Afrikaans press.

Therefore, the section of the press which caters primarily to the opposition section of the ruling caste is read by increasing numbers of members of the subordinate castes. Furthermore,

27. Theo E. G. Cutten, *A History of the Press in South Africa* (Cape Town: National Union of South African Students, 1935).

since English is a universal language and Afrikaans is exclusive to South Africa, foreign correspondents and diplomats take their South African news mainly from the English press. For these reasons the government is anxious to deemphasize the teaching of English in black schools, to censor the English press, to make television and radio instruments of propaganda, and to disseminate large quantities of printed propaganda among the black communities of South Africa and in foreign countries. Thus the initial fragmentation of the modern communications system in South Africa was beginning to be overcome by the ascendancy of the English-medium press; but the government has been trying to check this process by state control and refragmentation.[28]

The oldest newspapers in South Africa are English-language papers founded in the nineteenth century. The Argus Printing and Publishing Company has control of six dailies — the Cape Town Argus (founded in 1857), the Johannesburg Star, the Durban Daily News, the Pretoria News, the Bloemfontein Friend, and the Kimberley Diamond Fields Advertiser — and also two weekend papers, the Durban Sunday Tribune and the Cape Herald. The South African Associated Newspapers Group (SAAN) includes four dailies — the Johannesburg Rand Daily Mail, the Port Elizabeth Eastern Province Herald, the Port Elizabeth Evening Post, and the Cape Times — and two weekend papers — the Sunday Times and the Sunday Express, both of Johannesburg, and the weekly Financial Mail. The Natal Mercury, a daily, is 40 percent owned by SAAN. There are also two independent English dailies — the Pietermaritzburg Natal Witness and the East London Daily Dispatch. The Argus and SAAN groups are extensively linked to each other. They have

28. On the South African press generally, see Alex Hepple, Censorship and Press Control in South Africa (Johannesburg: The Author, 1960); A. S. Mathews, The Darker Reaches of Government (Cape Town: Juta, 1978); John Dugard, Human Rights and the South African Legal Order (Princeton: Princeton University Press, 1978).

cross-cutting shareholdings, with Argus holding 40 percent of SAAN equity, and SAAN a somewhat lower stake in the Argus group. The Argus also has two directors on the SAAN governing board. Both these publishing groups are related to mining and industrial interests.

In 1980 these papers had a total daily circulation of about 900,000, and a weekend circulation of about 1,300,000.[29] The core of the circulation consists of English-speaking white South Africans, but since they numbered fewer than 1,700,000 men, women, and children, it is evident that the English press was read by many Afrikaners and Blacks. Until it was banned in 1981, the Johannesburg *Post* had an almost totally black readership; the *Cape Herald* is read almost entirely by Coloured people. None of these papers is directly linked with a political party. Nevertheless, they all oppose the National party, with degrees of vehemence ranging from the generally mild criticism of the Argus newspapers to the more fundamental opposition of the *Rand Daily Mail* and the *Cape Times*. The only English-medium newspaper which supports the government is *The Citizen*, which is published in Johannesburg. This newspaper was founded in 1975 through the clandestine involvement of the Department of Information in an attempt to counteract the influence of the established English press. When government involvement was revealed, it was taken over by the Afrikaans group, Perskor.

There are two Afrikaans press groups, Perskor and Nasionale Pers. Nasionale Pers owns the Cape Town daily *Die Burger* (founded in 1915), the Bloemfontein daily *Die Volksblad*, the Transvaal daily *Beeld*, and the Port Elizabeth daily *Oosterlig*. Perskor owns the Johannesburg dailies *Die Transvaler* and *Die Vaderland*, and the Pretoria dailies *Hoofstad* and *Oggenblad*. The two groups have equal shares in the weekly *Rapport*. In 1980 the combined circulation of the Afrikaans dailies was

29. *Financial Mail* (Johannesburg), September 5, 1980, p. 1132.

350,000 and the weekend circulation 580,000.[30] Since the Afrikaner population was nearly 2,300,000 men, women, and children, this means that many Afrikaners were still not buying Afrikaans papers and that very few Blacks or English-speaking Whites bought them. Until 1979 most of these newspapers had senior Nationalist politicians on their controlling boards. However, in the aftermath of the Muldergate scandal (see below),

30. Ibid. In 1980 the average circulation figures were as follows:

DAILIES

English		Afrikaans	
Star	184,000	Die Transvaler	75,000
Rand Daily Mail	131,000	Die Burger	72,000
Post (Tvl.)	112,000	Die Vaderland	60,000
Argus	106,000	Beeld	64,000
Daily News	92,000	Volksblad	25,000
Cape Times	67,000	Hoofstad	15,000
Natal Mercury	63,000	Oggendblad	6,000
Pretoria News	27,000	Oosterlig	10,000
Natal News	18,000		
Friend	6,000		
The Citizen	54,000		
Daily Dispatch	31,000		
Diamond Fields Advertiser	7,000		
Eastern Province Herald	28,000		
Evening Post	23,000		

WEEKLIES

Sunday Times	461,000	Rapport	417,000
Sunday Post	118,000	Burger (Weekend)	85,000
Sunday Tribune	127,000		
Argus (Weekend)	122,000		
Cape Times (Weekend)	91,000		
Sunday Express	90,000		
Cape Herald (Weekend)	68,000		
Weekend Post	44,000		
Natal Daily News (Weekend)	26,000		
Pretoria News (Weekend)	12,000		

The figures for The Citizen, Die Transvaler, and Die Vaderland are falsely inflated. See p. 142 on the rivalry between Perskor and Nasionale Pers.

Prime Minister Pieter W. Botha prohibited cabinet ministers from serving on these boards.

Traditionally the Afrikaans language newspapers gave enthusiastic support to the National party. However, in recent years editors have become increasingly independent of the party machine, and they do not hesitate to criticize government policies. A notable example of this is W. de Klerk, editor of *Die Transvaler*, who has crusaded for a dismantling of racial segregation in sport and other aspects of social life, and who has also opposed the increasing restrictions on press freedom. This more critical approach partially reflects conflict between Perskor and Nasionale Pers, which represent different factions within the National party. Their rivalry came to a head in 1978 in the competition for the succession to John Vorster. Perskor, based in the north, supported Connie Mulder, but he became discredited as the information scandal unfolded, and Nasionale Pers, based in the south, supported Pieter W. Botha, who became prime minister. Circulation rivalry between these two groups is intense; in 1980 the Audit Bureau of Circulation showed that Perskor had given falsely inflated figures for *Die Transvaler*, *The Citizen*, and *Die Vaderland* over a period of months. Some rivalry also exists between newspapers in the English language, particularly on the Witwatersrand, where there are three English dailies.

The effects of the greater circulation of the English press on intrawhite politics are negligible, for most Afrikaners who read English papers have an ingrained resistance to alien political views. In addition, the proportionate circulation of the English press among white South Africans has begun to decline as a result of the increase in the Afrikaner proportion of the white population, the rise of Afrikaner industrial and financial power, and the further consolidation of Afrikaner political control.

African readers are catered to, not only by the English dailies, which tend to have special editions aimed at African readership, but also by periodical publications produced especially for them. Formerly, several papers were under African control, but they have all either ceased publication or have been acquired by white companies. In 1980 the Argus group published the biweekly Durban *Ilanga*, in English and Zulu, and three weeklies, partly in English and partly in Sotho, Tswana, and Zulu for Lesotho, Botswana, and Swaziland, respectively. Another publication controlled by English-speaking white South Africans is the monthly pictorial *Zonk*. Perskor, publisher of *Die Transvaler*, also publishes *Bona*, an illustrated monthly, in Zulu, Xhosa, and Sotho editions and *Imvo*, which was previously a Bantu Press publication and originally an independent Xhosa newspaper, founded in 1884.

With the continuous growth in the African market as a result of industrial expansion and urbanization, there is the keenest competition for this readership. Prior to their banning in 1977 and 1981, respectively, *The World* had a daily circulation of over 150,000 and the *Post* of over 112,000. In 1977 the *Post* took over the place previously filled by *The World*. It had the same editor, Percy Qoboza, and was a vigorous opponent of racism, whether black or white. At the other extreme, *Bona* and the other Nationalist-controlled publications emphasize African traditional culture and either overtly support apartheid or, at least, refrain from criticizing it. There are also a small number of weekly and fortnightly newspapers owned by Indian and Coloured people. The Indian papers are all published in Natal.

More effective as a radical critic of white supremacy was a paper which had many names during its career. The *Guardian* was founded in Cape Town in 1937 by members of the Communist party of South Africa. It survived a series of bannings by adopting a succession of new names—*Clarion*, *Advance*, *New Age*, and finally *Spark*, which ceased publication in 1963. *The World*, too, was an articulate voice for black political aspirations. It provided energetic coverage of the civil unrest in 1976, but the government detained its editor, Percy Qoboza, and many reporters, and closed the newspaper down.

The National party regards the English South African press as one of its most dangerous opponents, and it has taken a series of steps to restrict its operation by legislation, intimidation, and prohibition. Since 1950 Parliament has passed over ninety laws that curb freedom of the press. Some of these laws contain extremely wide-ranging provisions. For example, the Internal Security Act as amended, originally known as the Suppression of Communism Act (1950), makes it an offense to further any of the aims of communism. This act also gives the state president the power to ban newspapers which, in news or comment, he deems to further communism or to endanger public security or public order. Similarly, the Terrorism Act of 1967 makes it an offense to publish information which "aids, advises, encourages or incites people to terrorism," and "terrorism" is defined so widely that it includes any act which "embarrasses" the state. Similarly, the Defence Act of 1957 as amended bans the publication of information "calculated to prejudice or embarrass the government in its foreign relations," or which "alarms or depresses" the public. In addition, information relating to the composition, movement or disposition of the Defence Force may not be published without permission from the minister of defence. Journalists may not enter any area defined as an "operational" area, nor may they report on anything which takes place in such an area without permission from the minister. Laws also prohibit press scrutiny of the police, prisons, or acts of sabotage on key installations, or the publication of information relating to the procurement or manufacture of petroleum products.

Furthermore, during the nationwide unrest of 1976 the government invoked the Internal Security Act to detain fourteen black journalists who were reporting on clashes between police and demonstrators. As white journalists were unable to enter black areas, this inhibited further reporting on the subject. During the unrest in 1980, several African and Coloured townships were declared "operational" areas and were thus closed to the press.

Under the Publications and Entertainments Act of 1963, the government appointed a Publications Control Board which may ban any book considered "undesirable" in the sense, inter alia, that it is "on any grounds objectionable." This was revised by the Publications Act of 1974, which makes it possible for the police to mount search operations against various organizations involved in publication. Literature may be seized and submitted to a committee for a judgment on its desirability, and the decision of the committee is binding on the courts. Inevitably, such police action serves as a restraint on publication which is further complicated by the vagueness surrounding the standard of undesirability. The act also empowers the minister of the interior to prohibit the importation, distribution, or holding of publications which are "indecent or obscene" or in any way prejudicial to the safety of the state, and it may impose guilt retrospectively.[31] In recent years it has been frequently invoked in actions against student publications.

Under these laws the *Guardian* and its successors have all ceased publication. *The World* and *Weekend World*, South Africa's largest circulation black newspapers, were banned in October 1977. *Pro Veritate*, the journal of the Christian Institute, was closed down when the institute itself was banned. The University of Cape Town's student newspaper, *Varsity*, was banned from 1979 to 1980. In 1979 the black newspaper *Voice* was banned on the grounds that it was calculated to "undermine or harm peaceful race relations, prejudice peace and good order, harm the safety of the State, create artificially exaggerated grievances and deliberately feed black frustrations to the point of explosion."[32] This order was temporarily lifted as the result of

31. Mathews, *The Darker Reaches of Government*, p. 227.
32. *Survey of Race Relations, 1978*, p. 135.

an appeal by the newspaper's board of management on the condition that it make available to the director of publications a copy of each newspaper within twelve hours of publication. The government has detained Percy Qoboza, former editor of the *World*, and held him without trial for five months; and it has banned Donald Woods, former editor of the *Daily Dispatch*, and several newspaper reporters.

"Search and seize" police operations against student publications are commonplace following the conviction of Sean Moroney, editor of *Wits Student*, in 1976 on two counts of producing editions of a newspaper that were subsequently banned. In the first six months of 1980 the publications committee banned over thirty student publications. It has also banned many thousands of books, including works by foreign authors of international repute such as D. H. Lawrence, John O'Hara, John Steinbeck, Henry Miller, Christopher Isherwood, Vladimir Nabokov, and Mary McCarthy. The list includes numerous works of black South Africans, who can now find only an overseas audience, and also, ironically, a number of writings of Afrikaners. André Brink and Etienne le Roux have had books banned, and Brink has accused the censorship system of "killing the Afrikaans language. . . . Mediocrity has become the yardstick . . . the system has no place for the talented and gifted . . . this extreme puritanism that is being thrust upon us goes hand in hand with increasing totalitarianism."[33]

No film may be shown in South Africa which has not been approved by the Directorate of Publications. Cinemas are segregated and different standards are applied to censoring of films for Whites, Coloureds, Asians, and Africans. In effect, white committees decide what films the other defined races are allowed to see. Film censorship is severe, and many films freely available in North America and Europe are either prohibited or severely cut. In 1974, 127 films were prohibited and 383 were

33. *Sunday Tribune*, 27 November 1977.

approved subject to the excision of specified portions; 347 were approved for specific groups and only 207 were unconditionally approved.[34]

Finally, the government has embarked upon a lavish propaganda campaign, both inside and outside South Africa, through the radio and television systems that it controls and through various publications. It has an internal and external radio service in twenty-five languages, including nine South African languages. Ever since 1936 the South African Broadcasting Corporation (SABC) has been a public corporation with a monopoly of broadcasting in South Africa, controlled by a board of governors appointed by the head of state on the advice of the minister of posts and telecommunications. The SABC was originally modeled on the BBC and was politically neutral, providing parallel services in English and Afrikaans. But under Dr. Piet J. Meyer, an interned Ossewabrandwag leader during the Second World War who was chairman from 1961 to 1979, it was transformed into an organ for National party propaganda. The liberal approach to race relations, anti-apartheid South Africans, the English South African press, the United Nations, and the independent States of Africa and Asia are persistently excoriated. The SABC 1977 annual report stated that the television service "made the point of stressing the need for spiritual, economic and military preparedness."[35] The government's radio and television monopoly is an important instrument of political control, and is to be extended by the introduction of a television channel which will broadcast in Zulu, Xhosa, North and South Sotho, and Tswana.

The government also allocates considerable resources to printed propaganda. During the 1970s the Department of Information provided secret funds in support of projects which had not been authorized by Parliament. These included *The Citizen*

34. Dugard, *Human Rights,* p.199.
35. *Survey of Race Relations, 1978,* p. 135.

newspaper, the periodical *To The Point*, and advertisements placed by "fronts" in British and American newspapers in defense of the South African government. The government continues to fund numerous publications for consumption in South Africa and abroad, notably *South African Digest* and *Panorama*. This propaganda is most sophisticated. It emphasizes the economic strength of South Africa and the material well-being of Africans in the Republic compared with Africans in other parts of Africa, and eulogizes the "homelands" policy.

Nearly all the modern communications media in South Africa are controlled by Whites. Those which are in the public sector, such as the radio and television services, are used as instruments of government propaganda. Those which are in the private sector, such as the daily and most of the periodical press, still reflect the variations of interest and opinion within the white caste, but the lead in circulation of the English-medium press is gradually being narrowed and the capacity of the English-medium press to oppose the caste system is restricted by legislation. Black South Africans have to depend mainly on white-controlled media for their political information; but just as the English-medium press has never determined the political conduct of a significant number of its Afrikaner readers, so the white-controlled communications media are not likely to determine the political conduct of their black audiences. That is determined primarily by the realities of the daily life of Blacks in the Republic. Nevertheless, the legislative restrictions on the privately controlled media do have the effect of seriously impeding the flow of communication between black leaders and their followers—indeed, they make it extremely difficult for black leaders to emerge and to build up and maintain a following.

THE ARTICULATION OF INTERESTS

In South Africa the articulation of interests does not conform to the normal pattern of modern countries where the basic criterion of articulation is economic interest: in South Africa the primary criterion is race. South African interest groups may be classified in three categories, distinguished by their ethnic scope. There are *community* groups, which are confined to members of only one community and which pursue the interests of that community (e.g., Afrikaner, Malay, Xhosa). There are *caste* groups, which include members of the different communities within the same caste (white, Coloured, Asian, African). And third, there are a few *national* groups, extending to all the castes and communities in the country.

South African interest groups may also be classed according to the strength of their channels of systematic influence over the authoritative political structures, especially Parliament, the cabinet, and the bureaucracy. There are interest groups whose influence is dominant; others whose influence is slight; and others whose means of exerting systematic influence are virtually nil.

Afrikaner community groups are dominant in all areas in which they exist, and where they are lacking white caste groups are dominant. Those of slight influence are white English-speaking community groups and also white caste groups where they exist alongside Afrikaner community groups. All groups with black members—whether based on the community, the caste, or the national principle—have virtually no systematic means of influencing the authoritative political structures. The institutions that the government has created for the subordinate castes do have some effect on the government in that they are able to influence administrative practices at the lower level of local government. But systematic influence over the government of South Africa is virtually monopolized by the white caste and dominated by its inner oligarchy—the Afrikaner community.

Afrikaner Associations
Within Afrikanerdom there is a hierarchy of organizations pursuing political, economic, and cultural goals. Afrikanerdom is

politically unified in the National party (dealt with in the next section); it is religiously united in the Dutch Reformed churches; it finds cultural expression through the Federasie van Afrikaanse Kultuurverenigings (FAK), and it functions in the economic field through the Afrikaanse Handelsinstituut. Cross-cutting membership between these groups ensures a high degree of group cohesion, so the typical Afrikaner is a member of one of the Reformed churches, he supports the National party, he belongs to one or more Afrikaans cultural organizations, and he may be a member of the Handelsinstituut or the Broederbond.

The Afrikaner Broederbond (Brotherhood) is at the apex of these organizations, and it exists to ensure Afrikaner solidarity and group cohesion in all aspects of Afrikaans social life. In the past the Broederbond played an important part in developing political, cultural, and economic organizations, by setting up institutions in all the fields which were traditionally the domain of English speakers.[36]

The Broederbond is a secret society. Before 1978, when a *broeder* defected and provided the *Sunday Times* with extensive documentation on its activities, there was only sketchy information about it. Founded in 1918, it made a decision to operate in secret in 1921.[37] There is an elaborate selection procedure, which may take up to two years before a new recruit is inducted. Names of prospective members are suggested at local cells. If unanimous approval is given, the candidate's name is put to the national level. If there is no dissenting voice, the person may then be invited to join. A prospective candidate may be excluded if his home language is English, or even if his wife is English-speaking, if he ever showed signs of disloyalty to the

36. T. Dunbar Moodie, *The Rise of Afrikanerdom: Power, Apartheid and the Afrikaner Civil Religion* (Berkeley: University of California Press, 1975); I. Wilkins and H. Strydom, *The Super-Afrikaners: Inside the Afrikaner Broederbond* (Johannesburg: Jonathan Ball, 1978); J. H. P. Serfontein, *Brotherhood of Power* (London: Rex Collings, 1979). A semiofficial history is provided by A. N. Pelzer, *Die Afrikaner Broederbond: Eerste 50 Jaar* (Cape Town: Tafelberg, 1979).
37. Wilkins and Strydom, *The Super-Afrikaners*, p. 41.

National party, or if he is not an active member of one of the Reformed churches. The recruit is told:

The Afrikaner Broederbond was born in the deep conviction that the Afrikaner nation with its own nature and task was called into being in this country by God's hand and is destined, for as long as it pleases God, to remain in existence. The members of the Afrikaner Broederbond are mission conscious Afrikaners who strive to represent the best that is in our nation.

The recruit is also required to promise to "strive for the welfare and advancement of all interests of the Afrikaner nation."[38] The Broederbond is, therefore, a self-perpetuating association of Afrikaner elite. With a membership of twelve thousand operating through more than eight hundred cells, some of its main concerns have been to place zealous Afrikaner Nationalists in key positions and to found special organizations to meet new needs of the Afrikaner people.

A typical cell will include among its members a doctor, a town councillor, a headmaster, businessmen or farmers, the chief of police, a *predikant*, and senior members of the local branch of the National party. This enables the Broederbond to exercise influence on town councils, school boards, church bodies, business or farming bodies, and the National party. Above the local cells there are a general council, an executive council of "Twelve Apostles," and a "Trinity" headed by a "Supreme Chief."

Almost all Nationalist members of Parliament are members of the Broederbond; all prime ministers since 1948 have been members; all but one minister in the 1980 Botha cabinet were members.[39] In 1978 others included the heads of all the Afrikaans-medium universities and leading Afrikaner professors, schoolmasters, businessmen, churchmen, lawyers, bankers, policemen, and other highly placed Afrikaners such as the

38. Serfontein, *Brotherhood of Power*, p. 227.
39. The exception is the English-speaking Owen Horwood.

general manager of the South African Railways, the head of the South African Broadcasting Corporation, the chairman of the South African Atomic Energy Board, six board members of the parastatal Iron and Steel Corporation, and the managing director of SASOL—the company that produces oil from coal.[40]

Over the past fifty years the Broederbond has been a bone of contention in white South African politics. In 1935 Prime Minister J. B. M. Hertzog denounced it as "a grave menace to the rest and peace of our social community," and in 1944 Prime Minister J. C. Smuts called it "a dangerous, cunning, political Fascist organization" and ordered civil servants who were members to resign either from the Broederbond or from the service.[41] In 1965 a judicial commission, appointed by the prime minister— himself a member—exonerated the Broederbond from engaging in subversive activities or exerting an undesirable influence.[42]

Today the National party and the Broederbond are mutually supportive organizations. Cross-cutting membership at the higher organizational levels ensures that the cabinet and the National party caucus have direct secret access to all portions of the Afrikaner elite. In addition, the Broederbond provides a testing ground for policies and is a generator of ideas for governmental initiatives. Although it has often been accused of being a sinister movement with designs on ultimate political power, it is unlikely that its present function is more than to ensure Afrikaner group cohesion.[43]

In 1929 the Broederbond was instrumental in founding the FAK, whose object is to maintain and further Afrikaans language and culture.[44] The FAK, in turn, has seen to the creation of exclusive Afrikaner associations in a wide variety of specific

40. Wilkins and Strydom, The Super-Afrikaners, pp. 13–15.
41. G. Carter, The Politics of Inequality: South Africa since 1948 (London: Thames and Hudson, 1958), pp. 251–52.
42. Africa Digest (London) 12, no. 5 (April 1965): 133.
43. H. Adam and H. Giliomee, Ethnic Power Mobilized: Can South Africa Change? (New Haven: Yale University Press, 1979), pp. 250–53.
44. On the FAK, see Carter, Politics of Inequality, pp. 256–58.

fields—in some cases by founding new associations, in others by capturing control of bodies that had previously embraced a wider membership and a wider ideal, and in others by seceding from such bodies.

During the 1930s there was a series of secessions. Typical was the secession leading to the establishment of an exclusive Afrikaner student association. In 1924 Leo Marquard, an Afrikaner with wide loyalties who had recently returned from holding a Rhodes scholarship at Oxford University, had convened a conference that resulted in the founding of the National Union of South African Students (NUSAS). For some years NUSAS was supported by the student bodies in all the universities, but in 1933 an agitation commenced against NUSAS in the four Afrikaans-medium universities. Late that year Afrikaans students met in Bloemfontein under the chairmanship of P. J. Meyer, heard an address from D. F. Malan (later prime minister) on "Nationalism as an Outlook on Life," and founded the Afrikaanse Nasionale Studentebond (ANS), which soon received the support of the students' representative councils in the Afrikaans-medium universities.

To the seceding Afrikaners, NUSAS was not truly a national association because it conveyed "nothing national in the Afrikaans sense," while to NUSAS the seceding Afrikaners were not national but merely sectional. During the Second World War, ANS hoped for a German victory in the expectation that it would hasten the founding of a republic in South Africa. In 1940 it issued a manifesto in favor of an authoritarian South African Republic, with Christian National Education, a state-controlled press and radio, and Afrikaans as the only official language. After the defeat of Nazi Germany, ANS passed into oblivion.

However, in 1948 a new group, the Afrikaanse Studentebond (ASB), was founded. Its declared objects were to combine all Afrikaner students into one organization, to further their common interests, and to maintain and expand "white

Christian civilization in opposition to Communism."[45] In 1968 Stellenbosch University disaffiliated from the ASB because the ASB insisted that all students at Afrikaans universities be automatic members of the organization. In 1980 there was a break away from the ASB and the formation of a rival Afrikaans student body which aimed to establish contact with NUSAS and black student organizations. However, the ASB has the support of the majority of Afrikaner university students and it has steadfastly endorsed the government's racial policies. Consequently, it is a recruiting ground for the Afrikaner political elite.

On the other hand, NUSAS, which had previously equivocated on the question of the admission of black student bodies, opened its membership to several black institutions after the Second World War. Later, NUSAS organized a series of spectacular demonstrations against the closure of the established universities to black students, and became one of the most forthright critics, not only of the Afrikaner Nationalist government, but of the entire system of white supremacy. In the mid-1960s NUSAS lost significant support on the English-speaking campuses when its officials were harassed by the government and some were found guilty of acts of sabotage. NUSAS still aspires to be a national group and is imbued with a social philosophy diametrically opposed to that of the government. The government intimidates NUSAS and hopes to neutralize it. The founding of the black student movement, South African Students' Organization (SASO), in 1968, brought about the disaffiliation of all black universities from NUSAS. Since then, infiltrated by the security police and harassed by the government, NUSAS has become a de facto all-white organization and is under pressure not only from the South African Right but also from the international student Left. The government dealt it a further blow in 1974 by prohibiting it from receiving funds from

45. Neville Rubin, *History of the Relations between NUSAS, the Afrikaanse Studentebond and the Afrikaans University Centres* (Cape Town: NUSAS, 1960), p. 12.

abroad.[46] By the end of the 1970s it had been reduced to educational activities in the white English-speaking universities and occasional symbolic protests against official policies.

A similar secession led to the establishment of an Afrikaner association for the study of racial questions in South Africa. In 1929 the South African Institute for Race Relations had been created for this purpose, and since the 1930s it has built up a deserved reputation for open-minded scholarship and as an agent for the improvement of human relations across community and caste lines, through its conferences, its publications, and its casework. The institute's membership is open to South Africans of all races, but in practice the bulk of its members have always been English-speaking whites and its leadership lies mainly, but by no means exclusively, in the same community. In 1935 a group of Afrikaner intellectuals broke away from the institute on the grounds that it was too liberal, and they founded a rival Afrikaanse Buro vir Rassestudies (Afrikaner Bureau for Racial Studies). This was a body which, in 1937, searching for a "slogan" different from "segregation" with which to "label the racial policy of the Afrikaner," used the word "apartheid," and thereby played some part in the spadework that eventually led to the formulation of the policy of the National party for the decisive election of 1948.[47] By the time of that election, however, the Buro itself was moribund.

Four months after the election another group of Afrikaner intellectuals founded the Suid-Afrikaanse Buro vir Rasse-Aangeleenthede (South African Bureau for Racial Affairs, SABRA), with financial aid from the FAK.[48] Among the founders

46. Affected Organisations Act, 1974.
47. N. J. Rhoodie and H. J. Venter, *Apartheid: A Socio-Historical Exposition of the Origin and Development of the Apartheid Idea* (Cape Town: HAUM, 1959), p. 171.
48. On SABRA until 1958, see Carter, *Politics of Inequality*, pp. 266–72; and Rhoodie and Venter, *Apartheid*, pp. 169–75. There is no adequate recent account of the organization. SABRA publishes the *Tydskrif vir Rasse-*

were Professor N. J. J. Olivier of Stellenbosch University, Professor W. W. M. Eiselen of Pretoria University (soon to become secretary of native affairs), Professor J. C. van Rooy of Potchefstroom University (then head of the Broederbond), and Professor H. B. Thom of Stellenbosch University (a later head of the Broederbond). In the mid-1950s the minister of Bantu affairs, H. F. Verwoerd, used SABRA as a vehicle for the communication of his separate development policies to Afrikaner intellectuals. In the process he came into conflict with Professor N. J. J. Olivier on the question of policies to be adopted in the treatment of urban Africans and Coloureds. Olivier was driven out of SABRA, and the organization was transformed into an instrument of the National party. Under the somewhat more pragmatic race policies of Prime Ministers B. J. Vorster and P. W. Botha, SABRA lost much of its ability to exert direct influence on the government, and today it enjoys little standing in the National party.[49]

Other exclusive Afrikaner associations that have been founded by secession from more broadly based associations are the Voortrekkers (from the Boy Scouts), Noodhulpliga (from the Red Cross), and Afrikaner teachers' associations.

The Reddingsdaadbond ("Rescuing" Association, RDB), which was founded at the time of the celebrations of the centenary of the Great Trek in 1938 to aid the Afrikaners in their second Great Trek from the rural areas to the industrial towns, carried the process of fission into the economic field.[50] Two generations ago Afrikaners controlled a very small proportion of the wealth of South Africa, for most of the powerful enterprises

aangeleenthede (Journal of Racial Affairs) and a Nuusbrief (Newsletter), both of them bimonthly since 1949, and a number of monographs. On the South African Institute of Race Relations, see Carter, pp. 336–37. The institute publishes Race Relations News (monthly, 1938–), A Survey of Race Relations in South Africa (annually, 1929–), and numerous pamphlets and books on a wide range of South African topics.

49. For an example of this, see the editorial comment in Die Burger, 25 September 1980.

50. On the RDB, see Carter, Politics of Inequality, pp. 255–61.

were of British or Jewish origin and remained under the control of South Africans of British or Jewish descent. However, there already were a small Afrikaner life assurance society and a small Afrikaner trust and assurance society. The RDB saw to the founding of other Afrikaner financial institutions and to the channeling of Afrikaner business into the Afrikaner institutions. By the 1950s the RDB had completed its task of sparking Afrikaner economic advance, and its role was superseded by Afrikaner business institutes, and directly by the government.

Now, largely as a result of the National party's control of the state since 1948, the Afrikaners have made great economic advances. The most powerful Afrikaner financial enterprises are Volkskas (People's Bank), Sanlam (a life assurance society), the Trust Bank, Saambou (a building society), and Santam (a trust and assurance society). Afrikaner companies are also making headway in the mining and industrial sectors—the rise of the Rembrandt Tobacco Company under Anton Rupert, with ramifications in four continents, is a striking example of Afrikaner enterprise. Professor J. L. Sadie estimates that the share of exclusively Afrikaner enterprise in the private sector of the economy rose from 24.8 percent in 1948−49, to 27.5 percent in 1975.[51] These figures exclude the income derived from ISCOR and SASOL, parastatals which are de facto controlled by Afrikaners. Professor David Welsh has estimated that if the trends of the past twenty years continue unchanged, Afrikaners will control 34 percent of the private sector by the year 2000.[52] Afrikaner enterprises and Afrikaner chambers of commerce and industry are able to exert considerable influence over the government, especially since many Afrikaner politicians have become directors of companies. A most significant development was the

51. Adam and Giliomee, Ethnic Power Mobilized, pp. 170–71.
52. D. Welsh, "Political Economy of Afrikaner Nationalism," in A. Leftwich, ed., South Africa: Economic Growth and Political Change (London: Allison and Busby, 1974), p. 253.

establishment of the mining finance house, Federale Mynbou, in 1953. In 1963 it took over General Mining and Finance Corporation with assets of R250 million from Anglo-American Corporation. In 1976 General Mining acquired control of Union Corporation, which made it the third largest of South Africa's finance houses and the largest mining house with assets totaling R750 million.[53] Nevertheless, while the Afrikaner share is growing, English-speaking white South Africans still have higher average incomes than Afrikaners, and the government is also influenced by industrial organizations that are predominantly under their control. Of these, the Transvaal and Orange Free State Chamber of Mines is by far the most powerful, embracing as it does all the great gold-mining corporations in the country.

Trade Unions

In the field of labor, professional, and sports associations, the primary problem confronting Afrikaner Nationalists has not been British influence as such, but rather the problem of black infiltration into associations that in virtually every case were initially confined to the white caste. Here, until very recently, Afrikaner Nationalists have given priority to transforming national groups into caste groups and preventing caste groups from developing into national groups, for the caste line has been even more important than the community line, though in some cases (as we shall see) Afrikaner community groups have been sponsored.

Trade unionism was introduced to South Africa at the turn of the century by white immigrants from Europe and Australia. From an early stage most white South African trade unionists were more concerned to maintain their caste privileges than they were to create a united workers' front against management, and successive governments responded to their demands. Consequently, serious legal impediments were placed in the way of

53. Adam and Giliomee, *Ethnic Power Mobilized*, pp. 169–72.

black—and especially African—trade unionists: the pass laws (in conjunction with endemic underemployment of Africans) have meant that African workers have always had to weigh the advantages of joining trade unions against the danger that they would thereby lose their jobs and their access to the towns; breaches of contracts and strikes by African workers were, until the lifting of the Master and Servants legislation in 1975, generally held to be criminal offenses; and the definition of *employee* in the Industrial Conciliation legislation excluded most African workers, so that African trade unions were not able to participate in the national system of collective bargaining. The result was that by 1948 there were segregated white unions, segregated Coloured, Asian, and African unions, and a few mixed unions in which Coloured, Asian, and even in some cases a few African members had equal rights with Whites; among the trade-union leaders were a few who were committed to the idea of uniting the industrial workers of all races.[54] This confused situation was anathema to the National party, which has striven to prevent the rise of a working-class movement transcending the color bar.

During the 1930s ardent Afrikaner Nationalists founded a Blankewerkersbeskermingsbond (white workers' protection association) and launched a vitriolic campaign against the radical trade-union leaders, whom they denounced as Jews, Communists, and *Kaffir-boeties* (literally, Kaffir-brothers). Thus the newly urbanized Afrikaners, who were becoming the majority of the white workers in most industries, found it necessary to choose between the race principle and the class principle. Until 1948 the struggle was bitter and inconclusive, but since then the racial principle has triumphed, thanks largely to government support. Within a year of coming into power the Nationalists gained control of the important Mineworkers' Union. Other unions were purged of their radical leaders under the Suppres-

54. On trade unionism before 1948, see H. J. Simons, "Trade Unions," in Ellen Hellman, ed., *Handbook on Race Relations in South Africa* (Cape Town: Oxford University Press, 1949).

sion of Communism Act and its amendments, which empowered the government to impose severe restrictions on Communists and defined a Communist so loosely as to include anyone who encouraged in any way the achievement of *any* of the objects of communism, which was also loosely defined. By 1956, fifty-six trade-union leaders had been ordered to resign from their unions, and the back of the radical leadership of the trade unions had been broken.[55]

The Industrial Conciliation Act of 1956 struck powerfully at the very existence of mixed trade unions. No mixed unions that did not exist in 1956 were to be registered; the existing mixed unions were encouraged to split into uniracial unions; and those which remained mixed were compelled to have separate branches for white and for black members and to have all-white executive committees and were prohibited from holding mixed meetings, conferences, or congresses. The same act placed still further obstacles in the way of African trade unionists by prohibiting Africans from representing employees in industrial councils or in disputes referred to conciliation boards, and prohibiting employers from collecting trade-union dues from African employees. Under these pressures several of the mixed unions split. On the other hand, notwithstanding the government's wish to prevent such contacts and the existing legal impediments, cooperation between white and Coloured and Asian branches continued in the surviving mixed unions, and there were also several cases of cooperation between white and Coloured and Asian unions.

By 1977, 172 trade unions were officially registered for participation in the statutory industrial bargaining system. Eighty-three of them had white members only, forty-eight had Coloured members only, and forty-one had white, Coloured, and Asian members. The main coordinating bodies were the all-

55. On trade unionism from 1948 to 1969, see M. Horrell, *South Africa's Workers* (Johannesburg: SAIRR, 1969), and H. J. Simons and R. E. Simons, *Class and Colour in South Africa 1850–1950* (Harmondsworth: Penguin Books, 1969).

white Confederation of Labour (CONFED, 25 unions with about 200,000 members) and the Trade Union Council of South Africa (TUCSA, about 228,000 members in 63 unions—12 white, 23 mixed white, Coloured, and Asian, and 21 Coloured and Asian, plus 7 unregistered African unions). No African worker had a say in the collective bargaining system and, not surprisingly, less than 1 percent of the African workers were unionized.[56]

By that time, following four years of intermittent strikes by Africans, the government had decided to reexamine the whole question of labor relations, and during 1979 it made substantial changes in the industrial relations system, after receiving a report from a commission chaired by Professor N. Wiehahn. The commission recognized that there were anomalies in South African labor relations: black and and white workers were part of the same economic system and often did the same jobs, but negotiations with African and other workers took place in different ways. Africans negotiated through a committee system which gave them very little power, and other workers through the authoritative industrial councils. This put multinational companies in a difficult position because they were unable to accede to pressures from overseas interests to set up and negotiate with African trade unions in their South African operations; and there was also the danger that nonunionized Africans would develop negotiating machinery which would bypass and undermine the existing conciliation procedures. The Wiehahn Commission recommended that African workers be brought under control by legislation, which it referred to as coming under the "protection" of the law.[57] The commission also recommended that job reservation should be abolished, that all trade unions (including African) should register, and that each union should be free to prescribe membership qualifications as it saw fit.

56. *Survey of Race Relations, 1977,* pp. 284–88.
57. *The Wiehahn Commission: A Summary* (University of Cape Town: South African Labour and Development Research Unit, 1979), p. 1.

During 1979 Parliament passed legislation giving effect to these recommendations. Unions may apply for registration and all registered unions have access to the industrial courts and the right to strike after a thirty-day notification period. In the same year, the government passed further legislation as a result of the recommendations of another commission, chaired by Dr. P. J. Riekert, making it a criminal offense, subject to a large fine, for employers to hire Africans who do not possess residential rights in the cities. The effect of these laws is that the government dominates the African labor market by controlling mobility and the procedures for mediating industrial conflict.[58]

Sports Associations

The shift in the government's attitude toward nonracial sports since the late 1950s is a case study in white South Africa's desire to reestablish international sporting contacts without appearing to deviate from its principles of racial segregation. It has devised a policy of "multinational" sport which allows South African athletes to participate in international competitions within the framework of apartheid, with each "nation" participating separately.[59] However, this has not appeased foreign critics, and in 1980 and 1981 the government was moving cautiously toward further dismantling of the legal barriers against nonracial sports.

White South Africans are extremely proud of their sportsmen's achievements in international competition, so that this aspect of the government's policy is peculiarly vulnerable to international pressure. In 1956 the International Table Tennis

58. In chapter 5 we discuss (inter alia) the possibility of black trade unionism serving as a basis for black resistance politics.

59. J. Brickhill, Race against Race (London: International Defence and Aid Fund, 1976); J. Kane-Berman, Sport: Multi-Nationalism versus Non-Racialism (Johannesburg: SAIRR, 1972); R. E. Lapchick, The Politics of Race and International Sport: The Case of South Africa (Denver: University of Denver Press, 1974).

Federation expelled the white South African group because of racial discrimination and recognized the South African Table Tennis Board, which represented Blacks but was pledged to nonracialism. The Federation of International Football Associations suspended its recognition of the all-white Football Association of South Africa in 1961; in 1967 a New Zealand rugby tour of South Africa was called off because of South Africa's refusal to admit Maoris; and in 1968 the MCC cricket team was not allowed to tour South Africa because it included Basil d'Oliveira, a former South African who was classified as Coloured. Subsequently, South Africa suffered further setbacks at international levels—netball, cross-country running, pentathlon, gymnastics, and others. South Africa has not participated in the Olympic Games since 1964. The escalation of international sport boycotts against South Africa has left it virtually isolated in most sporting activities, and has forced it to stage its own athletics and rugby meetings with invited individuals.

Blacks may now compete with Whites for places on national and provincial teams in most sports, including cricket, rugby, and tennis, but the de facto exclusion of Blacks from club-level sport continues. Here not only sporting legislation applies, but the provisions of the Liquor Act (which denies Black and White access to the same facilities without special permit) and the Group Areas Act (which restricts mobility). Some sections of overseas opinion consider that this is a significant move toward breaking down racial discrimination, but others demand more far-reaching changes. In 1981, New Zealand was wracked by violent disturbances in protest against the visit of a South African rugby team, and in the United States the team was only able to play in private.

A Racial Hierarchy of Associations
The dominant cultural, economic, and social groups with political influence are, therefore, those that belong to the Afrikaner

community—the Broederbond, the FAK, and the Afrikaner chambers of commerce and industry, and specific white caste groups operating in areas where there are no Afrikaner community groups, including many of the professional and sports associations and some industrial associations such as the Chamber of Mines and the white trade unions. These groups monopolize all the regular channels of political influence in South Africa, not only because they are the beneficiaries of discriminatory legislation, but also because all significant political decision-making roles in the country are performed by Whites, and most of them by Afrikaners.

This fact is as true of the army and the navy, the police and the bureaucracy, as it is of the cabinet, the judiciary, and the central and provincial legislatures. Indeed, the elite of the Afrikaner community includes the leaders of most of the Afrikaner interest groups and the decision-makers in nearly all of the authoritative governmental structures; together they form a single social unit. Despite considerable differences of interest and attitude among them, the unit is still compact enough for effective pressures often, perhaps usually, to be transmitted in the course of normal social contacts, though when formal contacts are requested access is readily granted. Thus the process of interest articulation in South Africa is dominated for the most part by the overriding ethnic interest of the bulk of the Afrikaner community; in fact, the associational interest groups within that community are all dedicated to the proposition that the political summum bonum is the welfare of the Afrikaner community.

For English-speaking community groups, and for white caste groups that stand in opposition to Afrikaner community groups, effective access to governmental decision-makers is much more difficult. They do not have normal social access because their leaders are not part of the self-consciously Afrikaner community, but they are not suppressed or entirely ignored because they are members of the white caste—and voters. On some issues, where the interests of such groups coincide with the interests of corresponding Afrikaner community groups, their claims are effectively transmitted to the government by the Afrikaner group leaders. For example, the claims of English-speaking white teachers' associations for salary increases and improvements in working conditions are effectively transmitted by the Afrikaner teachers' associations, whose interests on these issues are virtually identical. On the other hand, in cases where the interests of such groups conflict with those of Afrikaner groups, the former have to resort to indirect methods to make their influence felt at all.

Consequently, English-speaking white interest groups have become expert organizers of public statements, mass meetings, petitions, solemn processions, and symbolic devices designed to draw the attention of the government and the electorate to objections to contemplated legislation. The English-medium universities resorted to most of these methods, including processions of their governing bodies, faculties, and students through the streets of Cape Town, Johannesburg, and Durban, in an attempt to dissuade the government from enacting the legislation that made it unlawful for them to admit black students; the students of those universities organized a series of ceremonies in which a torch was used as the symbol of freedom.

South African conditions have brought into being an organization that has adopted original techniques of protest, the Black Sash. This is an organization of women founded in the 1950s to protest a particular piece of legislation, the Senate Act which led to the removal of the Cape Coloured voters from the common roll. When the Senate Act was passed, the Black Sash did not dissolve but remained in existence to serve as a reminder to the government and the electorate of what had been done, and to protest later legislation restricting the liberties of South Africans. Wearing white dresses and black sashes and standing silently with bowed heads in public places, such as the entrance to the Parliament buildings, the members of the Black Sash certainly succeeded in producing reportable news. In 1973 this passive form of political protest in the vicinity of Cape Town parliament was declared illegal. Further legislation in 1976 led to the prohibition of all Black Sash demonstrations of more than one person. However, it is doubtful whether these specific but extraparliamentary techniques materially influenced the course of events in South Africa. Over the years their edge grew blunt through continual use without appreciable success. The Black Sash now concentrates on helping individual victims of oppressive laws.[60]

The government steadfastly restrains all organizations with black members (whether national, black caste, or community organizations) from exerting effective influence through any channels other than those of its own making. By the end of 1960 it had banned not only the multiracial Communist party and Congress of Democrats, but also the African National Congress and the Pan-Africanist Congress. Since then, it has systematically banned all black organizations with political aspirations except those which operate the "homeland" institutions and the bodies the government itself has created in the "white areas."

The mode of articulation of interests reflects the structure of South African society. The picture is not a tidy one, for there are divisions of interest even within the Afrikaner community, and many Blacks now regard the entire system as illegitimate. South Africa is the nearest approach to a pigmentocracy which has existed in an industrialized society, and it remains to be seen whether the pigmentocratic order can survive in the domestic and global conditions of the late twentieth century. Historians of the future may find that the most significant South African associations of the 1980s were not the Afrikaner ones that are interwoven with the present political system, but the plethora of

60. See Cherry Michelman, *The Black Sash of South Africa: A Case Study in Liberalism* (London: Oxford University Press, 1975). The Black Sash also publishes a monthly journal, *Black Sash*.

African associations which seem to be impotent today but may
be carrying the seeds of South Africa's political system of tomorrow.

THE AGGREGATION OF INTERESTS

If a South African were asked to classify his party system, his
answer would most likely depend upon his prescribed status in
South African society. An Afrikaner would probably label it a
two-party system, pointing out that South Africa is ruled by a
cabinet responsible to an elected legislature, and that the opposition of today has the prospect of becoming the government of
tomorrow. An English-speaking white South African would be
inclined to state that though the forms of a two-party system do
exist, in reality South Africa has become a one-party state, in the
sense that since 1948 the National party has entrenched itself in
power by legislation and administrative action, that it has increased its majority in most elections, and that it seems de facto
to be irremovable by constitutional means. A black South African would probably say that South Africa is an authoritarian
state, ruled by a government responsible to a racial oligarchy,
and that the existence and maneuvers of the political parties
within the oligarchy are of trivial importance. There is some
truth in each statement, and a comprehensive definition should
include all of the three ingredients. South Africa has a two-party
system tending toward a one-party system within a racial oligarchy or pigmentocracy.

The National Party
The ruling party is the party of the Afrikaner nation, born in the
rejection of fusion with the South African party, nourished in
anglophobia and negrophobia, and elevated and sustained by
the whole network of exclusive Afrikaner associations and in-

stitutions.[61] In 1963, J. C. Greyling, National party member of Parliament for Ventersdorp, declared that "the National Party is no party; it is the personification of the efforts and thought of the whole nation."[62] He was right in two respects. In one sense the National party is more than a party. It deems itself to be the only legitimate political home for an Afrikaner, irrespective of wealth, occupation, or class. The Afrikaner who does not support the National party is not a true Afrikaner but a traitor.

Daniel F. Malan taught the Afrikaner people the lesson of political solidarity. Disunited, they were the prey of the British government, of British South Africans, and of traitors; united, they rule South Africa. That lesson has sunk deep into the Afrikaner mores and is transmitted not only by the party itself but also by many organs of the state, notably the public schools, and by the whole gamut of Afrikaner organizations, from the Dutch Reformed churches to the voluntary associations. Many families that were Smutsite in previous generations have become supporters of Verwoerd, Vorster, and Botha in the present generation. Defectors to the Left are few, because the rebel faces the terrible punishment of ostracism by his community and the punishment is extended to his entire family. Of those who do rebel, some return, chastened, to the fold; others, smeared and

61. On the National party—its historical origins, its ideology, and its structure—see Carter, *Politics of Inequality*, esp. chap. 8; J. Albert Coetzee, *Politieke Groepering in die Wording van die Afrikanernasie* (Johannesburg: Voortrekker Pers, 1941); G. Cronjé, *'n Tuiste vie die Nageslag: Die blywende oplossing van Suid-Afrika se Rassevraagstukke* (Johannesburg: Publicité Handelsreklamediens, 1946), and *Regverdige Rasse-Apartheid* (Cape Town: Citadel Press, 1947); D. W. Krüger, *The Age of the Generals* (Johannesburg: Dagbreek, 1958); S.W. Pienaar and J. J. Scholtz, *D. F. Malan as Redenaar* (Cape Town: Tafelberg, 1964); N. M. Stultz, *Afrikaner Politics in South Africa 1934–1948* (Berkeley: University of California Press, 1974): F. A. van Jaarsveld, *The Awakening of Afrikaner Nationalism, 1868–1881* (Cape Town: Human and Rousseau, 1961); Adam and Giliomee, *Ethnic Power Mobilized*; Moodie, *The Rise of Afrikanerdom*; and, for a class analysis, Dan O'Meara, "White Trade Unionism, Political Power and Afrikaner Nationalism," *South African Labour Bulletin 1*, no. 10 (1975): 31–51.

62. *House of Assembly Debates, 1963*, col. 6136.

derided, are ejected from the entire complex of Afrikaner institutions and associations—indeed, from the *volk* itself—and they have either to live in social isolation or to essay the difficult and often uncongenial task of trying to integrate themselves into the English-speaking white community. Consequently, only the exceptionally noble or the exceptionally frustrated Afrikaner has the courage to rebel and the stamina to persist in a state of public rebellion against organized Afrikanerdom. Indeed, the only recent rebellion that has had a measure of success was a rebellion from the Right. During the late 1960s a group of Afrikaners known as *verkramptes* broke away from the party in the name of Afrikanerdom to form the Herstigte Nasionale party (Reestablished National party, HNP). They accused the National party of deviating from the pristine principles of Afrikanerdom by allowing limited interracial sport and by tolerating a breakdown of job reservation. Although they have never won a parliamentary seat, they provide a focal point for reactionary Afrikaners, and in the 1981 general election they received over 13 percent of the votes cast—sufficient to limit the capacity of the government to institute significant reforms.

In another sense the National party is less than a party, because the "nation" for which it stands is only a fraction of the population of South Africa. It has never made any attempt to identify itself with the Blacks, and toward the English-speaking Whites it has always been ambivalent. On the one hand, it is concerned to preserve Afrikanerdom, pure and unsullied by alien influences; on the other hand, it requires white allies against the Blacks. In practice, until the end of the Second World War the primary emphasis was given to the reestablishment of *Afrikaner* unity, and little more than lip service was paid to the idea of *white* unity; but since that time the later idea has been more urgently expressed.

There are two reasons for this change of emphasis. Afrikanerdom's very success in gaining control of the political and bureaucratic machinery, in increasing its share of the national economy, and in severing South Africa's last political links with Britain has enabled it to view with equanimity the prospect of white unity. In the early twentieth century, white unity might have spelled the absorption of Afrikaners by English-speaking South Africans; today it is more likely to involve the absorption of English-speaking South Africans by Afrikaners. Furthermore, the unity of all white South Africans is now perceived as being essential if they are to survive the internal and external challenges to white supremacy. Consequently, though anglophobia persists as a deep-rooted element in the Afrikaner psyche and still breaks surface from time to time, most of the leaders, including Prime Minister Pieter W. Botha, present the party as the only true political instrument for all white South Africans.

Before 1965 very few English-speaking voters actually supported the National party. The results of the Republican referendum of 1960 and the general election of 1961 are probably to be interpreted as meaning that the party then had the support of nearly 85 percent of the Afrikaner voters and less than 10 percent of the English-speaking voters. Since then, appreciable numbers of English-speaking Whites have voted Nationalist. Over 30 percent of the English-speakers who voted supported the National party in the 1977 election. English-speaking support for the ruling party dropped quite dramatically after the Muldergate scandal, but may rise again during the 1980s.

Membership in the National party is open to white South Africans who are at least eighteen years of age, accept the party statement of principles, and pledge themselves to accept party discipline. A high proportion of the Afrikaner people— probably between one-third and one-half of those who are qualified—are members. The inducements are many. Only members may participate in primaries or be elected as party officers, and party membership is often a recommendation for employment, as well as a satisfaction of the individual's need to belong to a prestigious corporate group. Indeed, the party is a manifestation of the Afrikaner community, organized for political purposes. For many Afrikaners, it is as natural to belong to the party as it is to belong to a Dutch Reformed church.

The party is efficiently structured, with a particularly strong grass-roots organization. There are local groups or cells under elected groups leaders; successively above them are the branches (usually corresponding with polling districts), the divisions (corresponding with parliamentary constituencies), and the provinces. At each of these levels there is political activity of a far more continuous character than is to be found in most countries; before an election there is intense activity for several weeks, absorbing the time and the energy, not merely of a few zealots, but of a high proportion of the members. It is true that the many electoral gains since 1948 have diminished the need for political effort; it has become a foregone conclusion that the party will acquire a large parliamentary majority, and in recent elections there were many uncontested seats. But tension is maintained by other factors: the desire to break previous records of seats and majorities, the anxiety to discredit the latest crop of defectors—especially defectors to the Right—and, above all, the deepening consciousness of the hostility of the Blacks and of the outside world. The tension is also promoted by the Afrikaans press, which devotes a high proportion of its space, year in and year out, to party polemics.

We have already seen how numerous organizations act as agents for the promotion of Afrikaner self-consciousness in every sphere of human activity. The party itself has one important subsidiary—the Nasionale Jeugbond (National Youth League)—which draws young Afrikaners into the party and trains them for party service so successfully that many of the Nationalist members of parliament received their political initiation in the Jeugbond. That many Nationalists tend toward extremism is largely to be attributed to the Jeugbond.

The structure of the National party is federal, the organization in each province having great autonomy. The body that elects all officeholders and lays down policy is the provincial party congress, whose meeting is the main feature of the annual party activity, bringing the representatives of the divisions or the branches into contact with the provincial leaders. Between congresses, control over the provincial party is exercised by the provincial leader and the provincial steering committee, elected by the congress. They determine the extent, the manner, and the timing of the application of a policy laid down by congress and operate the party machinery—appointing and dismissing officials, disciplining individuals, determining whether candidates are eligible for office and (in the Transvaal) repudiating the decisions of branches at their discretion.

Linking the provincial organizations is a Federal Council, comprising seven representatives from each province, appointed by the congresses, one representative of the Jeugbond, and the national leader. But this unwieldy body rarely meets. Each province has its own organization and party newspaper. The coordinating power between the provincial organizations is de facto exercised by a steering committee of the four provincial leaders—consisting in 1981 of Pieter W. Botha (Cape), Andrés P. Treurnicht (Transvaal), C. V. van der Merwe (Orange Free State), and Owen P. F. Horwood (Natal)—who meet informally as required to deal with overall problems of strategy and tactics, subject when possible to confirmation by the provincial congresses.

The other coordinating bodies are the cabinet and the parliamentary caucus. The caucus, consisting of the National party members of the parliament, meets weekly during parliamentary sessions, under the control of whips whom it elects. The cabinet decides policy on important matters and then explains that policy to the caucus, which usually accepts it without criticism and proceeds to discuss the tactics for giving effect to the policy in parliament. The caucus also has the crucial power of electing the national leader, and for this purpose it is convened out of session if necessary.[63]

In form, therefore, the National party is federal and democratic. Since 1948, however, there has been a centralizing and authoritarian trend within the party. The continuity of Nationalist rule has promoted the shift of power from the organs of the party, as such, to the cabinet; this shift has been accentuated by the personalities of the prime ministers and the deepening crisis of the regime.

During his premiership, Malan had tremendous prestige as the man who had reunited national Afrikanerdom and led it to the unexpected electoral victory in 1948; throughout the party it was acknowledged that Malan was without peer as tactician and debater. With Strijdom, the center and gravity in the party began to move from the Cape to the Transvaal—from the Afrikaner community that had experienced a continuity of political development ever since 1806 and had become conditioned to the process of discussion and compromise, to the community with a stormy political history and in which the authoritarian leadership of Paul Kruger was regarded as a model. This movement continued under Verwoerd, prime minister from 1958 to 1966, who, more than any other individual, set his stamp upon the modern South African political system.

Verwoerd was born near Amsterdam in 1901 and migrated to South Africa as a child. After studying at Stellenbosch University, he declined a scholarship to Oxford, giving preference to study in German universities. In 1927 he returned to Stellenbosch as professor of applied psychology—a science of which he became a superb exponent. His first political activity was as organizer of a national conference on the poor white problem and as leader of a deputation to ask Prime Minister Hertzog to refuse admission to Jewish refugees from Nazi Germany. In 1937

63. Adam and Giliomee, *Ethnic Power Mobilized*, pp. 198–200.

he followed in the footsteps of Malan by leaving his profession to become the founder-editor of a newspaper, *Die Transvaler*, in which he was an uncompromising advocate of Afrikaner nationalism and a supporter of the Nazi cause in the Second World War. He entered the Senate in 1948 and two years later acquired the key portfolio of Native Affairs; he then proceeded to lay the legislative and administrative foundations of the policy of apartheid. By 1958 Verwoerd was the natural candidate of the Transvaal Nationalists for the succession to Strijdom, and in the second ballot in the caucus he defeated T. E. Dönges by 98 votes to 75. He attributed that victory and his survival after an assassination attempt in 1960 to the will of God. However, the vagaries of the divine will were revealed in 1966 when he succumbed to an assassin's knife in Parliament.

Verwoerd's achievement lay in two things: the first was that he was able to fulfill Afrikaner nationalism's yearning for a republic, and the second was to spell out the ideological justification for "separate development" and its practical implementation in the "homeland" policy.[64] He brought an unyielding and autocratic style of rule to the National party and the country as a whole. He was not prepared to tolerate discussion within the National party which hinted at a political assimilation with the Coloureds into white political structures, and he reacted vigorously against the opponents of the "separate development" policies. As the pressures against the National party's policies increased, both internally and from abroad, he allowed the police to apprehend and hold suspects without access to the courts.

Verwoerd's successor in office was Balthazar Johannes Vor-

64. On Verwoerd, see G. D. Scholtz, *Hendrik Frensch Verwoerd 1901–1966* (Cape Town: Perskor, 1974): Alex Hepple, *Verwoerd* (London: Penguin, 1967); Jan Botha, *Verwoerd is Dead* (Cape Town: Books of Africa, 1967); A. H. Pelzer, *Verwoerd Speaks* (Johannesburg: Afrikaanse Pers Beperk, 1966); H. Kenny, *Architect of Apartheid: H. F. Verwoerd—An Appraisal* (Johannesburg: Jonathan Bell, 1980).

ster, who was born in 1915. From the age of nineteen, he studied at the University of Stellenbosch, where one of his lecturers was Verwoerd, with whom he developed a lifelong connection in politics. From his university days he was an ardent Afrikaner Nationalist, and at the outbreak of the Second World War he was one of the founders of the Ossewabrandwag (Oxwagon Guard), a right-wing movement which opposed South Africa's fighting with Britain against Nazi Germany. Because of this political involvement he was detained without trial for three months and then held at Koffiefontein Internment Camp for a further seventeen months. When later he was instrumental in detaining political opponents without trial, Vorster stated: "I had no real hard feelings about my own internment. I had come out in opposition to the government of the day, that government identified me as a threat to established order and so it neutralized me, it did what it felt was necessary at the time. I adopted the same approach."[65] After the war he made an unsuccessful attempt to enter Parliament in 1948 but eventually succeeded in 1953. His links with Verwoerd bore fruit in 1958 when he was appointed deputy minister of education, arts, and science and of social welfare and pensions. In this role he had the important task of implementing the Bantu Education Act of 1953, which was one of Verwoerd's keys to the implementation of the "separate development" policy.

Later, as minister of justice, Vorster saw to the enactment and enforcement of a series of drastic penalties against opponents of the regime (see chap. 5). He dismissed accusations that he was using totalitarian methods and claimed that he had found his form of house arrest justified in the Bible, of which he read a chapter a night.[66] He denounced liberalism as the precursor of communism: "[T]he difference between the communists and the

65. J. d'Oliveira, *Vorster the Man* (Johannesburg: E. Stanton Publishers, 1977), p. 130. See also B. M. Schoeman, *Vorster se 1000 dae* (Cape Town: Human and Rousseau, 1974).
66. D'Oliveira, *Vorster the Man*, p. 133.

liberalists is getting smaller and smaller, so that a person will eventually need a magnifying glass to see the differences."[67] This classic equation, favored by the extreme Right in international politics, suggested to the outside world that a totalitarian government was developing in South Africa, and that Vorster was instrumental in bringing it about. It also endowed communism with the lustre of being in the forefront of opposition to white domination in South Africa, and ascribed to it the acknowledged virtues and values of Western liberalism.

The prestige that Vorster acquired among Nationalists for crushing the incipient black revolt during the early 1960s was sufficient to ensure his election as leader of the party and prime minister after the assassination of Verwoerd in 1966. One of his first actions as prime minister was to establish a special intelligence unit (the Bureau of State Security) directly responsible to himself, under Hendrik van den Bergh, a former fellow member of the Ossewabrandwag and fellow wartime internee. Ironically, BOSS (as it became known) set about investigating, not only the liberal and socialist opponents of the National party, but also right-wing Afrikaner dissidents who thought that Vorster was deviating from Afrikaner Nationalist principles.

Following the widespread black revolts in 1976, Vorster reacted with predictable harshness and blamed the unrest on Marxist agitators and the African National Congress. Also, without informing the cabinet, he approved of vast increases in the activities of the Department of Information, allowing it to indulge in a series of secret operations inside and outside the country using funds from a secret defense account. However, "Muldergate" (named after the minister of information, Dr. Connie Mulder) became a public scandal after the auditor-general made a critical report.[68] As the scandal began to break, all concerned attempted to cover up. Vorster himself resigned as

67. *Die Vaderland*, 23 October 1962.
68. See Mervyn Rees and Chris Day, *Muldergate: The Story of the "Info Scandal"* (Johannesburg: Macmillan, 1980).

prime minister and was elected state president, an office that provided some immunity from criticism; but when a commission of inquiry revealed his involvement, he resigned from that office too. Muldergate also terminated the careers of General van den Bergh, head of BOSS, Dr. Mulder, hitherto a potential prime minister, and Dr. Eschel Rhoodie, secretary of the Department of Information, who was extradited from France and charged on five counts of fraud.

After bitter in-fighting, the parliamentary caucus elected Pieter Willem Botha leader of the party, and hence prime minister, in succession to Vorster. Born in 1916, Botha has been a politician throughout his adult life: a National party organizer at the age of twenty, a member of parliament for a Cape constituency since the Nationalist triumph in 1948, and minister of defence since 1966. His defense portfolio increased in power and prestige as warfare escalated in Angola, Mozambique, and Rhodesia-Zimbabwe. He is no less dedicated than his predecessors to maintaining white supremacy and the preeminence of the Afrikaner *volk*; but he is somewhat more aware than they were of the need to adapt to changing circumstances inside and outside the country, especially by providing members of the Coloured and Asian communities with some say—but not a decisive say—in the political process, as explained in chapter 3.

Vorster's administration had already begun to reduce the scope of "petty apartheid"—for example, by opening selected hotels and restaurants to black people who could afford to patronize them. Hard-core racists resented even these concessions. As early as 1969 several members of Parliament were expelled from the National party and formed the Herstigte Nasionale party on a platform of undiluted apartheid. Although this party won no parliamentary seats during the 1970s or in 1981, its very existence causes ministers to look over their shoulders for signs of defections to the Right and limits their capacity to introduce substantial reforms.

Criticism from the other side is more muted. Despite the

social penalties, in each generation a number of distinguished Afrikaners have defected from the ranks. In 1963, for example, several ministers of the Dutch Reformed churches founded a Christian Institute of Southern Africa, in conjunction with white and black ministers of other churches, with the aim of uniting all South African Christians and making Christianity a living force in South Africa. However, when such people seem likely to become serious threats, the government isolates them and silences them. Thus in 1977 it banned the Reverend C. F. Beyers Naude, head of the Christian Institute, and the institute was closed down later that year. Intolerance of white as well as black dissidents has become an increasing feature of the Nationalist regime.

Opposition Parties

The Progressive Federal party (PFP) is an amalgam of supporters of the former Liberal party, left-wing members of the former United party, and a few former National party supporters. Since the first Progressive party member, Helen Suzman, was elected to parliament in 1961, the party has grown in strength. In 1974 several members of parliament resigned from the United party to form the Reform party which, in its turn, amalgamated with the Progressive party to become the Progressive Reform party (PRP). When the United party disbanded in 1977, many of its former members joined the PRP, which then changed its title to the Progressive Federal party. In the 1977 election it won seventeen seats in parliament and became the official Opposition; in 1981 it won nine more seats. The PFP draws its parliamentary support from upper-income, English-speaking constituencies. Very few Afrikaners support the party. Nevertheless, in 1980 a third of the PFP parliamentarians were Afrikaners, including the leader of the party, Frederick van Zyl Slabbert, a former sociology lecturer and professor at the universities of Stellenbosch, Cape Town, and the Witwatersrand.

The party's identification with the principles of a laissez-faire capitalism unfettered by race restrictions has made it attractive to some private capital interests. It enjoys the support of many leading businessmen, notably Harry F. Oppenheimer, chairman of the powerful Anglo-American Corporation, one of the largest finance houses in the world. In addition, most sections of the English-speaking press give it their support.

The PFP opposes the racially discriminatory practices of the government. Initially it proposed a limited extension of franchise rights based upon educational and financial criteria. Since 1974 it has adopted a policy of universal franchise, the basis of which would be decided by negotiation among elected representatives of the various population groups; this might be a one-man–one-vote or a qualified franchise system, or some combination of the two. It also recommends a constitutional framework which, while making it possible for all South Africans to participate in the political decision-making process, would eliminate the possibility of a reversal from white domination to black domination.[69]

In the 1960s and 1970s the PFP consistently protested against the enactment of legislation which extended the powers of the executive at the expense of the judiciary and the legislature. In a period of the rapid erosion of the power of Parliament, the independence of the courts, and the freedom of the press, the PFP identified itself strongly with the three pillars of Western democracy: press freedom, judicial independence, and the accountability to Parliament of the executive arm of government. In spite of its protests and its significant support from business quarters, the PFP has been unable to stop, or even to slow down, the movement away from accepted Western democratic principles in South Africa. Its inability to gain enough electoral support to become a potential ruling party shows that the National party remains the most effective spokesman for the pre-

69. F. van Zyl Slabbert and David Welsh, *South Africa's Options* (Cape Town: David Philip, 1979).

sumed interests of the majority of the white group, and indicates that the initiative for political change within the present constitutional system still rests with the National party.

Consequently, so long as the system is not destroyed by economic disaster, or by revolution from within, or by attack from without (or some combination of these forces), the National party seems likely to rule South Africa, provided only that it can stop the drift to the right-wing Herstigte Nasionale party. With its highly articulated supporting organizations, its control of the bureaucracy, the police, and the army, and its tough experienced leadership, it appears impregnable. Indeed, whatever our attitudes may be regarding the morality, the wisdom, and the long-term practicability of making the preservation of white supremacy the primary goal of politics in an industrialized state in the last quarter of the twentieth century, we should recognize that in the South African context the National party is a remarkably efficient instrument for that purpose.

5

The Internal Opposition

Oppositions to a caste system vary in scope, objective, and method. In scope, opposition may be national or sectional. National opposition, in the fullest sense, derives support not only from all the castes but also from all the major classes within each caste, whereas sectional opposition is limited in terms of caste, or class, or both. In objective, an opposition may be reformist or revolutionary. A reformist opposition is concerned, in the short run, to ameliorate the conditions of the subject castes and, in the long run, to persuade the members of the ruling caste, operating through the existing constitutional machinery, to admit members of the other castes to share in power, and thus gradually to erode the caste system by a process that maintains the institutional continuity of the state. In contrast, a revolutionary opposition is concerned, not with mitigating the effects of the caste system, but with destroying the system—that is, not operating through the established constitutional machinery (whose legitimacy it denies), but overthrowing it and starting again with a clean slate. Finally, a revolutionary as well as a reformist opposition may confine itself to nonviolent methods to advance its purposes, such as strikes and passive resistance to caste laws and customs, but may also resort to organized violence.

During the last seventy years there have been three main phases in the opposition to the caste system in South Africa. For a long while the principal opposition was sectional in scope (being limited to elite groups in each caste), reformist in objective, and nonviolent in method. Then between about 1948 and 1960, though remaining nonviolent, it became revolutionary in objective and very nearly national in scope. Since 1960 the most unequivocal opposition has been an underground and predominantly African movement, pursuing revolutionary goals by violent as well as nonviolent means; but black people have also created a series of organizations with varying degrees of revolutionary potential within the framework created by the government.

The two great changes in the character of the principal opposition were both reactions to the persistent and increasingly unequivocal determination of the controllers of the authoritative governmental institutions to maintain white supremacy at all costs. The postwar shift from sectional to national scope and from reformist to revolutionary objective was a reaction to the prolonged refusal of South African governments to grant any of the reforms that had been demanded, culminating in the 1948 election of a government committed absolutely to the maintenance of white supremacy. The shift to violence was a reaction against the government's systematic and violent suppression of all black organizations outside the institutions of apartheid, which reached its climax in the banning of both of the major African political organizations in 1960.

OPPOSITION BEFORE 1948

The sectional, reformist opposition to the caste system had roots in the Cape Colony, where the laws had been for the most part color-blind and Blacks had been admitted to the franchise on the common voters' roll equally with Whites, subject to economic and educational qualifications. After 1910, as segregationist laws and practices became more and more pervasive in the Cape Province and the other three provinces of the Union, Blacks — and also a few Whites — opposed the trend.

Among the Whites, opposition was generally confined to the professional classes in the major cities, especially to lawyers, clergy, and university teachers in Cape Town and Johannesburg. In 1929 some of them founded the South African Institute of Race Relations to collect and publish information about race relations in South Africa and to arrange conferences for the discussion of South Africa's racial problems. Thus, white people who were dismayed by the segregationist trend were drawn into regular contact with one another and a body of relevant empirical data was accumulated.

In 1939 R. F. A. Hoernlé, a former professor of philosophy at Harvard University who had been head of the department of philosophy at the University of Witwatersrand since 1923, analyzed the segregation policy of the government of the day:

"Segregation" stands for a policy offensive to all non-Europeans in South Africa, viz. for a policy of exclusion, forced upon them by the white group, from the status and privileges which the white group insists upon reserving for itself. This is segregation as an instrument of domination; segregation *which retains the segregated in the same social and political structure with the dominant white group*, but subjects them to the denial of important rights and keeps them at a social distance implying inferiority.[1]

The Whites who represented Africans in Parliament under the Representation of Natives Act of 1936—notably Edgar H. Brookes, Margaret Ballinger, and Donald B. Molteno— persistently exposed the harshness of the laws as they bore upon the black people. There were even leading white politicians, responsible to white electorates, who were uneasy about the segregation policy. When he was out of office in 1929, J. C. Smuts himself admitted that the entire basis of that policy would fall away if significant numbers of Africans were incorporated in the

1. R. F. Alfred Hoernlé, *South African Native Policy and the Liberal Spirit* (Johannesburg: Witwatersrand University Press, 1945), p. 168. Italics as in the original. See also the same author's *Race and Reason* (Johannesburg: Witwatersrand University Press, 1945).

industrial process in the cities; in 1945 J. H. Hofmeyr, Jr., deputy prime minister of South Africa, advocated "an unwearying activity towards the removal of inequalities of opportunity."[2]

Doubts about the segregation policy were also expressed in a series of reports by government commissions. In 1932 the Holloway Commission reported that to treat all Africans as residents of the reserves, with no rights other than those of visitors in white areas, was "impracticable" and "unfair."[3] In 1946 the Social and Economic Planning Council reported that there would always be large numbers of Africans in the white areas, however efficiently the economy of the reserves might be developed.[4] The Fagan Commission reported in 1948 that "the idea of total segregation is utterly impracticable" and that the process of urbanization of Africans was an inevitable and irreversible phenomenon.[5]

Despite these doubts, up to the crucial general election of May 1948 all governments had maintained far-reaching legal discriminations against Blacks—especially Africans—in the white areas, and no white political organization existed which presented a clear-cut challenge to the system. The white liberals were equivocal when it came to propounding policies. Continuously preoccupied with the business of trying to ameliorate the effects and to expose the fallacies of the existing system, they failed to create a picture of their ultimate goal for South African society or to suggest how radical reforms might be realized.

Political activity among the subordinate castes began to-

2. Jan C. Smuts, *Africa and Some World Problems* (Oxford: Clarendon Press, 1930), pp. 94–98; Jan H. Hofmeyr, *Christian Principles and Race Problems: Hoernlé Memorial Lecture, 1945* (Johannesburg: SAIRR, 1945), p.31.

3. Union of South Africa, *Report of Native Economic Commission, 1930–1932: U.G. 22/1932* (Pretoria: Government Printer, 1932), p. 101.

4. Union of South Africa, *Social and Economic Planning Council Report No. 9: The Native Reserves and Their Place in the Economy of the Union of South Africa: U.G. 32/1946* (Pretoria: Government Printer, 1946), p. 3.

5. Union of South Africa, *Report of the Native Laws Commission 1946–48: U.G. 28/1948* (Pretoria: Government Printer, 1948), p. 19.

ward the end of the nineteenth century.[6] Before 1948, the principal organizations were the African National Congress (ANC,
founded in 1912), the South African Indian Congress (SAIC,
founded in 1920 as an amalgamation of preexisting Natal and
Transvaal organizations), and the African Political Organization
(APO, whose members were Coloured people). All three organizations comprised small groups of Western-oriented middle-
class elements and lacked mass support. Their purpose was to
realize the promise inherent in the Cape colonial laws: first, by
gaining full equality with Whites for the Black middle classes
which they represented and, later, by extending the benefits of
equality to the masses of the people. The precedent they had in
mind was the step-by-step extension of the parliamentary franchise to all classes and both sexes in Britain. By rational argu-
ment and pressure within the framework of the constitution,
they sought to persuade the existing electorate to reverse the
segregationist tide.

Throughout this period the successive presidents-general
of the ANC were John L. Dube, a Congregational minister with an
American education, Sefako M. Makgatho, a teacher and
Methodist lay preacher with a British education, Zaccheus R.
Mahabane, a Methodist clergyman, Josiah T. Gumede, a teacher,

6. On black political activity before 1948, see Mary Benson, The African
Patriots: The Story of the African National Congress of South Africa (London:
Faber, 1963); Gail M. Gerhart, Black Power in South Africa: The Evolution of an
Ideology (Berkeley: University of California Press, 1978); Thomas Karis and
Gwendolen M. Carter, eds., From Protest to Challenge: A Documentary History
of African Politics in South Africa 1882–1964, 4 vols. (Stanford: Hoover Institu-
tion Press, 1972–77); Leo Kuper, "African Nationalism in South Africa, 1910–
1964," in Monica Wilson and Leonard Thompson, eds., The Oxford History of
South Africa, vol. 2 (Oxford: Clarendon Press, 1971), chap. 8; Z. K. Matthews,
Freedom for My People: The Autobiography of Z. K. Matthews (London: Rex
.Collings, 1981); Edward Roux, Time Longer than Rope: A History of the Black
Man's Struggle for Freedom in South Africa, rev. ed. (Madison: University of
Wisconsin Press, 1964); A. P. Walshe, The Rise of African Nationalism in South
Africa: The African National Congress, 1912–1952 (Berkeley: University of
California Press, 1971).

Pixley Seme, a lawyer with American and British education, and Alfred B. Xuma, a medical doctor trained in the United States. With the exception of Gumede, who came to regard Russia as the "new Jerusalem," these leaders concentrated on educating the white electorate concerning "the requirements and aspirations of the Native people," enlisting the support of sympathetic white organizations, promoting unity among all African peoples, and, above all, redressing African grievances "by constitutional means."[7] Accordingly, the ANC protested each installment of segregationist legislation, from the Natives Land Act of 1913 through the Representation of Natives Act of 1936, usually making its protests in South Africa but sometimes sending delegations overseas—to England in 1913 and to Versailles in 1919. Though the ANC usually acted alone, its leaders were as a rule in close touch with white liberals, and on occasion they sponsored multiracial conferences, as in 1926.

By 1948 it was clear that this type of opposition was barren. Instead of being admitted to equality, the black middle classes were being subjected to additional forms of discrimination. All the reformist opposition had achieved was a succession of rearguard actions, each ending in defeat.

Sporadic efforts were also made to create revolutionary movements. The most spectacular was founded by Clements Kadalie, an African from Nyasaland, who created an Industrial and Commercial Workers Union (ICU) with the help of a small group of white socialists and organized a series of industrial strikes starting in 1919.[8] Like its contemporary, the Universal Negro Improvement Association of Marcus Garvey in the United States, however, the ICU was poorly organized, and it disintegrated in the late 1920s, partly from internal weaknesses and partly in consequence of official suppression.

7. *The Constitution of the African National Congress*, 1919, "Objects," clauses 4 and 11, cited in Karis and Carter, *From Protest to Challenge*, 1:77– 78.
    8. Roux, *Time Longer than Rope*, pp. 161–205; 251–63; Clements Kadalie, *My Life and the ICU* (London: Frank Cass, 1970).

The Communist party of South Africa was founded in 1921 by a small group of Whites. It was the only political organization in South Africa that recruited members from all the racial groups and had a multiracial executive. But it suffered from ill-judged directives from Moscow, like other Communist parties outside Russia, and from a series of internal schisms; it never gained a wide following. Nevertheless, it exerted a considerable influence on the ICU, and by 1948 Communist ideas were attracting several of the younger and most frustrated members of the ANC and the SAIC.[9]

WHITE CRITICS OF THE SYSTEM

In May 1948 the white electorate rejected any possibility of seeking an accommodation with the reformist opposition to the caste system along the lines that had always been demanded by the reformers, in favor of the doctrine of "apartheid" or "separate development" as propounded by the National party—that is to say, in favor of the perpetuation of the caste system within the white areas of South Africa on the ground that Blacks would be able to fulfill their legitimate aspirations in their own areas.[10] Since then, as the tensions within South African society have mounted, an ever-higher proportion of the white electorate has supported the NP or parties still further to the right; at the same time, however, a small but continuously augmented stream of white people has become critical of the racist structure of South African society. These critics are drawn from both the Afrikaner

9. Roux, chaps. 15 ff.; A. Lerumo, *Fifty Fighting Years: The Communist Party of South Africa 1921–1971* (London: Inkululeko Publications, 1971); H. J. Simons and R. E. Simons, *Class and Colour in South Africa 1850–1950* (Harmondsworth: Penguin Books, 1969).
    10. Newell Stultz, *Afrikaner Politics in South Africa 1934–1948* (Berkeley: University of California Press, 1974).

and the English-speaking communities, and many of them are professional men of standing. They point to the glaring gulf between the theory and practice of apartheid, to the continuous increase in the numbers of Africans in the white areas, to the absence of any adequate substitute for participation in the political process for Coloureds and Asians, and to the harshness of the methods employed to maintain the caste system. They conclude that the government's policy is morally indefensible and, in the long run, disastrous. Though they have not been very effective in creating voting power, they have built up an impressive critique, not only of the day-to-day performance of the government, but also of the caste system.

For example, in 1957 the historian Leo Marquard compared the situation in South Africa with the postwar situation in tropical Africa:

Our problem is fundamentally the same as that of any other colonial power: how to terminate colonialism reasonably and peacefully. Our problem is not unique unless we want to make it so. Nor is the solution unique. It is to renounce political power over colonial subjects. For Europe, this takes the form of withdrawing political authority; for us it must take the form of sharing political authority with our colonial subjects. [11]

John R. Dugard of the University of the Witwatersrand has said, "some might argue that some laws are so lacking in minimum moral content that they do not deserve the name 'law.' "[12] And Philip V. Tobias, dean of the faculty of medicine and head of the department of anatomy in the same university, has declared bluntly that "science provides no evidence that any single one of the assumptions underlying South Africa's racial legislation is justified."[13]

11. Leo Marquard, South Africa's Colonial Policy (Johannesburg: SAIRR, 1957), pp. 25–26.

12. John R. Dugard, "The Legal Framework of Apartheid," in Nic Rhoodie, ed., South African Dialogue (Johannesburg: McGraw-Hill, 1972), p. 99.

13. Philip V. Tobias, The Meaning of Race (Johannesburg: SAIRR, 1961), p. 22.

Most Christian churches in South Africa have made official pronouncements critical of the caste system.[14] David Russell, an Anglican priest, and Cosmos Desmond, a Roman Catholic priest, were prohibited from disseminating their views because they had publicized the widespread poverty and social dislocation in the "re-settlement" areas. The Reverend Theo Kotzé, a minister in the Methodist church and an official of the ecumenical Christian Institute, was also silenced in 1977. In two notable cases church ministers were imprisoned in the name of security legislation. In 1971, Gonville ffrench-Beytagh, Anglican dean of Johannesburg, was sentenced to a five-year term of imprisonment for being found guilty on a charge under the Terrorism Act. He appealed successfully and was released. In 1980, David Russell was sentenced to jail for attending a church synod outside the area to which he was confined by a banning order.

Several Dutch Reformed clergy, too, have had the courage to stand up against the caste system, notably Professor B. B. Keet of Stellenbosch and C. F. Beyers Naudé, former moderator of the Nederduits Gereformeerde Kerk (NGK, the largest of the Dutch Reformed churches) and former head of the Christian Institute. Beyers Naudé's trenchant criticism of the inhumanity of the apartheid system was a source of division within his church. In 1977, when he was silenced and the Christian Institute was declared unlawful, the black branch of the Dutch Reformed church supported him, but few voices from the white NGK were raised in his defense. Woord en Daad (Word and Deed), a small group of theologians from the Gereformeerde Kerk, a sister church of the NGK, has been outspoken in its criticism of racism, though generally supporting separate development. From

14. John de Gruchy, *The Church Struggle in South Africa* (Cape Town: David Philip), chap. 3; Andrew Prior, ed., *Catholics in Apartheid Society: Essays on the Catholic Church in South Africa* (Cape Town: David Philip, 1982).

within this theological circle a radical critique of apartheid emerged in 1978.[15]

The South African Council of Churches (SACC), which was organized in the 1960s to encourage interchurch cooperation, has played a significant role in the emerging church-state conflict. In 1968 it issued a document entitled *Message to the People of South Africa*, which declared that separate development is a "pseudo gospel" in conflict with Christian principles and called upon those in authority to dismantle the apartheid social structures. The *Message* was a turning point in church-state relations. The Afrikaans-speaking branches of the Reformed churches repudiated it, and Prime Minister Vorster threatened those who promulgated it. Since 1968 there has been an uneasy relationship between the state and the SACC. In 1980 Prime Minister Botha threatened to take action against the council because of its strong criticisms of the government.

In 1970 the executive council of the World Council of Churches voted to extend nonmilitary assistance to African guerrilla movements. The decision was a shock to white Christians and an encouragement to black Christians, and it precipitated a crisis in the churches in South Africa. Archbishop Denis Hurley said this about the decision:

White South Africans were horrified to think that a responsible and widely representative Christian group could judge that there was so much 'institutional violence' in South Africa that practical encouragement could be given to movements designed to overthrow it by force. The average white South African would not know what you were talking about if you accused his country of 'institutional violence.' This is the measure of the Church's failure to communicate Christian concern to the majority of their white members.[16]

Several South African judges, after retirement from the

15. "The Koinonia Declaration," *Journal of Theology for Southern Africa,* September 1978.

16. Denis Hurley, "The Churches and Race Relations," in Rhoodie, *South African Dialogue.*

bench, have also become forthright critics of the caste system, and by the early 1980s active judges, too, were criticizing decisions of the executive branch of government.[17] Likewise, several talented white writers, journalists, and playwrights, such as Alan Paton, André Brink, and Athol Fugard, have written penetrating protest literature. A number of white critics have been imprisoned, and one, Rick Turner, a University of Natal political scientist, was assassinated in his home in 1977.[18]

All the politicians who were elected to Parliament by African voters under the Representation of Natives Act were critical of the caste system. Margaret Ballinger, who was a Native representative from the introduction of that form of representation in 1937 until its abolition in 1960, regarded the government arguments in support of apartheid as grossly misleading. Helen Suzman, the only Progressive party member of Parliament from 1961 to 1974, vigorously opposed every major racial bill and has become an internationally respected critic of apartheid.

Thus the dominant caste carries within itself a sense of guilt, which is articulated by a number of clergy, lawyers, scholars, and authors. Nevertheless, the prospect of dismantling all the legal barriers between the castes—in education, property ownership, residence, mobility, employment, and sexual and other social relations—does not correspond with the perceived interests of any class in white South African society. There are many enlightened businessmen who experience their share of guilt and are concerned to acquire legitimacy in the eyes of the outside world and the majority of the local population, to preserve industrial peace, and to recruit enough skilled workpeople to operate the increasingly complex equipment of modern industry; but their capacity for radical action is impeded by their

17. For example, A. van de Sandt Centlivres, *Thomas Benjamin Davie: The First T. B. Davie Memorial Lecture* (Cape Town: University of Cape Town, 1961); O. D. Schreiner, *South Africa—United or Divided?* (Johannesburg: SAIRR, 1964).

18. *Richard Turner, The Eye of the Needle* (Johannesburg: SPROCAS, 1972).

socialization and participation in the existing system, with its gross inequalities and its endemic racism. Such people provide the economic basis for the Progressive Federal party and like-minded voluntary associations, which are committed to change by gradual and peaceful methods and expend a great deal of intellectual energy in searching for constitutional devices that might provide permanent safeguards for the Whites as a collective group within an otherwise democratic system. That they cannot discard their racial categories is not surprising. Dominant classes do not voluntarily surrender their powers and privileges.

Those Whites who act in the belief that the reformist route is barren in South Africa tend to be rejected by both poles in South African society. Their fellow Whites treat them as traitors; while all but a few proven white revolutionaries are isolated from the mainstream of black political activity, as it, in turn, has moved from reformist to revolutionary objectives, and from nonviolent to violent methods. In short, white critics of the caste system have made an impressive diagnosis of the malady affecting South Africa, but they cannot agree among themselves which remedy to prescribe and they lack the means to apply any remedy at all.[19]

BLACK REVOLUTIONARIES

The origins of a shift from a reformist to a revolutionary policy in the principal black organizations can be traced to the war years, when African urbanization and proletarianization were accelerating and a new generation of African intellectuals, losing patience with the established leadership, formed a pressure

19. P.L. v.d. Berghe, *The Liberal Dilemma in South Africa* (London: Croom Helm, 1979).

group within the African National Congress.[20] The core of the group were four Africans working in Johannesburg: Anton Lembede from Natal, who had obtained a B.A. degree by correspondence and worked as a teacher and law clerk; Walter Sisulu from the Transkei, a laborer; Oliver Tambo from Pondoland who, after taking a B.A. degree at Fort Hare, was working as a teacher and later qualified in law; and Nelson Mandela, who became the chief spokesman for the ANC in a period of intense confrontation with the state.

Mandela was born in Umtata, Transkei, in 1918. Neither his father nor his mother had gone to school. He is a member of the Thembu ruling family and uncle of Kaizer Matanzima, the president of the Transkei. After attending Healdtown, a Methodist school, he went to Fort Hare College to study for a B.A. degree, but was suspended in his third year for organizing a boycott of the Student Representative Council when the government deprived it of its power. He then went to Johannesburg, where he completed a correspondence B.A. degree from the University of South Africa. In Johannesburg, which was in the midst of the wartime industrial boom, Mandela experienced the realities of massive proletarianization of the black population: teeming urban slums, with poverty aggravated by the color bar, pass laws, and police harassment. In the city he met Walter Sisulu, who encouraged him to complete his law studies, and in 1952 he went into practice with Oliver Tambo.

These men formed the nucleus of an ANC Youth League in 1944 and gained control of the ANC in 1949 when the national conference adopted their program, which sanctioned the use of

20. Benson, *African Patriots*, chaps. 9–15; E. Feit, *South Africa: The Dynamics of the African National Congress* (London: Oxford University Press, 1962), chap. 1; A. Luthuli, *Let My People Go: An Autobiography* (London: Collins, 1962), chaps 9–10; Gerhart, *Black Power*, chap. 3; Walshe, *Rise of African Nationalism*, chaps. 1, 2; Karis and Carter, *From Protest to Challenge*, vol. 2, pt. 2.

strikes, civil disobedience, and noncooperation to coerce the government to remove discriminatory laws. At the same time, they secured the election of Sisulu as secretary-general of the ANC and caused the president-general, Dr. Alfred B. Xuma, to be replaced by Dr. James S. Moroka. In 1952 they came to the conclusion that Moroka was not the dynamic leader they were looking for and replaced him with Albert J. Luthuli, a devout Christian, who had been a teacher and then the elected chief of an African community at Groutville, Natal. The South African Indian Congress had already undergone a similar change, with the emergence of Dr. Gangathura Naicker as president of its Natal section and Dr. Yusuf M. Dadoo as president of its Transvaal section.

The first systematic campaign against the Afrikaner Nationalist government was undertaken by the African and the Indian congresses in concert in 1952, when large numbers of volunteers went out of their way to defy discriminatory laws and some eight thousand were arrested. By the end of the year, however, rioting occurred in Port Elizabeth, East London, Cape Town, and Johannesburg, contrary to the intentions of the organizers, who called the campaign off in 1953 after Parliament enacted severe penalties for protest actions.[21]

The next major campaign was almost national in scope. The ANC, the South African Indian Congress, the South African Coloured People's Organization, the predominantly white Congress of Democrats, and the multiracial South African Congress of Trade Unions cooperated in a campaign designed to enlist the support of the black masses and the sympathy of the outside world. Throughout the country, local groups compiled lists of grievances and elected delegates to a "Congress of the People." On June 26, 1955, three thousand delegates (over two thousand Africans and two to three hundred each of Coloured people,

21. Leo Kuper, *Passive Resistance in South Africa* (London: Jonathan Cape, 1956). See also Benson, chaps. 16–17; Luthuli, chaps. 11–13; Gerhart, chaps. 4–5; and Karis and Carter, vol. 2, pt. 3.

ans, and Whites) met at Kliptown near Johannesburg and adopted a "Freedom Charter," which begins:

> We, the people of South Africa, declare for all our country and the world to know:
> That South Africa belongs to all who live in it, black and white, and that no government can justly claim authority unless it is based on the will of the people;
> That our people have been robbed of their birthright to land, liberty and peace by a form of government founded on injustice and inequality;
> That our country will never be prosperous or free until all our people live in brotherhood, enjoying equal rights and opportunities;
> That only a democratic state, based on the will of the people, can secure to all their birthright without distinction of colour, race, sex or belief;
> And therefore, we, the people of South Africa, black and white together—equal, countrymen and brothers—adopt this FREEDOM CHARTER. And we pledge ourselves to strive together, sparing nothing of our strength and courage, until the democratic changes here set out have been won.[22]

The government responded by enacting further repressive legislation and, in December 1956, by arresting 156 persons, including the leaders of the organization forming the congress alliance, and charging them with high treason, in the form of a conspiracy to overthrow the state by violence and replace it with a state based on communism. Sixty-five of those arrested were released after the preliminary examination; thirty of the accused were acquitted and discharged on March 29, 1961; and the case against the remaining sixty-one accused was then withdrawn.[23]

The failure of both the passive resistance campaign of 1952–53 and the Congress of the People campaign of 1955–56, at a time of continuous economic diversification, led to new divisions within the ANC. There were those who agreed with

22. Full text in Karis and Carter, 3:205. On the Congress of the People campaign, see also Benson, chap. 18; Feit, chaps. 3–5; Luthuli, chap. 15.

23. On the treason trial, see Benson, chap. 20; Lionel Forman and E. S. Sachs, *The South African Treason Trial* (London: Calder, 1957); Luthuli, chap. 16; Gerhart, chap. 5.

Albert Luthuli, Walter Sisulu, and Nelson Mandela that the congress should continue to cooperate with other bodies and to confine itself to nonviolent methods; others contended that the alliance with the Indian, Coloured, and white congresses had weakened and distracted the ANC, and that there were excessive communist influences in each of the congresses. What was needed, they believed, was a purely African movement, dedicated simply and solely to the emancipation of the African majority of the population of South Africa by whatever means necessary. Failing to gain control of the ANC, the latter group seceded in 1959 and founded the Pan-Africanist Congress. The PAC leaders were younger than the ANC leaders. The president was Robert Sobukwe, who was born in the eastern Cape Province in 1924, was educated at Fort Hare, and since 1953 had been a languages assistant in the Department of Bantu Studies at the University of the Witwatersrand; the secretary was Potlako Leballo, born near the Lesotho and Orange Free State border in 1922, and since 1954 a full-time politician and chairman of the ANC branch in Orlando township near Johannesburg.[24]

In an attempt to keep the initiative, the ANC planned a new campaign against the pass laws, which was to have started at the end of March 1960. But the PAC forestalled the ANC, taking the first step in its national campaign on March 21, 1960. On that day large numbers of Africans presented themselves at police stations in various parts of the country without passes, thus inviting arrest in the hope of clogging the machinery of justice and causing a labor dislocation. At the police station at Sharpeville, near Johannesburg, the police resorted to shooting at the crowd, killing 67 Africans and wounding 186, most of whom were shot in the back. Both the ANC and the PAC called for a day of mourning a week later, and there were widespread work stoppages especially in Cape Town, Johannesburg, and Port Elizabeth. In Cape Town an impressive demonstration took

24. On the origins of the PAC, see Benson, chaps. 21–22; Feit, chap. 3; Luthuli, chap. 18; Gerhart, chap. 6; Karis and Carter, vol. 3, pt. 2.

place on March 30, when some 20,000 Africans marched in orderly procession under the leadership of twenty-three-year-old Philip Kgosana to the center of the city, near the Houses of Parliament, which were in session.[25]

The government struck back fiercely; it declared a state of emergency; it mobilized the armed forces, including the reserves; it outlawed the ANC and the PAC; it arrested 98 Whites, 36 Coloured people, 90 Asians, and 11,279 Africans under emergency regulations. It jailed another 6,800 Africans for pass and other offenses, while the police beat up hundreds of Africans and compelled them to return to work. Subsequently, the PAC leaders were sentenced to imprisonment without the option of a fine—Sobukwe to three years, and Leballo and others to two. These stern measures broke the campaign. They also deprived Africans of their last means of lawful country-wide opposition to the South African political system and engendered in many hearts a hatred which had not previously existed.[26]

Mandela and other ANC leaders went underground; there they organized a sabotage group, Umkhonto we Sizwe (the Spear of the Nation), which made its first strike against a government installation on December 16, 1961. In 1962 Mandela left the country and toured independent Africa, addressing a conference of the Pan-African Freedom Movement in Addis Ababa. In Algeria he underwent a military course and made arrangements for ANC recruits to receive military training. After returning to South Africa, he eluded the police for several months, but was eventually arrested and sentenced to life imprisonment.

In his testimony before the court Mandela said this about Umkhonto:

25. Muriel Horrell, comp., *Days of Crisis in South Africa* (Johannesburg: South African Institute of Race Relations, 1960). Also Benson, chap. 23; Luthuli, pp. 217–23; Gerhart, pp. 244–45.

26. Benson, chap. 23; Luthuli, pp. 223–28; Gerhart, chap. 7.

I, and the others who started the organization, did so for two reasons. Firstly, we believed that as a result of Government policy, violence by the African people had become inevitable, and that unless responsible leadership was given to canalize and control the feelings of our people, there would be outbreaks of terrorism which would produce an intensity of bitterness and hostility between the various races of this country which is not produced even by war. Secondly, we felt that without violence there would be no way open to the African people to succeed in their struggle against the principle of White supremacy. All lawful modes of expressing opposition to this principle had been closed by legislation, and we were placed in a position in which we had either to accept a permanent state of inferiority, or to defy the Government. We chose to defy the law.

. . . Our problem was not whether to fight, but was how to continue the fight. We of the ANC had always stood for a non-racial democracy, and we shrank from any policy which might drive the races further apart than they already were. But the hard facts were that fifty years of non-violence had brought the African people nothing but more and more repressive legislation, and fewer and fewer rights.[27]

Two other revolutionary movements emerged during this period. Poqo (pure, simple) was an offshoot of the PAC, and the African Resistance Movement was a multiracial organization consisting mainly of young white professional men and students.

Umkhonto intended to disrupt communications and power lines and destroy government offices, hoping that public order would gradually collapse, guerrilla warfare would begin, and white supremacy would be overthrown. Poqo planned some sort of mass killing of white people and the abrupt termination of white supremacy. Of these two, it is likely that Umkhonto had the more effective leadership and that Poqo created the more effective grass-roots organization, though the claim of Leballo to 150,000 members in March 1963 was certainly grossly inflated. The African Resistance Movement may apparently be traced back, under various aliases, to 1961 or earlier, but it only became

27. Karis and Carter, 3: 772, 776.

active in 1963, when it committed acts of violence in the hope of frightening the government into making concessions.

During a three-year period starting in December 1961, there were over two hundred acts of sabotage in South Africa. Most of these were attacks in which time-bombs, made of imported ingredients, were used on post offices and other government buildings, and on railway and electrical installations in and near the main industrial centers, especially Johannesburg and Cape Town. Until 1963 most of these acts were probably committed by members of Umkhonto; in 1964, by members of the African Resistance Movement.

Poqo was responsible for attacks on African chiefs and policemen (three African police were killed in Langa township, Cape Town, in 1962) and for the murder of five Whites near a bridge over the Bashee River in the Transkei in February 1963.[28] The most dramatic incident attributed to Poqo took place at Paarl, thirty-five miles from Cape Town, on the night of November 21, 1962. Corrupt and insensitive local officials had applied the government's policy of limiting the number of African women residents to an absurd degree. A particularly explosive situation resulted, and Poqo organizers found a ready response in the Mbekeni location, which housed about thirty families and two thousand men. After five Africans and three Coloured women had been murdered in Mbekeni, the police made arrests, whereupon about a hundred Africans marched into the white town, attacked the police station, burned two shops, damaged houses, and killed a white girl and a white man before they were dispersed by police.[29]

The most dramatic act of violence in 1964 was committed by John Harris of the African Resistance Movement, who caused a time-bomb to explode in the concourse of the Johannesburg

28. Muriel Horrell, *Action, Reaction and Counteraction* (Johannesburg: SAIRR, 1963), pp. 40–55.

29. Ibid., pp. 47–51; South African Institute of Race Relations, *Survey of Race Relations, 1962*, pp. 16, 238, and *1963*, pp. 14–20.

railway station, killing one woman and seriously injuring fourteen other people.

To these acts of violence the government responded by banning Umkhonto, Poqo, and the African Resistance Movement, by enacting still more repressive legislation, and by further large-scale arrests. Poqo was broken by mid-1963; the collapse of Umkhonto was hastened by a police coup in July 1963, when seventeen men were arrested in a house at Rivonia near Johannesburg; and most of the saboteurs of the African Resistance Movement were arrested in July and August 1964. Nearly all who evaded arrest or escaped from detention fled the country, with the result that by the end of 1964 scarcely any active revolutionaries remained at large in the Republic.[30]

After 1964 there was a decade of comparative quiescence, during which the ANC and PAC regrouped outside South Africa with assistance from the Organization of African Unity (see chap. 6). In 1973 the ANC sent a number of trained men to join with the Zimbabwean guerrillas as a step toward the liberation of South Africa, but most of them were killed or captured by the Rhodesian security forces. By the end of the 1970s, however, ANC cadres were infiltrating South Africa from the north and making their presence felt by attacking police stations, exploding bombs in public places, and depositing caches of arms, some of which were discovered by the South African police. In two dramatic episodes in 1980, they seized control of a bank in Pretoria city and gravely sabotaged the strategically important SASOL plants at Sasolburg in the Orange Free State and at Secunda in the Transvaal.

By that time the ANC had gained important allies among a new generation of black youths inside South Africa embittered by the government's rigid educational system. For some years after the government created segregated university colleges for

30. *Survey of Race Relations, 1964*, pp. 25–33, 93–95.

Blacks under the Extension of University Education Act of 1959, black college students recognized the long-established, white-controlled National Union of South African Students (NUSAS) as the appropriate channel for expressing their grievances; but in 1968 Steve Biko, a twenty-two-year-old student, led a breakaway and founded an exclusively black South African Students Organization (SASO). SASO accused white organizations such as NUSAS of paternalism—making it impossible for Blacks to think and act for themselves—and rebutted the white liberal policy of integrating Blacks into a white society. Initially, the Nationalists welcomed the breakaway and the liberals deplored it. For the former it was a vindication of their race policies; for the latter, another example of racism.

Adapting ideas and terminology derived from the civil rights struggle in the United States and the decolonization movement in tropical and North Africa, SASO regarded racial oppression as, in the first instance, a psychological problem. It argued that Blacks should cast off their dependence on white organizations which claimed to work for their benefit. It also stood for the unity of all the subject castes against their white oppressors. As Steve Biko put it: "We are oppressed not as individuals, not as Zulus, Xhosas, Vendas or Indians. We are oppressed because we are black. We must use that very concept to unite ourselves and to respond as a cohesive group. We must cling to each other with a tenacity that will shock the perpetrators of evil."[31]

Starting in the black colleges as an intellectual movement, SASO soon developed wider concerns, and in 1972 it was instrumental in launching the overtly political Black Peoples Convention (BPC), an umbrella alliance incorporating SASO

31. Steve Biko, *I Write What I Like*, ed. A. Stubbs (London: Heinemann, 1979), p. 97. On the Black Consciousness Movement, see Gerhart, *Black Power*, chap. 8, and Noel C. Manganyi, *Alienation and the Body in Racist Society* (New York: NOK publishers, 1977).

and several other black organizations. The government reversed its initial enthusiasm for SASO when it saw the organization's growing militancy, and in 1973 it banned several SASO leaders, including Biko. In 1974 the BPC and SASO organized rallies to celebrate the installation of the Frelimo government in Mozambique, whereupon the government arrested nine leaders and charged them with fomenting disorder under the Terrorism Act. All nine were found guilty and sentenced to imprisonment on Robben Island for periods ranging from five to ten years.

The new interpretation of the role of Blacks in a white-dominated society lay behind serious uprisings in 1976. In June of that year thousands of black schoolchildren demonstrated against the imposition of Afrikaans as a medium of instruction in black schools in Soweto, the largest African township serving Johannesburg. There were two proximate reasons for the protests: most young Africans saw Afrikaans as the language of the oppressor and were reluctant to learn it; they also considered that its imposition would jeopardize their careers by making their studies more difficult. A young African student was shot by police during a demonstration on June 16, and this incident triggered nationwide protests. A government commission subsequently reported that between June 1976 and February 1977 at least 575 people had been killed, including 494 Africans, 75 Coloureds, 5 whites, and 1 Indian, and that 134 of the victims were under eighteen years of age. In addition, nearly 4,000 people were injured.[32]

In 1977, ruthless action brought this particular sequence of events to a close. The Security Police arrested and interrogated Steve Biko, who died on September 12 after being brutally ill-treated. One month later the government arrested numerous black leaders and made the BPC and all its member organ-

32. *Africa Research Bulletin: Political, Social and Cultural Series (ARB)*, March 1980, pp. 5613–14, summarizes the report of the official South African commission on the Soweto riots by Judge Petrus Cillie.

izations unlawful. Many BPC supporters fled the country to join forces with the ANC cadres abroad.[33]

However, the "October massacre" of 1977 did not eradicate the revolutionary spirit engendered by the Black Consciousness movement. Despite persistent intimidation and harassment, new leaders and new organizations openly rejected the legitimacy of the regime.[34] The main African activity was in Soweto, where Ntatho Motlana, a medical doctor, chaired a Committee of Ten, which founded a Soweto Civic Association in opposition to the government-created Soweto Urban Bantu Council. In Port Elizabeth a similar Black Civic Organization (PEBCO) came into being. In 1979, the Committee of Ten was a prime mover in the creation of the Azanian People's Organization (AZAPO). The inaugural conference of AZAPO was attended by two hundred delegates from black organizations throughout the country. As summarized by the South African Institute of Race Relations, AZAPO's declared aims and objectives are:

1) "to conscientise, politicise and mobilise" black workers through the philosophy of black consciousness [and] to strive for their legitimate rights;

2) to work towards the establishment of an educational system that would respond creatively towards the needs of Azanians;

3) to promote an interpretation of religion as a liberatory philosophy relevant to the black struggle;

4) to promote and encourage research into various problems affecting the people;

5) to expose the oppressive exploitative system in which black people are denied basic human rights; and

6) to work towards the unity of the oppressed for the just distribution of wealth and power to all people of Azania.[35]

---

33. *Africa Research Bulletin,* Sept. 1977, pp. 4567–68, October 1977, pp. 4607–11, November 1977, p. 4637, and December 1977, pp. 4677–78.

34. *Survey of Race Relations, 1978,* pp. 33–35; *1979,* pp. 47–51; *1980,* pp. 56–59.

35. *Survey of Race Relations, 1979,* pp. 50–51. *Azania* is the word the PAC uses for South Africa.

AZAPO refuses to cooperate with Blacks who participate in government-created institutions, such as the "homeland" leaders; and also with white liberals and white workers, who are regarded as being part of the system of oppression.

As was to be expected, the government soon began to arrest AZAPO leaders, but their ideas persist among many members of the black population, Coloured and Asian as well as African. Among the most outspoken Africans who are neither in prison nor in exile is Bishop Desmond Tutu, secretary-general of the South African Council of Churches.

During 1980 there were disturbances in numerous towns and villages throughout the country. Particularly significant was the fact that a high proportion of the Coloured people, whom Whites had always assumed to be sure allies when the chips were down, rose in protest against the discriminations in their educational system. The government later admitted that thirty-four people had died in riots in the southwestern Cape in the month of June alone. By September 1980, secondary education for black children was at a virtual standstill throughout the Cape Province as a result of student boycotts, and some of the black universities were also closed.[36]

Thus, by the beginning of the 1980s South Africans of all three subordinate castes, especially those of the younger generation, had taken a vital step away from deference toward defiance. Their actions, in conjunction with the growth of guerrilla activity by armed infiltrators, were causing considerable alarm in the white establishment. Soon after he became minister of defence in August 1980, General Magnus Malan declared, "[W]e are already in a state of total conflict."[37] No doubt that was a calculated overstatement. But it was not wholly unjustified.

---

36. *Africa Research Bulletin*, September 1980, p. 5808.
37. Ibid., p. 5802.

BLACK RESISTANCE WITHIN THE SYSTEM

The South African government's "homeland" strategy is to deflect African political claims from the center to the periphery and to divide the Africans among ten separate territories, each dominated by conservative politicians and dependent on South Africa's economy. The effects of this strategy are uncertain. It may probably be counted a success in the Transkei, Bophuthatswana, Venda, and the Ciskei, whose chiefly politicians have accepted "independence" on South Africa's terms. Others may follow, but not all the "homelands" leaders are being so complaisant.[38]

Chief Gatsha Buthelezi, the leader of KwaZulu, has declined to accept "independence" on the South African government's terms and has created what is potentially the largest and most powerful African organization that has existed in South Africa since Whites conquered the region in the nineteenth century. This movement, Inkatha, derives most of its support from the Zulu people who, in South African law, constitute the largest ethnic group in the country (5.2 million compared with 4.3 million Whites). In 1979 Inkatha claimed a paid-up membership of 250,000, second only to the National party, which claimed 400,000 in that year.[39]

Buthelezi has become forthright in his denunciation of the South African system. In 1975 he told Prime Minister Vorster that Blacks sought fulfilment "not in unreal separate freedoms,

38. The fourth "homeland" government to accept independence on South Africa's terms was the Ciskei, which did so in 1981 despite the fact that a commission appointed by itself advised it not to do so. *Ciskei Commission Report* (Silverton, Transvaal: Conference Associates, 1980).

39. The full title is Inkatha Yenkululeko YeSizwe. *Inkatha* refers to the soft pad Zulu women wear on their heads to alleviate the discomfort of carrying water-pails, and it symbolizes a means of obtaining relief from discrimination. The official journal *Inkatha* is published irregularly at Ulundi, capital of KwaZulu.

but in one South Africa, and in the only seat of power: Parliament."[40] A year later, addressing some ten thousand people in Soweto, he said that South African Blacks despised what some people euphemistically called "separate development." South Africa was one country, with one economy and one destiny. It must move toward majority rule: "It is this single principle that is central to any question to do with southern Africa's policies. . . . We Blacks are concerned first and foremost with liberation. . . . We want to be free from oppression. . . . We want to be free to be equal to all other men. We want to be free to participate in majority decisions about the future of our country and our common destiny with other South Africans."[41] However, Buthelezi also stands for nonviolent methods of effecting change, and he has spoken out against an economic boycott of South Africa.

With views such as these, and the Inkatha movement behind him, Buthelezi is the most powerful African in South Africa. He aspires to the leadership of the entire liberation movement. Opinion polls show that he has considerable support among urban Africans.[42] He has opened Inkatha to non-Zulu members and has formed a "Black Alliance" with Indian and Coloured leaders as well as with leaders of other "homelands." He has also established contact with the exiled ANC. Nevertheless, Buthelezi is subject to attack from both sides: by the South African government for his radicalism; and by AZAPO and other radical black organizations who dismiss him as a collaborator with apartheid.[43]

40. *Africa Research Bulletin*, January 1975, p. 3495.
41. *Africa Research Bulletin*, March 1976, p. 3959.
42. In 1977, a survey of the attitudes of urban Africans undertaken on behalf of the Arnold Bergstraesser Institute in Germany found that they regarded Buthelezi as the most popular political leader in South Africa; he was supported by 43.8 percent of those polled.
43. On Buthelezi and KwaZulu, see Lawrence Schlemmer and Tim J. Muil, "Social and Political Change in the African Areas: A Case Study of KwaZulu," in Leonard Thompson and Jeffrey Butler, eds., *Change in Contemporary South Africa* (Berkeley: University of California Press, 1975); Jeffrey Butler, Robert I. Rotberg, and John Adams, *The Black Homelands of South Africa* (Berkeley:

Black urban workers are another potential source of challenge to a political system that excludes the entire black population from a say in the authoritative political process. This potential has increased with the remarkable economic growth of recent years. The white population is not numerous enough to perform all the skilled roles in the burgeoning economy as well as to satisfy the personnel demands of the bureaucracy and the military. Furthermore, technological change requires the possession of greater skills, including literacy, among an ever-larger proportion of the labor force. Consequently, it has ceased to be practicable to treat all Africans as interchangeable labor units. Employers require more and more African workers with more and more skills. The more skills they possess, the more indispensible they become. And the more indispensible they are, the greater their capacity to exert power.

As explained in chapter 4, the government is attempting to deal with this problem by coopting black workers into trade unions that will operate according to the principles of the industrial conciliation system, and by providing a section of the African population with rather more secure residential rights in the urban areas than previously, thus promoting the growth of a black petite bourgeoisie with a stake in the system.

By 1979 about eighty-five thousand African workers were unionized, and although they formed only 1 percent of the labor force and were absent from such key economic sectors as mining and agriculture, their impact has been considerable. The dilemma facing black trade unions is whether to collaborate with the government by registration, in exchange for important concessions such as the right to organize, bargain, and strike, or to refuse such collaboration and risk official harassment. Some, such as the clothing workers, have registered, while others fear that by doing so they will lose control over their more militant

---

University of California Press, 1977); *Africa Research Bulletin*, August 1980, p. 5774; and Gatsha Buthelezi, *Power Is Ours* (New York: Books in Focus, 1979).

members. Thus the government has driven a wedge between the militant and the moderate workers and unions, just as it has between the militant and the moderate "homeland" leaders.[44]

While there is considerable growth potential for the African labor movement, its effect on the political system is diminished by the state's extensive controls. Workers may find themselves arrested or banned under widely framed security legislation; they may lose the right to reside in the towns if they are dismissed during a labor dispute; and they are deterred from striking by the existence of vast numbers of unemployed Africans eager for work. However, as the economy continues to expand, more Africans must be trained to perform skilled functions and their replacement will become costly. This will increase their bargaining power, give them the ability to wrest concessions from management, and possibly create a base from which to make political demands.

The strengths as well as the weaknesses of African labor are illustrated by recent events. During 1979 there was a sustained strike in the Ford motor plant at Port Elizabeth; in 1980 and 1981 thousands of black workers went on strike up and down South Africa. In nearly every case they were protesting low wages and in several cases they achieved their objective, but their demands often included the recognition of unregistered black unions and the reinstatement of dismissed workers. There were two important stoppages in July 1980. At the construction site of SASOL 3, more than eighteen thousand black workers were laid off for several days, when rioting broke out because of suspicions that troops had killed a black worker.[45] In Johannesburg, ten thousand black municipal workers formed a breakaway union and struck over pay demands and the dismisssal of workers who had earlier gone on strike. The Johannesburg city council broke that strike by sacking over a thousand men and having armed

44. *Survey of Race Relations, 1979*, pp. 264–86.
45. *Africa Research Bulletin*, June 1980, pp. 5712–13.

police load them onto buses and ship them off to "homelands,"
and soon afterward the government arrested the strike leaders.
As *The Economist* commented:

> Even by South African standards, it was a savage reaction to a
> strike. It has prompted speculation that the recent labour reforms may
> have been fatally discredited. Their most significant feature was that
> they gave blacks collective bargaining rights. . . . There are clear signs
> here of a strategy of slowly building a black power base—and it is
> because the government fears such a development that it decided to
> make a stand in Johannesburg. But, as a result of that stand, the new
> machinery is now in danger of being labelled part of "the system."[46]

OFFICIAL REPRESSION

To appreciate the problems which opponents of the caste system
face in South Africa, we must understand the techniques
employed by the government to maintain that system. When it
came to power in 1948, the National party took over a considerable coercive apparatus: segregationist laws which had accumulated over the previous half-century, including laws giving the
administration wide powers over Africans;[47] white police,
magistrates, and other officials who were almost to a man in
complete sympathy with the caste system and were accustomed
to using force to suppress the slightest sign of physical opposition; and black police and African chiefs who were reliable
agents, being utterly dependent on the government for support
and maintenance. What has happened since 1948 may be regarded, in one sense, as a systematic expansion of the preexisting instruments for the suppression of opposition. However, the

---

46. *The Economist*, August 16, 1980, p. 34. See also an important thirty-
page special article by Simon Jenkins, "The Great Evasion: South Africa, A
Survey," *The Economist*, June 21, 1980.
47. Muriel Horrell, *Laws Affecting Race Relations in South Africa 1948–
1976* (Johannesburg: SAIRR, 1978). Chapter 1 is a concise account of legislation
before 1948.

expansion has been so far-reaching that South Africa has experienced a veritable counterrevolution.

The caste system in South Africa is supported by vast numbers of statutes and innumerable executive orders issued under powers delegated in statutes. The population register determines the racial category, and with it the rights, of every South African; marriage and sexual intercourse outside of marriage are unlawful between people of different races; the country is divided and subdivided into uniracial zones for landownership, residence, and the conduct of business; the movements of Africans outside the undeveloped "homelands" are rigorously controlled; there are separate educational systems for each race from kindergarten to university; and membership of the authoritative governmental institutions is confined to white people. Most of these laws carry severe penal sanctions. The result is a tremendous accumulation of legalized coercive powers in the hands of the executive government.[48]

Over Africans, the legal powers of the government are virtually unlimited. Inside those "homelands" which are not "independent," the government exercises control directly, or through the regional legislatures. Outside the "homelands," the government's powers over Africans are the cumulative result of a long series of interlocking laws, which reached their logical conclusion in the Bantu Laws Amendment Act of 1964. Despite a measure of security possessed by some Africans, such as those born in urban areas, this act gives the government the legal power to remove any African from any part of any white area at any time. Even if he was born there, has lived there as a law-abiding citizen throughout a long life, and has not been convicted of any offense, an African may only stay in a white area at the government's pleasure. This act is applied with the dual purpose of limiting the African population of the white areas to those who are working for white employers on contracts entered

48. Ibid. The later chapters review legislation from 1948 to 1976.

into through official labor bureaus and of removing any African as soon as he is suspected of making trouble. It is a simple matter for the government to expel an African from a white area if, for example, he has become politically active or in any way objectionable, and to banish him to a "homeland" where he has no following and no means of creating one.

The basic law designed to prevent political activity against the caste system by people of any race was the Suppression of Communism Act of 1950, which is now incorporated in the Internal Security Act of 1976. This legislation defines "communism" in sweeping terms and empowers the minister of justice to punish without trial anyone who in his opinion is likely to further any of the aims of "communism." The minister may "list" such a person, in which case he may not join certain organizations, communicate with another listed person, or publish anything at all; and nobody else may publish anything he has ever said or written. He thus becomes a nonperson. The minister may also "ban" such a person, which usually involves additional prohibitions plus the obligation to report regularly to the police. Besides banning him, the minister may place the "offender" under house arrest, confining him to his home during specified hours and denying him the right to receive visitors. The minister does not have to give reasons for these decisions, and the victim has no legal means of challenging them.

Later legislation closed the loopholes in the 1950 act and still further increased the powers of the executive government and its agents, including the police. The most notable of these laws are the Riotous Assemblies Act of 1956, the General Laws Amendment Act of 1962 (known as the Sabotage Act), the General Laws Amendment Act of 1963, and the Terrorism Act of 1967; but refinements were added during the 1970s, as in the Internal Security Act of 1976.

This mass of coercive legislation gives the government and ᐧ its agents, including the police, vast powers to arrest people without trial and to hold them indefinitely in solitary confinement without revealing their identities and without granting them access to anyone except government officials. The government may ban any organization. It may prohibit the holding of gatherings of any sort. It may make it unlawful for organizations it specifies to receive funds from abroad. It may detain postal articles. Most of these provisions are cast in terms that prevent the courts from enquiring into the ways in which officials use their delegated powers. Moreover, under the Public Safety Act of 1953, the government may declare a state of emergency in any or every part of the country and rule by proclamation, if it considers that the safety of the public or the maintenance of public order is seriously threatened and that the ordinary law is inadequate to preserve it.

All this amounts to a system of legalized tyranny comparable to that in the Soviet Union: legalized, because officials act according to laws enacted by due constitutional process; tyranny, in that the South African laws themselves override nearly all the liberties that exist in the countries from which the ancestors of the South African elite migrated—from habeas corpus to freedom of speech, publication, and assembly.[49]

The government has formidable instruments for enforcing these draconian laws. Whites have a virtual monopoly of modern weapons. Except for a few Blacks in the police and the army, scarcely any Blacks are licensed to carry arms, whereas most white men and many white women possess firearms and are experienced in their use. The army and the white members of the police force are well equipped with the most modern weapons, including up-to-date aircraft, helicopters, missiles, tanks, and quick-firing guns; they are trained and practised in

49. For commentaries by South African academic lawyers, see A. S. Mathews, *Law, Order, and Liberty in South Africa* (Berkeley: University of California Press, 1972), and idem, "The Terrors of Terrorism," *South African Law Journal*, vol. 91 (1974); Albie Sachs, *Justice in South Africa* (Berkeley: University of California Press, 1973); and John Dugard, *Human Rights and the South African Legal Order* (Princeton: Princeton Univerisity Press, 1978).

the handling of hostile crowds; and they can be quickly augmented by trained reserves. South Africa also possesses the technological ability to manufacture nuclear weaponry. Thus, in strictly military terms, the black numerical superiority in South Africa is more than offset by the immense white superiority in the possession of the instruments of violence.

Not the least of the government's agents of law enforcement is the large number of informers who operate in all the communities in South Africa. White supporters of the government infiltrate white associations and regard it as their duty to search out suspicious activities; while Blacks, some in the plainclothes branch of the police force and others who are employed in particular assignments, spy on black associations. These informers, reporting to police officers, petty officials, and chiefs who are vested with wide powers, constitute a serious deterrent to effective opposition.

All this organized state power is exercised with the primary purpose of eliminating opposition to the caste system. The Communist party, the African National Congress, the Pan-Africanist Congress, Umkhonto, Poqo, the African Resistance Movement, the Congress of Democrats, the Christian Institute, and seventeen Black Consciousness movements all have been declared unlawful organizations.

According to official statements, 105 people were charged under the Terrorism Act during 1978; of these, 5 had been detained incommunicado for 380 days before being charged, another 35 for more than 120 days, and another 52 for more than 30 days. In the same year, 30 people were charged under the Internal Security Act, of whom 4 had been detained for more than 136 days before being charged, and another 13 for more than 30 days.[50] In November 1978, 152 banning orders were in force, and during the first eleven months of 1979, 334 people were detained and 116 people were still in detention on

50. *Survey of Race Relations, 1979*, pp. 125–26.

November 30, 1979.[51] The principal prison for political offenders is on Robben Island, four miles north of Cape Town. In May
1979 it contained 447 political prisoners.[52] Official returns also
show that prisoners have been transported in closed vans for up
to 1,200 kilometers, "if necessary" restrained by handcuffs and
leg-irons, with up to 30 prisoners in a 5.5-by-2.4-meter van.[53] In
1978, according to the government, 161 people died in police
custody, 22 of them as suicides and another 22 as a result of
resisting arrest or attempting to escape.[54]

Behind these official statistics is a mass of private evidence
that the security police use extremely cruel techniques for inter-
rogating political prisoners and that many of the "suicides" are
police-induced. Much evidence of police brutality came to light
in the inquest into the death of Steve Biko in 1977. The autopsy
report showed that he had died from brain damage caused by
skull injuries; and police evidence showed that after receiving
such injuries he was transported naked in the back of a van for
750 miles on the night before he died. Despite these revelations,
the magistrate ruled that no one was criminally responsible for
his death, and no one was prosecuted for these events. Moreover,
it is not suggested that the Biko case was exceptional.[55]

By 1980 most of the other effective African leaders had died,
had been silenced by banning or imprisonment, or had left the
country. Albert Luthuli, winner of the Nobel Peace Prize and the
last president-general of the ANC, was banned from all political
activities and all South African towns for a year starting in 1952.
He was banned for two more years in July 1954; in December
1956 he was arrested and charged with treason, and was released

51. Ibid., pp. 137, 144.
52. Ibid., p. 119.
53. Ibid., p. 116.
54, Ibid., p. 112.
55. Survey of Race Relations, 1978, pp. 119–21; Africa Research Bulletin,
September 1977, p. 4637, December 1977, p. 4677, February 1978, p. 4751; UN
Centre against Apartheid, Repression in South Africa (New York: United Nations, March 1980).

in December 1957; he was confined to a small area in an African reserve in Natal for five years from May 1959; and he was confined there for a further five years from May 1964, when he was sixty-six years old. He died in 1966.[56] Walter Sisulu of the ANC was sentenced to six years' imprisonment in March 1963 for continuing to further the aims of the ANC and for enjoining people to stay at home during the demonstration of May 1961. Released on bail pending an appeal, he was placed under house arrest, but disappeared in April 1963 and remained at large until he was one of those persons arrested at Rivonia near Johannesburg on July 11, 1963, after which he was charged with sabotage and sentenced to life imprisonment. Nelson Mandela, who was the principal planner of the demonstrations of May 1961, evaded the police for six months after a warrant had been issued for his arrest; but he was arrested in November 1962 and sentenced to five years' imprisonment for incitement and for having left the country unlawfully, and he, along with Sisulu, was later charged with sabotage and sentenced to life imprisonment.[57]

Robert Sobukwe, former president of the PAC, was sentenced to three years' imprisonment after the events of March 1960, and immediately after the sentence expired on May 3, 1963, he too was taken to Robben Island and was imprisoned there under the General Laws Amendment Act of 1963. In 1969 he was released and allowed to live in Kimberley under restrictions imposed in terms of the Suppression of Communism Act. He died of natural causes in 1978.[58] Virtually all the other established leaders of the ANC and PAC are also under bans or serving

---

56. On Luthuli, see Karis and Carter, *From Protest to Challenge,* 4: 60–63; Edward Callan, *Albert John Luthuli and the South Africa Race Conflict* (Kalamazoo: Western Michigan University Press, 1962); Luthuli, *Let My People Go.* Callan includes his Nobel Peace Prize address of December 11, 1961, on pp. 55–63.

57. On Sisulu and Mandela, see Benson, *African Patriots,* pp. 104–10; Gerhart, *Black Power,* pp. 108–23; Karis and Carter, 4: 143–45 and 71–73.

58. On Sobukwe, see Karis and Carter, 4: 147-49; and the articles by Godfrey Pitje, Aelred Stubbs, and Helen Suzman in *South African Outlook,* August 1978.

prison sentences or in detention without trial, except those who
have left South Africa, where they have been joined by a flood of
recent emigrés. It is estimated that some 25,000 young Blacks
left South Africa after the 1976 disturbances.[59]

Emigrés who were politically active in 1980 include Oliver
Tambo, Thabo Mbeki, and Seretzi Choabi of the ANC, Vusumuzi
Make and Alias Ntloedibe of the PAC, Khotso Seathlolo of the
Youth Revolutionary Council (SAYRC), Ranwedzi Nengwen-
kulu and Barney Pityana of the Black Consciousness Movement
(BCMSA), and Joe Slovo of the CPSA.[60]

Part of the price South Africa has paid for the suppression of
opposition to the caste system has been a very general abroga-
tion of the rule of law.[61] The rule of law is now violated in South
Africa by many statutes empowering cabinet ministers, government officials, and police officers to deprive people of their
liberty and their property. In many cases the violation is compounded by the fact that a deprived person is not informed of the
precise nature of the charge made against him, nor of the names
of the persons initiating the charges, and is given no opportunity
to defend himself nor to appeal to a court of law against the order
of deprivation. This supersession of the rule of law has been so
gradual, so insidious, and yet so complete a process, that most of
the white inhabitants of South Africa have become conditioned
to it and accept it as a natural state of affairs.

Today the property and civil rights of all South Africans are,
in manifold ways, subject to the whims of persons who are not
judicial officers. The most devastating invasion of property
rights is the Group Areas Act, which has led to the expropriation
by administrative committees of land lawfully acquired by many

59. *Die Vaderland*, Nov. 21, 1977.
60. *Survey of Race Relations, 1979*, pp. 52–57; *1980*, pp. 60–64.
61. See note 55 above; also A. S. Mathews, *The Darker Reaches of Government* (Cape Town: Juta, 1978), chap. 7; Arthur Suzman, Q. C., "South Africa and
the Rule of Law," *South African Law Journal*, vol. 85 (1968); H. R. Hahlo and I. A.
Maisels, "The Rule of Law in South Africa," *Virginia Law Review*, vol. 52, no. 1
(1966); and Dugard, *Human Rights*, chap. 3.

thousands of people. The most devastating invasions of civil liberties are, of course, the General Law Amendment acts of 1962 and 1963, the Terrorism Act of 1967, and the Internal Security Act of 1976, and their amendments. They remove any doubt that may previously have existed concerning whether South Africa is a police state in the precise sense of the phrase, because they empower police officers to arrest whomever they wish without a warrant and to detain them indefinitely without trial and without access to legal advisers. In the government's determination to preserve white supremacy, which it equates with the safety of the state, the South African authorities have replaced the rule of law with the rule of cabinet ministers, public officials, and police officers.[62]

CONCLUSION

By 1981, a third of a century of Afrikaner Nationalist rule had accentuated the polarizing tendencies that have existed in South African society since the very beginnings of white colonization in the seventeenth century. The vast majority of the white population believe that their very survival depends on their retention of political hegemony. Although both reason and conscience prompt some members of both white communities to doubt the viability of a society structured on racial lines in the final decades of the twentieth century, there is nothing to suggest that they are able to build a political majority among an electorate that is racially defined. Meanwhile, all three subordinate castes are becoming increasingly alienated from a regime that denies them access to meaningful political power and economic welfare. International moral support, the collapse of white supremacy in Angola, Mozambique, and Zimbabwe, and the spread of the black-consciousness philosophy have produced a distinct shift from deference to defiance.

62. Dugard, chap. 3.

The Nationalist government tries to subvert black resistance with a mixture of manipulation and repression. In its "homeland" policy it exploits the old imperialist technique of divide-and-rule with great virtuosity. It seeks to control the minds of black people via the communications media and the educational system. And it continuously proscribes organizations and individuals who seem likely to become effective revolutionaries. Despite all this, new black opposition movements mushroom every time others are suppressed—many of them with some sort of foothold in the institutions the government itself has created. By 1981, numerous black people in schools, workshops, and "homelands" were committed to the transformation of South African society. Among a rapidly growing black population subjected to frequent indignities and conscious of the vast economic gulf between themselves and their white rulers, the very excesses of the repressive apparatus evoke militant reactions.

Nevertheless, there is still an abyss between black will and black achievement. Confronting a determined and cohesive white population which controls the commanding heights of the economy as well as the state apparatus, it is extremely difficult for black South Africans to create a revolution out of the disparate elements of which they are comprised, each possessing such distinct interests and perceptions: young and old; educated and illiterate; African, Coloured, and Asian; Zulu, Xhosa, and Sotho; student, industrial worker, farm laborer, and peasant; urban insider and urban outsider. Even so, time seems to be on the side of the Blacks. In 1981 Blacks outnumbered Whites by five to one; by 2000 the ratio is expected to be more than seven to one. Already the regime is hard pressed to man the bureaucracy and the army, as well as the economy, without admitting Blacks to positions of authority.

In 1981 there are two distinct tendencies among the Afrikaner Nationalist political elite in trying to cope with the increasing evidence that the overwhelming majority of the population of South Africa denies the legitimacy of the regime. Some, including Prime Minister Botha, are keenly aware of the dangers. In speech after speech Botha has harped on the necessity for change. He presides over the dismantling of many of the petty apartheid rules (rules that do not directly affect the distribution of power), and he is attempting to coopt the smaller subject castes by appointing Coloured and Asian members to the President's Council, to bring the African workers into the industrial bargaining system, and to provide somewhat greater security of urban domicile for Africans who have lived and worked in towns for long periods. Some observers consider that these decisions represent the beginning of a process of substantial change from a racist to a class society, and toward greater economic justice. Others construe them as amounting to nothing more than the latest of a long series of manipulative devices designed to preserve the essence of white power and privilege. The actual changes that have been made so far are compatible with the latter interpretation.[63] Even if Botha and his intimates, such as General Malan and Dr. Viljoen, wished to initiate a process of substantial change, they would be constrained by the voting power of right-wing Afrikaners, who have strong advocates not only in the Herstigte Nasionale party but also in the upper reaches of the National party.

Commenting on the prime minister's emphasis on the need for change, Andries Treurnicht, cabinet minister and Transvaal leader of the National party, is reported to have asked, "Why would you want us to change this paradise?"[64]

63. On this, we agree with the conclusions of Simon Jenkins in the article in *The Economist* cited in note 46 above.

64. *Manchester Guardian Weekly*, Nov. 16, 1980, p. 12, which cites Jean-Claude Pomonti in *Le Monde*.

6

The External Opposition

Before 1948 the South African political system was not exceptional, nor was it singled out for condemnation by foreign governments. Today it is exceptional. It runs counter to the almost universal renunciation of racist principles and dismantling of racist practices. It is almost universally condemned. And it is in some danger of coercion by the international community.

One factor promoting the growth of this formidable external threat has been the increasing rigidity and severity of the South African system, marked by the advent of the National party to power, the unfolding tf its policy of apartheid, and its resort to more and more ruthless methods of suppressing internal opposition. But this has not been the crucial factor. Even if the South African system had remained as it was in 1948, in the changed world of the 1980s it would have incurred severe condemnation and its survival would have been threatened.

First, the essential causes of this development are to be found in the shifts in the distribution of power and influence in the world. The power and influence of the erstwhile colonial states have shrunk; this is particularly true of Britain, which had a major responsibilty for the evolution of the South African system and continues to have a great stake in the South African economy. Furthermore, the official attitudes of the former colonial powers toward colonialism and racism have been radically transformed. Before 1948 they not only ruled colonies —and in them necessarily applied some measure of racial stratification—but they vindicated the colonial system. By the 1980s they had renounced colonialism and its concomitants, and such power and influence as they possessed were no longer overtly exerted in support of white supremacy in South Africa.

Second, as the United States assumed the responsibilities that went with its towering strength in the fluid years after the Second World War, it encouraged its principal allies—the erstwhile colonial powers—to dissolve their empires. At the time, the primary American motive was to open those territories to American trade. Later, however, as the civil rights movement gathered momentum, it served as a spur to the American government publicly to endorse the ideology of the African revolution by denying the validity of the doctrine of white domination, in South Africa as in the United States.

Third, whatever their practices may have been in Europe and Asia where they have long-standing interests and ambitions, the Soviet Union and the People's Republic of China were not inhibited by their possession of stakes in the colonial system in Africa from encouraging anticolonial revolutionaries. They disseminated Marxist-Leninist propaganda and gave support to liberation movements in Africa, actions which had the effect of spurring the Western powers into yielding to the demands of African nationalists for fear of being outbidden and losing their influence in the new Africa.

Fourth, the African elites throughout the continent became imbued with anticolonial and antiracist fervor. This was the psychological force behind the drive toward independence in each territory, and since independence was achieved it has remained a basic mystique in the policies of the successor states. To the rulers of the new African states, South Africa is not just a foreign country with a different way of life: it is anathema, because its government oppresses people whom the other rulers regard as kinfolk and because it is the one sovereign state in the world today which still practises racism without shame and even raises it to the level of a philosophy. Moreover, despite

many economic and political setbacks in the new states of tropical Africa, by the 1980s Nigeria wielded considerable power in
global politics as a major producer of fuel oil, and the destruction of South Africa's racist regime was a major goal of Nigeria's
foreign policy.

Fifth, the process of decolonization has moved rapidly in
southern Africa in recent years. In 1974 Mozambique and Angola won their independence from Portugal after protracted
guerrilla warfare; in 1980 Zimbabwe elected a black-controlled
government to bring to an end a seven-year war against white
rule; and South Africa's hold on Namibia was being loosened by
guerrilla warfare, and international political pressure. Indeed,
by the beginning of the 1980s the waves of the African revolution were pounding along the northern frontiers of the Republic.

Finally, the continual flow of refugees out of South Africa
has led to the creation, in capital cities of Africa, Western
Europe, and North America, of groups of emigrés committed to
the overthrow of the South African regime. Despite fierce internal disputes, these groups bring passion and a sense of urgency
to the interventionist lobbies, as well as invaluable experience of
the realities of life for the subject groups in South Africa.

EXTERNAL OPPOSITION BEFORE 1974

Since the end of the Second World War, South Africa's racial
policies have become notorious. As early as 1946 the General
Assembly of the United Nations took cognizance of complaints
by the Indian government that South Africa was ignoring
agreements it had made with India concerning the treatment of
Indians in South Africa. Soon after the installation of the National party government in 1948, the General Assembly began to
pass resolutions criticizing its entire apartheid policy. During
the 1960s, as more and more African states became members of

the UN, the General Assembly devoted more and more attention to the South African question. In 1962 it asked member states to break off diplomatic and economic relations with South Africa and created a permanent Special Committee on Apartheid "to keep the racial policies of the Government of South Africa under review."[1] Four years later it added a permanent Unit on Apartheid, which publishes a stream of literature. Meanwhile, in 1963 independent African states founded the Organization of African Unity (OAU), which set up a Liberation Committee with headquarters in Dar es Salaam. Condemnation of apartheid is a regular theme of Third World rhetoric. Indeed, it is one of the few subjects on which the governments of the Third World have been continuously unanimous.

Nevertheless, before 1974 the external opposition to the South African regime, though long on rhetoric, was short on substance. The Republic was in no danger of military attack. It was able to accommodate to the emergence of Botswana, Lesotho, and Swaziland as independent states under black control because it dominated their economies, and it was sheltered from direct contact with other black states by the existence of friendly white regimes in Angola, Mozambique, and Rhodesia.[2] Neither the Soviet Union nor the People's Republic of China was making a major contribution to the South African liberation movements. The United States and its allies were not hostile, for Americans and Europeans had substantial, profitable, and increasing investments in the country's burgeoning economy, and they set a high value on South Africa's mineral resources and the strategic significance of the sea route between the Atlantic and the Indian oceans round the Cape of Good Hope. Moreover, most American and European politicians possessed at least a residue

1. James Barber, *South Africa's Foreign Policy 1945–1970* (London: Oxford University Press, 1973), p. 272.
2. Kenneth W. Grundy, *Confrontation and Accommodation in Southern Africa: The Limits of Independence* (Berkeley: University of California Press, 1973).

of racist assumptions and a world view that gave great prominence to Soviet expansionism.

The case of the United States is of special interest because of
its preeminence in the Western alliance.[3] During the
Eisenhower administration the United States joined in the verbal criticism of South Africa's racial policies but continued to
cooperate with South Africa, even in military matters. United
States warships called frequently at South African ports, and in
1957 the United States and South Africa signed a twenty-year
agreement for cooperation in energy research, including the
development of nuclear power. On the other hand, the 1954
decision of the United States Supreme Court in the Brown case,
rejecting the concept of "separate but equal," was pregnant with
implications for American policy toward South Africa. Thereafter, American rhetoric became increasingly strident, especially
after the Sharpeville shootings in 1960. Nevertheless, the Kennedy and Johnson administrations did nothing to check American industrialists and bankers from becoming more and more
deeply enmeshed in the South African economy as it boomed
throughout the 1960s, and they offset the public rhetoric with
economic support and friendly private signals to Pretoria. In
1961, the United States government helped South Africa to
overcome the effects of the massive outflow of capital following
Sharpeville by approving loans by the World Bank and the
International Monetary Fund.

On July 20, 1963, Secretary of State Dean Rusk actually
endorsed the South African government's embryonic policy of
separate development in a long discussion with Willem Naudé,
the South African ambassador to Washington. After Naudé had

3. William J. Foltz, "United States Policy toward South Africa," Yale-
Wesleyan Southern African Research Program paper, July 30, 1980; Thomas
Karis, "United States Policy toward South Africa," in Gwendolen Carter and
Patrick O'Meara, eds., Southern Africa: The Continuing Crisis (Bloomington:
Indiana University Press, 1979); René Lemarchand, ed., American Policy in
Southern Africa (Washington, D.C.: University Press of America, 1978).

outlined the policy, Rusk suggested that the entire southern African region might become a "confederation" of "six or eight states largely black and possibly three states largely white." The Whites would provide "management, investment and various kinds of assistance," the Blacks "labor as well as other things." "The whites and blacks being in each other's states would be resident aliens without rights of participation as citizens." The delighted ambassador replied: "The Secretary had precisely, almost word for word, expressed the intent of the South African government."[4]

In 1969 the incoming Nixon administration made a series of reviews of United States policy in different parts of the world. The Southern African document, National Security Council Study Memorandum number 39 (NSSM 39), predicted that the Whites were in Southern Africa, including Angola, Mozambique, and Rhodesia, to stay, "and the only way that constructive change can come about is through them. There is no hope for the blacks to gain the political rights they seek through violence." Consequently, the memorandum recommended that the United States should continue its public opposition to racial oppression but ease up on political isolation and economic restrictions on the white states.[5] This is what happened. The White House declined to pressure the Senate to repeal the Byrd Amendment, which allowed Americans to import Rhodesian chrome in defiance of UN sanctions against Rhodesia. The United States also vetoed an Afro-Asian motion in the UN Security Council that would have extended the general mandatory sanctions from Rhodesia to Portugal and South Africa. Moreover, John Hurd, Nixon's choice as ambassador to

    4. U.S. State Department, "The South African Program of Grouping Independent Bantu States," July 20, 1963 (declassified 2/16/79), appended to Scott Delman, "The Subtle Sanction," Yale University history essay, December 12, 1980.
    5. Mohamad A. El-Khawas and Barry Cohen, eds., The Kissinger Study of Southern Africa (Westport, Conn.: Lawrence Hill, 1976), pp. 105–06.

South Africa, was callous enough to accept an invitation to join a South African cabinet minister in hunting small game on Robben Island, with the political prisoners serving as beaters.[6]

THREATS FROM SOUTH AFRICA'S NEIGHBORS

Events soon belied the premise of NSSM 39. For several years Portugal, a small and undeveloped European country, had been spending 40 percent of its national budget and 5 percent of its gross national product, and straining the loyalty of its young men, in efforts to suppress rebellions in its three African territories—Guinea-Bissau, Angola, and Mozambique. In April 1974 a group of officers ousted the Caetano regime and opened negotiations with the guerrilla movements in all three territories. Within a year Portugal transferred power to the guerrilla movements and the new governments promptly gained international recognition as members of the United Nations. The change in Mozambique led to an intensification of the war in neighboring Rhodesia-Zimbabwe, where Ian Smith's white regime had been trying to survive without international recognition since it declared its independence from Great Britain in 1965; and in 1980 Zimbabwe, too, passed under the control of the African organizations that had been fighting the white government.[7]

The new regimes in Luanda, Maputo, and Harare had all been supplied by the People's Republic of China and/or the Soviet Union and its allies. Moreover, a South African military force, with American connivance, had fought its way deep into Angola in support of the losing nationalist faction, and South Africa had also been an open supporter of the losing faction in Zimbabwe. Thus by 1981 the white buffers between South Af-

6. Foltz, "United States Policy," p. 24.
7. John Seiler, ed., *Southern Africa since the Portuguese Coup* (Boulder, Col.: Westview Press, 1980); Carter and O'Meara, *Southern Africa*.

rica and black Africa had fallen, to be succeeded by African regimes which South Africa had tried desperately to keep out, except only in Namibia.

These regimes—the products of wars of liberation waged by nationalist guerrilla movements supported by Soviet or Chinese aid—have a profound desire to eradicate the last racist regime from the African continent. Under present circumstances, however, they lack the means to do much about it by themselves. The inexorable first priorities of all three regimes are domestic. Each is hard pressed to consolidate its political authority and to create a viable economy. In their dealings with South Africa, Mozambique and Zimbabwe share the frustrations that have already been experienced by the black governments of Botswana, Lesotho, and Swaziland, and also Zambia and Malawi, as a result of their economic dependence on South Africa. The distribution of economic power in the region is illustrated by the relative strengths of the national economies: in 1975 South Africa had a GNP of $31,622 million and the eleven black southern African states, including Zaire and Tanzania, a combined GNP of about $17,000 million.[8] Scarcely one of them is self-sufficient in food supplies; nearly all are frequently obliged to purchase maize and other agricultural produce from South Africa, which has a large surplus in most years. Even Julius Nyerere, president of Tanzania and host of the African Liberation Committee, has admitted that his country must import maize from South Africa.[9]

Lesotho, Swaziland, and Botswana are locked into nearly

8. Kenneth W. Grundy, "Economic Patterns in the New Southern African Balance," in Carter and O'Meara, Southern Africa, p. 293. The South African figure includes the GNP of all the "homelands," including the Transkei ($159 million) and Bophuthatswana ($206 million). The other eleven states were Angola, Botswana, Lesotho, Malawi, Mozambique, Namibia, Rhodesia (now Zimbabwe), Swaziland, Tanzania, Zaire, and Zambia.

9. Jean-Pierre Langellier, "Tanzania—Africa's Conscience," The Manchester Guardian (weekly edition), November 9, 1980 (translated from Le Monde original).

total dependence on South Africa. They are members of a customs union with South Africa, from which they derive substantial proportions of their revenues. Many of their citizens survive by working in South African mining, manufacturing, and agricultural industries. All three countries are served by South African transportation links.[10]

Mozambique is also in large measure a client state. Thousands of Mozambique citizens work as migrant laborers in South African mines, though the number has declined since 1975, when South Africa decided to recruit more labor from its "homelands." In 1980, South Africa was buying all the electricity produced by the Cabora Bassa power station in northern Mozambique and providing the skilled personnel to man the project; South Africans were managing the railroad between Johannesburg and Maputo; and South Africa was supplying 25 percent of Mozambique's imports. Despite the ideological gulf, Mozambique signed an agreement with South Africa in 1979, providing for the transport of fifteen thousand tons of South African products through Maputo and Beira each day.[11]

Zimbabwe, too, is heavily dependent on South Africa. The seven-year guerrilla war between African nationalists and the white Rhodesian government so weakened the country, that the incoming Mugabe government could not break many of the economic links which had been built up over the previous century. In particular, the colonial heritage of rail communications made Zimbabwe depend largely on South African facilities for its foreign trade. Zambia is in a similar position. Years of depressed copper prices, inadequacies and closures of the rail

10. E. Philip Morgan, "Botswana: Development, Democracy, and Vulnerability," Richard Weisfelder, "Lesotho: Changing Patterns of Dependence," and Absolom Vilakazi, "Swaziland: From Tradition to Modernity," in Carter and O'Meara, Southern Africa.

11. Tony Hodges, "Mozambique: The Politics of Liberation," in Carter and O'Meara, Southern Africa; Keith Middlemas, "Independent Mozambique and its Regional Policy," in Seiler, Southern Africa; The Economist, August 16, 1980, p. 11.

links through Tanzania and Angola, and the costs of the war in Zimbabwe which had spilled over into its territory, have severely weakened its economy. In 1980 Zambia exported about half its copper, the source of 95 percent of its export earnings, through South African ports.[12]

The governments of the black states in the region are anxious to detach themselves from South Africa. In 1980, their leaders held a meeting for this purpose and announced that they hoped to create a communications network that would reduce their use of South Africa's railways and ports, pool their mining, industrial, agricultural, and energy expertise, and set up a regional bank. But these are long-term possibilities. Any effective detachment from their dependence on South Africa is likely to be a prolonged process, and a partial one at best.[13]

Under present circumstances, South Africa's neighbors are in no position to wage war against the Republic. But they are under continuous diplomatic pressure to provide facilities for South African insurgents. If they do so on a large scale, they risk ruthless reprisals, as illustrated by several devastating South African raids on SWAPO and ANC bases in Angola and Mozambique. Guerrilla activities launched from the north will probably continue to be a nuisance to the South African regime; but they are not likely to constitute a serious threat to its survival without major cooperation from industrialized countries.

THREATS FROM THE INTERNATIONAL COMMUNITY

The international community has repeatedly denounced South Africa's racial policies. In 1973, the UN General Assembly

12. Timothy M. Shaw and Douglas G. Anglin, "Zambia: The Crises of Liberation," in Carter and O'Meara, Southern Africa.
13. The Economist, August 16, 1980, p. 11; Financial Mail (Johannesburg), April 1, 1980.

adopted a resolution to form an International Convention on the Suppression and Punishment of the Crime of Apartheid, declaring apartheid to be "a crime against humanity" and making individuals, organizations, and states criminally responsible for involvement in apartheid. By 1980, fifty-eight states had agreed to be bound by the convention. Since 1974, South Africa has not been permitted to take part in the plenary sessions of the General Assembly, whereas the ANC and the PAC have been granted observer status not only in the Special Committee on Apartheid but also in plenary sessions. Following a World Conference for Action against Apartheid held in Lagos in 1977, the General Assembly in 1979 affirmed the legitimacy of the struggle against the apartheid regime, including armed struggle. The General Assembly has also passed numerous resolutions urging the Security Council to take effective actions against South Africa, from preventing South Africa from importing military materials to general mandatory sanctions. So far, however, the Security Council, constrained by the veto power of the permanent members, has limited its responses to rhetorical reaffirmations of its abhorrence of apartheid and racism—with one important exception. In 1977, in the wake of the death of Steve Biko and the suppression of numerous black-consciousness movements, the Security Council unanimously voted a mandatory arms embargo against South Africa—the first time it had taken such action against a member state under Chapter 7 of the UN Charter.[14] By 1981, moreover, there was a prospect of the imposition of general mandatory sanctions against South Africa, arising from the Namibian situation.

Namibia, with a population of about nine hundred thousand Blacks and one hundred thousand Whites, was on the brink of some form of independence by 1981. Colonized by Germany in 1884 and conquered by South African troops in the

14. United Nations, United Nations Today—1980 (New York, 1980), pp. 30–37.

First World War, "South West Africa" was then administered by South Africa as a mandated territory under the League of Nations. After the Second World War, the South African government refused to place the territory under the United Nations trusteeship system. Instead, it edged the territory toward incorporation in South Africa, giving its small white population representation in the Cape Town parliament and applying a modified version of the "homelands" policy. The UN never recognized South Africa's claims over the territory. In 1966 the General Assembly declared that the mandate was terminated, and the following year it established a UN Council for Namibia. In 1971, the Assembly's position was vindicated by an advisory opinion of the International Court of Justice to the effect that South Africa's control of the territory was illegal.

After 1974, large detachments of the South African army became engaged in military operations against guerrillas of the South West African Peoples' Organization (SWAPO) on either side of the Angolan border. The UN General Assembly recognized SWAPO as "the sole authentic representative of the Namibian people," and in 1976 the Security Council decided that there should be a general election under UN control to create an assembly which would draw up a constitution for an independent Namibia. Moreover, in 1978 the Security Council threatened South Africa with "appropriate actions" under Chapter 7 of the UN Charter, which empowers the Security Council to call on all UN members to cease diplomatic and trade relations with any country that threatens international peace and, in extreme cases, calls for the use of force, unless South Africa complied with the UN plan. Nevertheless, while entering into negotiations for the implementation of the UN plan, the South African government proceeded with its own effort to install and consolidate a "moderate" regime—a white-led alliance of parties representing the territory's eleven main ethnic groups.

In 1978 a general election was held under South African

control, and this Democratic Turnhalle Alliance won an overwhelming victory; but the election was held in defiance of the
Security Council and was boycotted by SWAPO.[15] This dead-
lock creates grave problems for the government of South
Africa—and also for the governments of Great Britain, France,
and the United States, with their veto powers in the Security
Council. If South Africa yields, SWAPO may win the UN-
supervised general election, which would complete the
semicircle of radically controlled states on South Africa's borders. But if South Africa continues to defy the UN, it will be
increasingly embarrassing for the Western powers to resist the
clamor for general mandatory sanctions from the entire Third
World, supported by the People's Republic of China and the
Soviet Union and its satellites.

The South African policies of the Western democracies
have continued to be equivocal. On the one hand, they all have
material ties with South Africa. They acquire from South Africa
a high proportion of their supplies of a wide range of
minerals—not only gold and diamonds, but also platinum,
vanadium, chrome, manganese, antimony, and the andalusite
group of metals. In the unstable world of the 1980s, Western
anxieties about Soviet expansionism are expressed in a determination to preserve access to these resources, several of which are
crucial to the armaments industry. Most Western countries also
have large, increasing, and profitable investments in South Africa and conduct a voluminous trade with that country. By 1980
their total investments in South Africa exceeded $25 billion and
provided an unusually high rate of return; and they were annually exporting to South Africa goods to the value of about $5
billion and importing from South Africa goods of still greater
value. The involvement of Great Britain, as a result of her previ-

15. Ibid., pp. 41–47; *Africa Research Bulletin*, October 1980, pp. 5858–59;
Gerhard Tötemeyer, *South West Africa/Namibia* (Randburg, So. Africa: Fokus
Suid Publishers, 1977); John Dugard, *The South West Africa/Namibia Dispute*
(Berkeley: University of California Press, 1973).

ous hegemony over the region, is especially great, amounting to about half the total foreign investment and a considerable share of the trade. However, many other Western industrialized countries, including Japan, have become deeply involved since the Second World War, and by 1980 West Germany and the United States were both surpassing Great Britain in the volume of their trade with South Africa.[16] Western politicians are well aware that their people have a stake in the stability of the South African political system. They are subject to pressures for the support of the status quo from their military bureaucracies and also from some of those national business interests that are most deeply involved—banks, computer and electronics industries, and automobile, oil, and mining industries.

On the other hand, there are countervailing forces in the West. In many of these countries South African emigrés, white as well as black, campaign against the South African regime. University students clamor for a boycott of companies that do business in South Africa. Churches single out the South African system as uniquely unjust, and the World Council of Churches supports a Program to Combat Racism, which provides financial aid to the ANC and the PAC. National and international trade-union organizations exert pressure for the recognition of the rights of black workers in South Africa.[17] This opposition does not rest exclusively on moral impulses. In countries with significant black populations there is a growing sense of identification with the black people of South Africa—a factor that has considerable political potential in the United States. Furthermore, the dependence of the West on oil supplies from OPEC—including Nigeria, the most powerful state in black Africa—obliges Western politicians to be wary of allowing their connivance with the South African regime to so alienate Third

16. Desaix Myers III, with Kenneth Propp, David Hauck, and David M. Liff, *U.S. Business in South Africa: The Economic, Political, and Moral Issues* (Bloomington: Indiana University Press, 1980), pp. 39–53.

17. Myers et al., *U.S. Business*, chap. 6.

World countries from the West that they become irrevocably allied with the Soviet Union.

Finally, despite the present weakness and disarray of the internal opposition, and the apparent inability of the OAU to impose its will on South Africa in the foreseeable future, the transformations in Angola, Mozambique, and Zimbabwe cast doubt on the capacity of the South African regime to survive in the long run on a racially stratified basis. Consequently, some well-informed western policymakers, to the right as well as the left of the ideological center in business as well as in govern-ment, regard as a Western interest the initiation of substantial changes by the South African regime, leading to the admission of the black population into effective participation in the central political system.[18]

The actions of Western countries have varied with the de-gree of their involvement in the South African economy. Private enterprise in most of the large Western states continues to take advantage of the opportunities created by the growth of the South African economy by increasing its investments in South Africa, and many Western governments continue to exercise diplomacy to moderate Third World demands for drastic action against South Africa. Great Britain, with its large-scale involve-ment, has used its veto power in the UN Security Council to block several anti–South African motions, and during the civil war in Rhodesia, British-dominated multinational corporations channeled oil fuel to Salisbury via South African intermediaries, despite the existence of general mandatory sanctions against the Smith regime. France has made similar use of her veto in the UN Security Council, and was a major supplier of arms to South Africa in the early and middle 1970s. However, Great Britain and France did not veto the resolution for a military embargo against

18. For example, Chester A. Crocker, "South Africa: Strategy for Change," *Foreign Affairs* 59, no. 2 (Winter 1980/81): 323–51; Clyde Ferguson and William R. Cotter, "South Africa—What Is to Be Done," *Foreign Affairs* 56, no. 2 (January 1978): 253–74.

South Africa in 1977. They are also party to the European community's code of employment policies for firms operating in South Africa. This code provides for equal pay for equal work, desegregation of the workplace, recognition of black trade unions, training schemes for black workers, and efforts to offset the effects of the migrant labor system.[19] However, the European community and its member states do not effectively enforce these recommendations, and while some European firms apply them, others do not. A few European countries that have never been deeply involved in the South African economy have gone further. The Scandinavian countries, in particular, are close to the Third World on this issue. For example, the Swedish government has prohibited the expansion of Swedish investment in South Africa and has supported the demand for the application of general mandatory sanctions.

Official relations between the United States and South Africa deteriorated in the late 1970s. The Carter administration came to power with the support of black Americans, and its world view was pluralistic rather than being centered on the East-West conflict. It attached weight to the increasing political and economic importance of Third World countries such as Nigeria, which became one of America's largest suppliers of crude oil and surpassed South Africa as a trading partner. It also reached the conclusion that African nationalism was the dominant political force throughout the African continent and would eventually triumph in South Africa. The shift in policy was symbolized by the appointment of two black Americans— Andrew Young and Donald McHenry—as ambassadors to the UN; and it became clear in 1977 when Vice-President Walter Mondale informed Prime Minister B. J. Vorster that the United States was committed to majority rule and regarded the policy of separate development as inherently discriminatory and morally indefensible. Spokesmen for the United States government also

19. *Africa Research Bulletin*, 1977, p. 4429B.

endorsed a code of conduct for U.S. firms in South Africa that was formulated by the Reverend Leon Sullivan, a black director of General Motors. This code includes desegregation in the workplace, equal and fair employment practices for all workers, equal pay for equal work, training facilities for black workers, the introduction of black workers into supervisory and management positions, and the improvement of the quality of life for Blacks outside the work environment in such areas as housing, transportation, schooling, recreation, and health facilities. Though some American subsidiaries have declined to adopt the Sullivan principles, and the effects of their formal adoption by others are not far-reaching, these actions convinced Pretoria that it could not rely indefinitely on the benevolent neutrality of the United States. They also gave encouragement to opponents of the South African regime.

The Carter administration's emphasis on human rights as a factor in foreign policy was resented by powerful elements in American society. Many Americans regard the maintenance of the South African connection as a vital national interest and are cynical about the use of economic sanctions as a diplomatic weapon, especially in the light of the survival of Rhodesia—a far weaker regime than the South African—for more than a decade after the imposition of mandatory sanctions. Consequently, the Carter administration cooperated with the European powers in parrying the demand for mandatory general sanctions against South Africa, and took the lead in protracted negotiations with South Africa on the future of Namibia. Even so, by the end of Carter's tenure time seemed to be running out for delaying tactics on the Namibian question, where South Africa was in blatant conflict with international law.[20]

The 1980 U.S. election portended a major shift in U.S. foreign policy. The campaign rhetoric of Ronald Reagan and his associates, followed by the appointment of Alexander M. Haig as

20. Foltz,"United States Policy"; Karis, "United States Policy."

secretary of state and Joanne Kirkpatrick as ambassador to the UN, showed that the new administration viewed the world in the perspective of Soviet expansionism and was far more tolerant of violations of human rights by right-wing regimes such as South Africa than by Communist regimes. In April 1981 the United States, joined by the conservative governments of France and Britain, vetoed a UN Security Council resolution that would have imposed general sanctions against South Africa for its continued blocking of the UN policy for Namibia; and in May one of the first foreigners to be received by President Reagan after he returned to the White House from the hospital following an assassination attempt was Roelof F. Botha, the South African foreign minister. This shift was approved not only by the major American business interests behind the Reagan administration but also by a large portion of the American electorate. However, the contrary point of view was lucidly articulated in May 1981, with the publication of the report of a commission financed by the Rockefeller Foundation and chaired by the president of the Ford Foundation. This report recommended that the Carter administration's pressures on South Africa should be intensified, not diminished. In particular, the United States should "promote genuine political power sharing in South Africa with a minimum of violence by systematically exerting influence on the South African government" and should "support organizations inside South Africa working for change."[21]

THE PROSPECT OF SANCTIONS

The possibility of imposing general mandatory sanctions against South Africa has been mooted ever since the Sharpeville shootings in 1960. As long ago as 1964 a London conference,

21. Foreign Policy Study Foundation, *South Africa: Time Running Out* (Berkeley: University of California, 1981).

sponsored by eleven Afro-Asian states, recommended economic sanctions against South Africa, and the convenor published the papers of the conference, which constitute an elaborate discussion of the prospects for coercion.[22] In the following year an Expert Committee composed of representatives of the members of the UN Security Council concluded that South Africa was not immune to danger from economic measures, but that their effectiveness depended on the universality of their application and the manner and duration of their enforcement.[23] Since then, the General Assembly has repeatedly voted resolutions for the imposition of full economic sanctions against South Africa, only to have them blocked by Western vetoes in the Security Council. Nevertheless, as we have seen, in 1977 the Security Council prohibited the export of military equipment to South Africa; and by 1981 the Namibian question was providing the Third World and Communist states with a strong legal basis for action. Moreover, even if the Namibian problem is overcome, pressures will continue for coercive action against an unreconstructed South Africa.

If general economic sanctions were imposed by the Security Council and effectively enforced, South Africa would be in serious trouble. The Republic is vulnerable to sanctions in a number of ways—above all, because of its dependence on imported oil fuel. In 1980 imported oil provided about 90 percent of South Africa's liquid fuel requirements. The government has managed to reduce the consumption of liquid fuel as a proportion of total energy consumption from 22.7 percent in 1973 to 21.1 percent in 1977, but it is probable that this is near the irreducible minimum of oil consumption. By the mid-1980s three SASOL plants are scheduled to be in full production and to provide between one-third and one-half of the Republic's 1980 liquid fuel requirements. To supply that shortfall, South Africa

22. Ronald Segal, ed., *Sanctions against South Africa* (Harmondsworth: Penguin Books, 1964).
23. *Africa Digest* 12, no. 6 (June 1965): 163–64.

would have to construct three to six additional SASOL plants. That would impose a severe strain on the economy. Moreover, it might take at least twenty years to build such plants, and still more to provide for the additional needs to sustain economic growth in the interval. Small quantities of liquid fuel can also be obtained from agricultural produce, but research and development for this is still in the embryonic phase. The conclusion is clear: in the absence of a discovery of natural oil inside South Africa, the country will continue to depend on imported oil for the foreseeable future, and is thus highly vulnerable to an effective oil embargo.[24]

The absence of published figures on oil importation, production, storage, and consumption makes it impossible to predict how long South Africa could survive such an embargo. For some time, the country could draw on its stockpile of oil, which is stored in disused coal mines in the eastern Transvaal. Rigorous rationing would also have some effect. Nevertheless, a strict oil embargo would soon damage South African transport and the mining and agricultural industries, and have a considerable impact throughout the entire economic system.

South Africa is also dependent on imported machinery and advanced technological equipment, and although the efforts that are already being made to substitute local products would be intensified, the cutting off of foreign supplies would create difficulties. The country would also suffer from the drying up of her export markets. Arnt Spandau of the University of the Witwatersrand has estimated that a 20 percent reduction of South Africa's exports would cost the country about $2 billion

24. A. Spandau, *Economic Boycott against South Africa: Normative and Factual Issues* (Cape Town: Juta, 1978); Martin Bailey and Bernard Rivers, *Oil Sanctions against South Africa* (New York: UN Centre against Apartheid, no. 12/78, June 1978); Martin Bailey, *Oil Sanctions: South Africa's Weak Link* (New York: UN Centre against Apartheid, no 15/80, April 1980); David M. Liff, *The Oil Industry in South Africa* (Washington, D.C.: Investor Responsibility Research Center, January 1979); Stanley Uys, "Prospects for an Oil Boycott," *Africa Report*, September–October 1980, pp. 15–18.

based on 1976 figures, or well over $3 billion in 1980, with damage to the balance of payments account.[25] Sanctions would also exacerbate the already serious unemployment problem, especially among Blacks. Spandau estimates that a 20 percent reduction in exports would increase unemployment by ninety thousand among Whites and three hundred and fifty thousand among Blacks, with serious consequences in terms of social unrest.[26] Finally, a cessation of fresh foreign investment would be damaging even if South Africa were able to export its gold at 1980 price levels, which did not seem likely in 1981.

However, all these projections are based on the assumption that sanctions would not merely be voted by the UN Security Council, but that they would also be effectively enforced. This is problematical. There are leaks in the arms embargo voted by the Security Council in 1977, and South Africa has had no difficulty in buying oil on the spot market (though at high prices) despite the oil embargo declared by the OPEC countries. The Western industrialized states would be far from enthusiastic about applying a cutoff of their mineral imports from South Africa. New sources would have to be found, or substitutions made, for a large number of minerals.[27]

The Soviet Union and its allies would have a greater interest in the enforcement of sanctions against South Africa. Since 1974, the Soviet Union has begun to play a significant role in southern Africa. It provided the guerrilla movements in Angola, Mozambique, and Zimbabwe with training, material, and financial aid during their military struggles; it equipped and funded the twenty thousand Cuban troops who have gone to Angola in support of the MPLA; it has treaties with the new regimes in Mozambique and Angola; and it provides the principal military and economic support for the ANC, the foremost South African black nationalist movement.

25. Spandau, Economic Boycott, p. 145.
26. Ibid., p. 140.
27. A. Koendermann, South Africa Digest, October 31, 1980.

This increased Soviet presence has led some commentators to conclude that the Soviet Union plans to gain control of South Africa's mineral wealth, on which the Western powers depend, and of the sea lanes around the southern end of the African continent, on which Western oil is transported from the Middle East.[28] This conclusion is enthusiastically endorsed by South African politicians and military strategists, who use it to solicit Western support against their black rivals.[29] Others argue more compellingly that there is no such grand design in Soviet African policies. They contend that the Soviet Union is primarily and obsessively concerned with two types of relationships: those with the states along its own borders from Eastern Europe through Turkey, Iran, and Afghanistan to China; and those with its rival superpower, the United States. Everything else is subordinate to those relationships. In this view, the Soviet Union seizes opportunities as they arise to make small-scale investments in anti-Western regimes and movements in southern Africa in order to outbid China and to weaken the United States and its allies. If, in due course, these investments prove profitable, so much the better. But, with problems such as Poland and Afghanistan on their own borders, the leaders in Moscow have no desire to extend the area of their major commitments to southern Africa.[30]

It therefore seems likely that, should the Security Council

28. David Albright, ed., *Communism in Africa* (Bloomington: Indiana University Press, 1980); W. Scott Thompson and Brett Silvers, "South Africa in Soviet Strategy," in Richard E. Bissell and Chester A. Crocker, eds., *South Africa into the 1980s* (Boulder, Colo.: Westview Press, 1979); W. C. T. van Rensburg, "Africa and Western Lifelines, " *Strategic Review* (Cambridge, Mass.), Spring 1978.

29. Republic of South Africa, *White Paper on Defence and Armament Production* (Pretoria: Government Printer, 1973), p.1.

30. David Albright, "Moscow's African Policy of the 1970s," in Albright, *Communism in Africa*; Colin Legum, "African Outlooks towards the USSR," in ibid.; Oye Ogunbadejo, "Soviet Policies in Africa," *African Affairs*, vol. 79, no. 316 (July 1980); Abbott A. Brayton, "Soviet Involvement in Africa," *Journal of Modern African Studies*, vol. 17, no. 2 (June 1979).

vote to impose general economic sanctions against South Africa, the white regime would manage to mitigate the effects by adopting various domestic expedients. Building on the experience of the former regime in Rhodesia, South Africa would probably develop an effective system of sanctions-busting, with considerable support—covert if not overt, unofficial if not official—from Western industrialized states, Israel, Taiwan, and even several African states.

In the final resort, South Africa would be a tough nut to crack by force. Before 1960, South Africa's military capacity was meager. Since then, spurred on by internal unrest, revolutions in neighboring territories, OAU and UN threats, the voluntary UN arms embargo of 1963, and the compulsory UN arms embargo of 1977, South Africa has moved toward becoming a thoroughly militarized state. The defense budget escalated from a mere R44 million in fiscal 1960/61 to R1,682 million in fiscal 1979/80, when it amounted to 16.6 percent of the total national budget and 4.2 percent of the GNP. These figures are not impressive by American, European, or Soviet standards, but in the southern African context they are overwhelming. The government is now able to mobilize four hundred thousand trained and disciplined personnel—nine times the combined armed forces of the other nine states in the southern African region. Those personnel are predominantly white men. Every white youth is subject to two years' military training and service. Recently, however, the government has been cautiously adding Coloured, Asian, and even African military units. The South African arms industry, which was nurtured by Western technology, is now dominated by a parastatal organization—Armscor—and produces a wide range of military equipment, including ammunition, armored vehicles, aircraft, and missiles. A nuclear explosion was reported off the South African coast in September 1979. Whether the report was accurate or not, there is no doubt that South Africa possesses enriched uranium and is capable of producing nuclear weapons. There is also an efficient communications system, including a radio command center near Cape Town, Decca navigational equipment covering the entire coastline, and an air-warning system along the northern border. Moreover, the military machine has gained considerable experience. South African officers have observed numerous colonial wars, including those in Kenya, Algeria, Portuguese Africa, and Zimbabwe, and in 1976 a force of over two thousand men penetrated five hundred miles into Angola, and withdrew for political rather than military reasons.[31]

In 1973, P. W. Botha, as minister of defense, expounded a "total strategy" for "the involvement of an entire country in . . . a conflict."[32] This concept has been regularly updated. With Botha as prime minister and General Magnus Malan as minister of defense, the government seems adequately prepared to cope with any military threat that is likely to emerge in the 1980s.

CONCLUSION

As we have seen, the South African political system is unstable. That in itself is not exceptional. In the world of the 1980s

31. Nancy Theis, "The Evolution of South African Defense Policies 1960–1980," Yale-Wesleyan Southern African Research Program paper, December 10, 1980; International Institute for Strategic Studies, The Military Balance 1979–1980 (London, 1980); Sean Gervasi, US Arms Transfer to South Africa in Violation of the UN Voluntary Arms Embargo (New York: UN Centre against Apartheid, 1978), and What Have South Africa's Traditional Suppliers of Arms Done to Abide by the Mandatory Arms Embargo against Apartheid South Africa? (New York: UN Centre against Apartheid, 1978); Asbjorn Eide, "South Africa: Repression and the Transfer of Arms and Arms Technology," in Mary Kaldor and Asbjorn Eide, eds., The World Military Order (London: Macmillan, 1979); Chester Crocker, "Current and Projected Military Balances in Southern Africa," in Bissell and Crocker, South Africa into the 1980s; Barbara Rogers and Zdenel Cervenka, The Nuclear Axis: The Secret Collaboration between West Germany and South Africa (New York: Times Books, 1978); Robert S. Jaster, South Africa's Narrowing Security Options (London: International Institute for Strategic Studies, 1980.)

32. Theis, "South Africa's Defense Policies," p. 26.

numerous national regimes are no more secure than the South African, and the global system itself has become closely integrated and highly volatile. However, since Zimbabwe passed under black rule in 1980, South Africa has become unique. It alone is dominated by an oligarchy defined by race. So the South African system is singled out for general opprobrium, even though many other regimes match it in their brutality toward dissidents.

Previous efforts by social scientists to make specific prognoses for the future of South Africa have not been very successful. In 1965, Pierre van den Berghe wrote that "conditions will have become favorable for these [revolutionary] developments within five years at most."[33] In 1971 Heribert Adam declared that more and more independent African states would soon "settle for peaceful coexistence" with the Republic.[34]

In this book, we have delineated the nature of the South African political system and the forces that bear upon it; but we do not claim to have the means to predict the resultant of those forces with any precision. An analyst might have identified a potential for revolution in France in 1788, in Russia in 1916, or in Iran in 1978, but nobody made, or could have made, accurate predictions of the timing of the subsequent upheavals or their outcomes. Looking at South Africa in the early 1980s, we see a racially defined oligarchy quite firmly in the saddle; but we also see cleavages within the oligarchy and a revolutionary spirit among the subject races, encouraged and assisted from outside the country. Whether those cleavages will open widely enough under pressure to lead to a transformation through interracial alliances,[35] or whether black South Africans and their allies will

33. Pierre van den Berghe, *South Africa: A Study in Conflict* (Middletown, Conn.: Wesleyan University Press, 1965), p. 263.

34. Heribert Adam, *Modernizing Racial Domination: The Dynamics of South African Politics* (Berkeley: University of California Press, 1971), p. 121.

35. This seems to be the opinion of Heribert Adam and Hermann Giliomee in their *Ethnic Power Mobilized: Can South Africa Change?* (New Haven: Yale Univerisity Press, 1979).

generate a revolution is problematic. If pressed, we would say that we expect there to be a continuation of the spiral of black resistance and white repression, probably with increased violence on the part of both sides in each episode, for an indefinite period; but sooner or later we would expect there to be a more or less radical transformation of South African society. It is beyond the capacity of human analysts to forecast the chronology, the means, or the results of the metamorphosis.

Index

African Liberation Committee, 15
African National Congress (ANC),
136; banned, 8, 10–11; purpose,
185–86; presidents-general,
185–86; Youth League, 192–94;
leaders' fate, 214–16; Soviet support, 240. *See also* Opposition
parties
African nationalists: objectives, 10–11
African people: view of South African
history, 33–34; how called,
34–35; increase of, 44; alien impact upon, 45–46; primary regional division of, 45–46; urbanization, 47; languages, 49; religion, 49; middle class, 49, 67;
conservatives and modernists, 49,
125–27; Cape Province voters, 85;
removed as voters, 85–86, 89–90;
"nations," 92. *See also* Caste system; "Homelands"
African Political Organization (APO),
185
African Resistance Movement, 198–
200
Afrikaanse Studentebond, 153–54
Afrikaans language: Soweto protests,
202
Afrikaner Broederbond, 131, 132; described, 150–52; Hertzog's and
Smuts's comments upon, 152
Afrikaner Bureau for Racial Studies,
155
Afrikaner nationalists: their traditional enemies, 32–33; church's

role for, 114; black campaigns
against, 194–96
Afrikaner people: Dutch colonial
period, 28; English compared to,
38–41; political parties, 76–77;
leadership, 129–36; civil service,
133; associations, 149–58
Anglicization, 32–33, 114, 131
Anglophobia, 131, 170
Angola: black regime established in,
16; invasion of, 134
Apartheid. *See* Separate development
Appellate Division, 81, 83. *See also*
Courts
Arms embargo: UN votes, 230, 234–
35; leaks in, 240
Arson: in universities, 124
Asian people: National party policy
toward, 7; defined, 34; increase of,
42–43; internal structure of, 43;
Coloured differentiated from, 44;
children's education, 118
Azanian People's Organization
(AZAPO), 202–03

Bantu: name discussed, 21n
Bantu Education Act, 116–17; rejec-
tion of, 119, 124; Vorster's im-
plementation of, 175
Bantu Laws Amendment Act, 68; ef-
fects of, 210–11
Bantu-speaking people: historical
background, 21–26
Bantustanization: described, 17
Bibliography: African political organ-

DATE			
APR 01 '91			
NOV. 19. 1996			
DEC. 17. 1996			
DEC 1 3 2004			